# Nicaragua

## A Country Guide

# Nicaragua
# A Country Guide

## Kent Norsworthy

with Tom Barry

The Inter-Hemispheric Education Resource Center

Albuquerque, New Mexico

Published by The Inter-Hemispheric Education Resource Center

ISBN: 0-911213-29-5

Library of Congress Catalog Card Number: 89-81689

**The Inter-Hemispheric Education Resource Center**
**Box 4506 * Albuquerque, New Mexico * 87196**

# Acknowledgments

Tom Barry was the primary author for the chapter on Foreign Influence and the sections on Popular Organizing, Labor and Unions, and Nongovernmental Organizations. Tom also was vital in research and editing assistance. Debra Preusch assisted in research and was the primary coordinator of the project. Thanks go to Beth Sims and Connie Adler for editing, Jenny Beatty for proofreading, and Jenny Beatty, John Hawley, Jodi Gibson, and Anna Darling for production and wordprocessing. Invaluable comments on the entire manuscript were provided by Lisa Haugaard, William I. Robinson, and Richard Stahler-Sholk. For comments on specific chapters I would like to thank Mario Arana, Yolanda Chávez, Ted Gordon, Paul Jeffrey, Manuel Orozco, and María Zúñiga. Above all I would like to thank Yolanda, Marcelo, and Nelson, without whose patience and support my efforts would not have been possible.

# Table of Contents

# The Resource Center

The Inter-Hemispheric Education Resource Center is a private non-profit research and policy institute located in Albuquerque, New Mexico. Founded in 1979, the Resource Center produces books, policy reports, and audiovisuals about U.S. foreign relations with third world countries. Among its most popular materials are *The Central America Fact Book* and the quarterly *Bulletin* mailed to subscribers for $5 annually ($7.50 outside the United States). For a catalogue of publications, please write to: The Resource Center, Box 4506, Albuquerque, NM 87196.

# Nicaragua

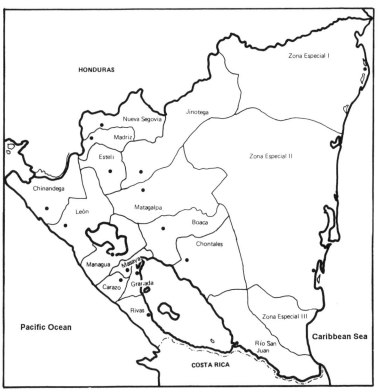

*Inforpress Centroamericana*

# Introduction

Ask Nicaraguans how they would compare themselves to their Central American neighbors and you are likely to be hit with a chorus of boasts and pejoratives. Not unlike their neighbors, Nicaraguans (known as *Nicas* or *Pinoleros*) consider themselves distinct.

The 3.5 million inhabitants of the largest country in Central America are proud of the attributes that set them apart, while often rejecting things foreign. Nicaraguans' sense of independence and nationalism rises from the country's long history of resistance to U.S. domination, dating back to the adventurism of U.S. filibuster William Walker in the 1850s and to the guerrilla war waged by Augusto César Sandino against the U.S. Marines in the 1920s and 1930s. Even President Violeta Chamorro, who hardly considers herself an anti-imperialist, brushed aside offers to send U.S. troops to restore order during a general strike in July 1990, asserting that Nicaraguans should be the ones to solve their own problems.

Nicaraguan nationalism also arises from a strong and self-confident popular culture. Cultural expressions from music to theater, dance, and painting are popular among all social sectors. Poetry and prose, however, reign supreme. Many Nicaraguans insist that their country has the highest per capita concentration of poets in the world! Indeed, in all corners of Nicaragua — from the remote mountain villages of Nueva Segovia to the halls of government in Managua — poets seem to be everywhere. In large part, the prominence of poetry can be traced back to Rubén Darío (1867-1916), the Nicaraguan who put his country on the map of international culture with his rich and intricate poems. Today museums, theaters, cultural events, and even the town where he was born are named after the hallowed Darío.

Baseball is the national pastime which comes closest to rivaling Nicaraguans' penchant for cultural production. On Sunday mornings virtually all open fields are occupied by baseball games — from the most impromptu and informal pickup contests where tightly wound rags and socks serve as a ball and 2-by-4s as bats to dozens of organized leagues for players of all ages and both sexes. On the pages of all three daily papers, national sports commentators dissect the every move of the few Nicaraguan players who have made it to the U.S. major leagues.

Other, less grandiose characteristics also set Nicaraguans apart. Informality is one. Dress codes for men — the necktie, for instance, standard attire in business, government, and academic circles throughout the continent — are largely relegated to a tiny, foreign-educated elite, while Nicaraguan women have much less affinity for high heels and lipstick than their neighbors in the region. Language too is affected. Words and phrases deemed too profane or slang to be used in a typical Costa Rican conversation, for example, are everyday fare for Nicaraguans, often making their way onto the airwaves and into popular slogans, billboards, and graffiti. Native Spanish speakers from other countries often lament the absence of a dictionary of "Nicaraguanisms," hundreds of words and phrases which have no meaning, or an entirely different one, outside the country's borders.

Complementing Nicaraguan informality is a strong drive to disagree. Nicaraguans love to argue and complain over just about anything, a characteristic magnified by the deep-bred cynicism produced by nearly 50 years of Somoza dictatorship. In part, this has translated into a widespread penchant among the population to oppose the powers that be, irrespective of political sentiments, voting behavior, or superficial allegiances. A popular refrain heard on the streets in the days after the February 1990 elections was, "We threw out Somoza, and now we've thrown out the Sandinistas. If doña Violeta doesn't deliver on her promises, we'll soon throw her out too." Indeed, if Chamorro's first 100 days in office proved anything, it was that the Nicaraguan people remain as militant and unpredictable as ever.

* * *

When arriving in Nicaragua, first-time visitors as well as foreigners and even Nicaraguans who have been away from the country for a prolonged period are immediately struck by several features. With few exceptions, the first is temperature. Since much of the country, including Managua, is just above sea-level, the tropical heat is stifling day and night, all year round. A brief rainy season provides little relief. To alleviate the heat, Nicaraguans are avid drinkers. In any city or town, water, soft drinks, and fresh-squeezed fruit juices, dispensed in little plastic bags, are never more than a few blocks away.

Decades of dictatorship, followed by eight years of war and U.S. financial aggression have taken a heavy toll: underdevelopment and poverty pervade the physical landscape throughout Nicaragua. Although the Sandinistas attempted to reduce inequalities through the redistribution of national wealth and income, they eventually realized that a small pie can be cut only so many times. In stark contrast to neighboring Costa Rica, and to a lesser extent Guatemala and El Salvador, even the most basic infrastructure is conspicuously absent. Outside of the cities there are few paved roads, other than the deteriorated two-lane highways which link the capital with Pacific ports and border crossings. Access to safe water is still a luxury. In Managua, less than half the population enjoys running water in their homes, in the countryside less than one in ten.[1] Outside of urban offices and the wealthier *barrios*, telephone service is practically nonexistent.

The extreme level of underdevelopment in Nicaragua today is the heaviest part of the legacy left behind by the Somoza dictatorship. Part of the reason why the Somozas generated such intense and widespread opposition among Nicaraguans of all stripes is that they ran Nicaragua as their personal fiefdom, monopolizing just about everything in the country worth owning. Evaluating the decade of revolutionary changes left behind by the departing government, Sandinista leader and guerrilla heroine Dora María Téllez reflected: "I say that if all we did was to make Nicaragua into a nation, that was still the most extraordinary thing we could have achieved."[2] This sentiment was shared by Chamorro and her allies who, if they were willing to recognize anything positive done by the Sandinistas, conceded their having constructed a modern state and a national identity where before there had been neither.

\* \* \*

Most of the above traits and characteristics can, to a greater or lesser degree, be found in all parts of the country. But Nicaragua, often characterized as three countries in one, is diverse and heterogeneous. The sparsely inhabited tropical lowlands of the Atlantic coast (divided into the North and South Autonomous Regions) cover more than half the national territory and are home to Nicaragua's five ethnic minorities (the indigenous Miskito, Sumu, and Rama, and the black Creoles and Garífuna). In the days of U.S. economic domination and the enclave economy, it was easier and quicker to travel from Nicaraguan Atlantic coast ports to New Orleans or Houston than inland to the national capital of Managua, a scant 250 miles away. Although a dirt road has been carved out of the dense jungles to connect the northern Atlantic coast with the rest of the country, the bulk of travel is still done by boat or plane. The Atlantic coast's isolation from the rest of the country and historic mistrust of the "Spaniards" from the Pacific side continue to act as barriers.

To the west of the Autonomous Regions, stretching from the Honduran border to the Río San Juan (which separates Nicaragua from Costa Rica), lies the broad central part of the country. This central region passes through the rugged mountainous departments of Jinotega and Matagalpa in the north, then descends through the low-lying hills and plains of Boaco and Chontales in the south. Home to the majority of the Nicaraguan peasantry, in the mid-1980s this area was the primary target for contra recruitment, military destruction, and more subtle efforts to win over a social base.

The rest of the country, stretching from the central mountains and lakes in the south to the Pacific coast plains, hosts the major cities, ports, industries, and large agroexport farms, as well as isolated pockets of the peasantry. The country's two traditional political parties, Conservatives and Liberals, historically were based in this region's two major towns, Granada and León. In the 1850s Managua became the capital and since then it has remained the country's largest city (current population one million) and hub of national political activity.

The choice of Managua as the seat of government turned out to be an unfortunate one. Despite the fact that the city sits beside the shores of giant Lake Xolotlán, Managua suffers from a chronic shortage of drinking water. Lake Xolotlán, contaminated in the 1960s and 1970s by industrial waste, is awash in floods every rainy season as runoff pours into the streets from the surrounding hill country. Furthermore, the capital was built atop a series of major earthquake faults. In 1972 on Nicaragua's traditional Christmas eve, the city was leveled by a massive earthquake. The only major multi-story building left standing, the 21-story former Bank of America building, is today the lone skyline element in a downtown area which has never been rebuilt.

* * *

The political history of Nicaragua throughout most of this century has been dominated by two forces: *somocismo* and *sandinismo*. The guerrilla struggle of nationalist hero Augusto César Sandino in the 1920s and 1930s succeeded in forcing the United States to withdraw its contingent of occupying Marines. Sandino's subsequent murder at the hands of Anastasio Somoza García, who had been installed by the departing Marines at the head of the Nicaraguan National Guard, paved the way for more than 40 years of Somoza family rule over the country—the longest and most corrupt dictatorship in Latin American history.

The Sandinista National Liberation Front (FSLN) grounded its fight against the dictatorship in the thinking and actions of Sandino. The essential elements of Sandino's campaign, rescued 30 years after his death by the FSLN, included anti-imperialism, the quest for national dignity and sovereignty, and a commitment to the worker and peasant majority. On this basis, the Sandinista guerrilla struggle proposed to overthrow the dictatorship, dismantle the exploitative structures and institutions of *somocismo*, break the country's dependence on the United States, and move toward the construction of a more just social and economic order.

* * *

Like the initial period after the 1979 Sandinista victory, Nicaragua in 1990 was enveloped in powerful changes. The National Organized Union (UNO)[3] government led by President Violeta Chamorro, in its drive to arrest the economic decline and reestablish agroexports and the private sector as the economy's motor force, has presided over a sometimes gradual, sometimes violent, process of rolling back the revolutionary transformations of the 1980s.

The process encountered resistance not only from the FSLN, which in the wake of its electoral defeat promised to "govern from below" and defend what it saw as the fundamental gains of the revolution, but also from tens of thousands of Nicaraguans who saw few signs of the peace, reconciliation, or economic prosperity which motivated them to vote for UNO.

But the frontlines of resistance were occupied by the country's labor unions and popular organizations. A major factor behind the failure of the Sandinistas' mixed-economy model was the refusal of the private sector to cooperate. In the 1990s, conversely, success of UNO's "social-market economy" appeared to hinge on the collaboration of the well-organized and highly class-conscious worker and peasant majority.

For the long haul, two key aspects of UNO's economic reforms, privatization and liberalization, appear likely to improve macroeconomic performance and generate some economic growth. But to the extent that these same policies lead to a reconcentration of land and wealth in the hands of the elite, they threaten to aggravate the very roots of poverty and injustice which gave rise to revolution in the first place.

Another painful lesson which the transition period drove home for many Nicaraguans who had voted for UNO was that the United States' commitment to democracy and reconstruction was but a small fraction of its commitment to destabilize the Sandinistas. Washington's economic aid to the Chamorro government turned out to be less than anticipated, and arrived much later than economic planners had hoped. Yet, at the political level, U.S. interference threatened to undermine the building of stable democratic institutions and the national consensus necessary to move the country forward.

\* \* \*

The following pages attempt to explain the key actors, events, and dynamics from two distinct periods. One is the period of Sandinista rule, from July 1979 until April 1990. The other deals with UNO's program of government and its performance during Chamorro's first 100 days in office. By the end of those 100 days it was all too clear that Nicaragua was still in the grips of what promised to be a prolonged transition. That transition was characterized by a constant jockeying for position as the country's major constituencies and power blocs—moderate and right-wing blocs within the government, FSLN, unions and popular organizations, armed forces, ex-contras, capitalists—struggled to define their stance in relation to the critical issues of the day.

## Chapter 1

# Politics

## Government

The Nicaraguan nation was born of Spanish colonial conquest. As in all of Latin America, the country's frontiers were carved out by European conquistadors, the indigenous population largely exterminated or crossbred with colonial settlers, and economy and society organized as a subordinate appendage of the colonial power. Colonialism gave way to formal independence in 1821, yet for much of the last century society continued to be dominated by the former colonial merchants and landed oligarchs. Nicaragua entered the 20th century facing sharp conflicts between these groups, which were frequently suppressed by U.S. interventions and later submerged by the advent of the Somoza dynasty.

Given this 500-year backdrop to government and society in Nicaragua today, it is curious, and perhaps a unique statement on this country, that three radically different governments have presided in the short span of the last 11 years: the Somozas, the Sandinistas, and the UNO coalition headed by President Violeta Chamorro. Each had a fundamentally different vision of how politics, the economy, and civil society should be organized.

The mass insurrection of 1979 swept away the Somoza family dictatorship which had ruled the country for 45 years. A provisional coalition government, led by the Sandinista National Liberation Front (FSLN), remained in place until the 1984 national elections when FSLN candidates won the presidency and two-thirds of the seats in the legislature. In 1990 the Sandinistas turned the government over to Violeta Chamorro, head of a 14-party coalition, the National Organized Union (UNO), dominated by conservative and center-right interests. Chamorro's inauguration was the first time in Nicaraguan history that power was transferred by peaceful means from government to opposition.

With the fall of the Somoza regime – which was formally installed with U.S. backing in 1936 and collapsed in July of 1979 – the new government inherited an underdeveloped state riddled with corruption.[1] The country's traditional politicians and state functionaries went about the business of government through backroom deals and inter-elite pacts aimed chiefly at dividing up the spoils and perpetuating the status quo. The country's legal system was designed to protect the interests of the economically powerful and their right to exploit the majority. Throughout Nicaragua there was a conspicuous absence among the broader population of participation in any type of democratic institution. And although the Somozas went through the motions of elections every so often, these were disregarded in and outside of Nicaragua as little more than hollow exercises staged by the dictatorship to legitimize dynastic rule. Nicaraguans had come to view government as of the few, by the few, and above all, for the few. These exclusionary politics engendered a powerful opposition to the Somozas, which eventually included virtually all of the country's political and social forces.

Precisely because Nicaragua had not been run as a nation, but as Somoza's personal estate, the 1979 insurrection was also a revolution that completely destroyed the institutions and the apparatus of Nicaraguan government. As the last Somoza fled Nicaragua and his National Guard disintegrated, Nicaragua slipped into a governmental vacuum with the disappearance of formal governing structures (executive, legislative, judicial) and the state apparatus, as well as the army and police force.[2]

The violent rupture with the Somocista past was the context in which the events of the immediate post-insurrection period unfolded and a new government was constructed. Just as quickly as the old order crumbled, the different sectors and classes that make up Nicaraguan society stepped into the vacuum, each entering into complex alliances and conflicts over how, and on what basis, to forge the new order. In fact, it was the complexity of achieving consensus around something that had broken so thoroughly with 500 years of history that explains why Nicaragua's alliances are so volatile and its conflicts so salient.

The FSLN, which began in 1961 as a relatively small political-military organization, led the armed struggle against Somoza. As it grew in influence in the 1970s, it won mass popular support and eventually assumed the leadership of the broad multiclass alliance that isolated the dictatorship. As the principal and best organized force in the period immediately following the overthrow, the Sandinistas spearheaded efforts to transform the Nicaraguan state and society.

In subsequent years the Reagan administration raved that the Sandinistas had "stolen" the revolution and arrogated the post-Somoza government. Yet as Somoza and the National Guard fled the country, the Sandinistas were the only real organized political and military force capable of leading the effort to set up a new state. They also enjoyed the support of the overwhelming majority of Nicaraguans. Moreover, the popular classes comprised the bulk of the anti-Somoza movement. The FSLN interpreted this groundswell of opposition as a popular insurrection, launched not only to get rid of Somoza but also to transform society in the interests of this poor majority. Later, as other sectors accumulated their own forces and as disputes emerged between different interests over how the country should be organized, the Sandinistas would become but one of several major groupings in society. But in 1979 it was only the FSLN that could fill the vacuum.

The FSLN was guided by its "Historic Program," drafted in 1969 as a statement of objectives for a post-Somoza society. The document called for a system based on political pluralism, a mixed economy, and international nonalignment. It stressed democratizing society and developing political pluralism in the framework of the "hegemony of the popular classes."[3] Perhaps, therefore, the most important changes to accompany the demise of the dictatorship were a fundamental reorientation of social priorities in favor of the poor and disenfranchised, a redefinition of values, and a redistribution of political power. For the Sandinistas, the guiding principle in political and economic decisions was the struggle to transform social and economic relations in the interests of the majority of the population. This led the FSLN to construct a concept of political pluralism as "participatory democracy" together with elements of traditional "representative democracy."

"Popular hegemony" in decision-making, according to this construct, was to be achieved at every level of society. Its expression was to include such features as popular participation in politics as expressed in the mass organizations, a new ideological orientation in the educational system and armed forces, and trade-union participation in the economy.[4] This Sandinista concept of political pluralism was summed up in an FSLN statement in 1980: "For the Sandinista Front, democracy is not defined in purely political terms, and cannot be reduced to the participation of the people in elections. It begins in the economic order, when social inequalities diminish, and from there spreads to the spheres of government and culture. In a more advanced phase, democracy means the participation of the workers in the running of the factories, farms, cooperatives, and cultural centers. In short, democracy is the intervention of the masses in all aspects of social life....It neither begins nor ends with elections."[5]

Thus while there was a strong commitment to political pluralism, its subordination to the class-based transformations of the revolutionary project implied clear limits. First, to the extent that representatives of the bourgeoisie felt their class interests threatened by the predominance of popular hegemony, they simply withdrew their political or economic support and participation from the project. Second, the FSLN invariably closed off political spaces to those who were seen as interested not in contributing to the new system, but to undermining or overthrowing it. These limits made themselves felt in the formative years of the post-Somoza government. An examination of the early 1980s reveals these limits, while also providing a comparison between the aftermath of the 1979 and 1990 transitions.

With the departure of Somoza, the Sandinistas attempted to provide continuity to the pre-triumph alliance by forming a coalition government, led by the Government Junta of National Reconstruction (JGRN). The five-member JGRN comprised three Sandinistas, including coordinator Daniel Ortega, and two representatives of the bourgeoisie, industrialist Alfonso Robelo and Violeta Chamorro, widow of one of the anti-Somoza struggle's martyrs, newspaper publisher Pedro Joaquín Chamorro. At the time, this 3-2 ratio probably gave the bourgeoisie greater formal representation than its proportionate support among Nicaraguans. But the Sandinistas viewed this as a way to encourage national unity and the participation of the private sector in the urgent task of reconstruction.

The JGRN, in turn, formed a cabinet, in which key economic ministries were given to representatives of the private sector. It also formed a Council of State as a transitional, co-legislative branch of government. Seats in the council were distributed to mass organizations, economic interest groups, and professional, political, and social associations. The JGRN said it had determined the distribution in accordance with the relative proportional representation of each group in the total population. The biggest single block was accorded to the Superior Council of Private Enterprise (COSEP), a conservative alliance of industrialists, financiers, and large-scale agricultural and commercial groups.

In early 1980 the JGRN and the leadership of the FSLN expanded the total number of seats in the council from 33 to 47, with the new ones awarded to recently formed popular organizations identified with the Sandinistas. The decision triggered a governmental crisis and the first major shakeup in the anti-Somoza alliance. Seeing their legislative strength diluted by the expansion of seats, the COSEP bench pulled out of the council. Early in 1980 Chamorro resigned from the junta, citing health reasons. Robelo resigned in April stating his opposition to the redistribution of council seats.

At root were fundamental issues linked to the increasingly clear class-based definition of the revolutionary project. In the political sphere, it quickly became evident that the bourgeoisie would not be given a share of political power commensurate with its economic clout. The Sandinistas felt it was important, indeed essential, that the bourgeoisie be represented in the government. But they made it clear that such a presence could not supplant "popular hegemony."

The Robelo and Chamorro resignations symbolized the decision among important sectors of the bourgeoisie to try to influence the shape and the structures of the emerging governmental system from the legal and extra-legal opposition, rather than sharing power with the Sandinistas. Robelo left the country shortly afterwards to become a leader of the *contrarrevolucionarios* or contras. Chamorro remained inside Nicaragua as publisher of the U.S.-funded *La Prensa*, the newspaper which served as the mouthpiece of the anti-Sandinista opposition.

Determined to pursue the course of national unity through multi-class alliances, the Sandinistas entered into lengthy negotiations with COSEP and invited two other representatives of the bourgeoisie, Arturo Cruz and Rafael Córdova Rivas, to take the places of Chamorro and Robelo in the JGRN.

In the wake of national elections held in 1984, both the structure of the provisional government and the informal nature of the coalition were dissolved. (See Parties and Elections) The Council of State gave way to a National Assembly in which all members were elected according to their party affiliation. The Assembly, where Sandinista candidates won some two-thirds of the seats, was charged with drawing up a constitution as the country's constitutive legislative branch. The JGRN gave way to a formal executive branch, in the presidential mold, headed by the victorious candidates President Daniel Ortega and Vice President Sergio Ramírez.

With the executive and legislative branches in place, attention turned in 1985 to drafting a new constitution. The Somocista constitution was scrapped after the insurrection, and the country had been guided juridically by outdated legal codes, legislation passed and put into effect without a constitutional framework, and by presidential decree. Throughout 1985 and 1986 the 202 articles of the new constitution were drafted with the assistance of a lengthy process of nationwide *cabildos abiertos* (town meetings). These public gatherings, presided over by representatives from the constitutional commission of the National Assembly, were used as key forums to enrich the draft constitution through direct, popular input.[6] The constitution was then ratified by the National Assembly and signed by President Ortega on January 9, 1987.

The document provides constitutional protection for the broad democratic rights introduced since 1979. It also legally enshrines the structures of participatory democracy alongside representative democracy, and constitutionally sanctions many of the fundamental social and economic transformations undertaken since then. For instance, it guarantees the traditional liberties, such as freedom of speech, assembly, and movement, as well as legally proscribing gender, racial, ethnic, and religious discrimination. Access to health care, education, a decent wage, and other social and economic benefits are considered constitutional rights in themselves, restricted only by the material limits of society. The document elevates the mixed economy — in which private, state, cooperative, and mixed enterprises are to coexist — to the constitutionally prescribed economic structure. In addition to providing the constitutional framework for periodic elections, as held in 1984 and 1990, it mandates that the population has the right, and the duty, to participate in decision-making at all levels of society.[7]

The formal structure of the government itself also is enshrined in the constitution. The system is essentially a hybrid, drawing on different aspects of the Latin American, Western European, and United States models.[8] Similar to many Latin American countries, national government is divided among four branches: executive, legislative, judicial, and electoral. The executive branch, which enjoys broad formal powers, consists of the president and vice president, elected by direct popular vote for a six-year term, together with an appointed cabinet.

Legislative power resides with a 90-member National Assembly, elected by universal adult suffrage (above 16 years) under a system of proportional representation.[9] Like the executive, assembly members serve six-year terms. Legislators are elected from each of nine political-administrative regions in numbers roughly proportionate to the population of each region.

An independent judicial branch headed by a seven-member Supreme Court is appointed by the National Assembly on the basis of nominations made by the president's office. The president then designates which of the seven will preside over the court. The five-member Supreme Electoral Council, an independent branch of the government, is charged with administering and overseeing elections.

The constitution also stipulates the creation of two new organs of government: Municipal Councils in 131 townships throughout the country and two Autonomous Councils in the Atlantic coast region. (See Native Peoples) These entities are empowered to exercise considerable authority over local social and economic issues, including taxation, control of local resources, and local branches of health, education, and other ministries. The municipal/autonomous structure, brought into being for the first time with the 1990 elections, allows for a decentralized system of government. The municipal councils are multiparty in composition, with parties assigned numbers of seats on the councils in proportion to votes won in local elections held every six years and overlapping with national elections. Mayors are appointed in turn by the municipal councils, and can be recalled or replaced by the councils.

By the time the Sandinistas turned over the government to UNO, the structures and institutions of a new, modern state had been erected. Among the institutions established were the executive, legislative, and judicial branches of government; local governing bodies; the legal, constitutional framework of society; and the basic autonomous agencies of the state, such as the army and police. The broad socioeconomic contours of society also had been defined around political pluralism and the mixed economy.

Given the February 25, 1990 electoral results, the question was whether the integrity of these new structures could withstand the transition to a new government with different ideological positions and an agenda different from the FSLN's. The question was put to the test during the two-month transition. After several weeks of negotiations, the outgoing Sandinista government and the Chamorro transition team signed the "Transition Protocol." This document, in essence, ratified that full governmental power would be transferred to those elected by popular vote. In addition, it affirmed that the new authorities would respect and operate within the parameters of the legal and constitutional order under which they had been elected.

Despite the unexpectedly smooth transition, major questions remained to be answered by the practices of the Chamorro administration and future governments. Are the structures and constitutional guidelines for running society sufficiently strong to sustain themselves through a variety of political regimes? Was the Sandinistas' decade-long tenure the formative years of a new Nicaraguan social and political order, or is that order still under such dispute that it could go through another fundamental redefinition? Although it provides a clear overall framework, the constitution itself is general, vague, or ambiguous on numerous substantial points. It is less a blueprint for governmental procedure than it is a document open to broad and even contrasting interpretations. For instance, what actually constitutes "popular participation" in decision-making? What is considered a "decent wage" or "decent housing"? What criteria should be fulfilled to justify denying economic rights on the basis of the nation's material limitations? In this regard, whether or not the structures erected in the 1980s have sufficient internal strength to sustain themselves will not be determined in juridical battles, but in the real political will of the different sectors in society and the balance of forces between them.

# Political Parties and Elections

The history of Nicaragua's traditional political parties is replete with infighting and divisions.[10] Between Independence in 1821 and World War II, nearly all Nicaraguans with a preference were either Liberals or Conservatives. The major conflicts of the day, which often led to coups, civil wars, and foreign interventions, were kept within the ranks of these two tendencies. A few new parties came on the scene in the 1940s in an effort to challenge Somoza's domination, but it was not until the 1980s that the political map would be fundamentally recast. With the onset of the Sandinista revolution, some parties entered into national unity alliances with the FSLN.[11] Others became part of the counterrevolutionary forces based in Honduras and Costa Rica. But most parties began a process of subdividing that would last throughout the decade. By the June 1989 deadline for party registration for the 1990 election the number of parties had risen to 20.

So splintered was the opposition that a U.S.-funded delegation sent to evaluate prospects for unifying the disparate groups described it as "centrifugal in dynamic [and] fratricidal in outlook."[12] Faced with this ominous panorama, the United States stepped in to, in the words of one State Department official, "micromanage the opposition" with the goal of unifying the anti-Sandinista forces.[13] Their efforts met with mixed results until June of 1989 with the formation of the 14-party UNO coalition and the nomination of Violeta Chamorro as the group's presidential candidate two months later.

Despite the creation of UNO, though, the factionalism of the opposition remained as a persistent feature even after the elections. In terms of the principal ideological currents, the Conservatives, Liberals, Social Christians, and Social Democrats each had representatives from at least two different factions elected to the National Assembly on the UNO ticket in 1990.[14] Two days after Chamorro assumed office UNO itself suffered a major internal division with eight parties supporting the hardline stance of Vice President Virgilio Godoy and six backing the more moderate positions of Chamorro. "UNO will continue in the opposition because this is not a new government but simply a new facade," asserted Godoy.[15]

The causes for this extreme atomization ranged from the tradition of strong-man politics or *caudillismo* to personal antagonisms and rivalries as well as actual political differences over strategy and social alliances (for example, urban vs. rural; professionals vs. producers; and traditional oligarchy vs. modernizing factions). But perhaps most important in the 1980s was the internationalization of Nicaraguan opposition politics. Being part of the opposition turned into a lucrative business. Although the combined organized strength of the parties remained relatively stagnant, there was an explosion of opposition "political leaders," each with his or her own "party." Political factions and power bases in the United States, Western Europe, and Latin America became the organizers, financiers, and advisers for dozens of anti-Sandinista groups inside Nicaragua. Washington and the U.S. Democratic and Republican Parties were the principal sources of external funds, but international Christian Democratic and Social Democratic parties were also active. (See U.S. Economic Aid)

Until the end of the 1980s the multiplicity of parties meant that the center of opposition activity in Nicaragua was not in the hands of a political party or coalition. Instead, the opposition was managed by a newspaper (*La Prensa*), a Cardinal (Obando y Bravo), and a businessmen's association (COSEP). Even UNO's upset victory at the polls in 1990 was hardly the product of the organizational strength of the parties that made up the coalition. With the exception of the Communists and Socialists, nearly all parties in UNO had been formed after 1985, albeit on the basis of long-standing traditional political currents, and had weak or nonexistent organizational bases and no proven independent electoral base.[16]

The secondary role played by the parties during UNO's electoral campaign was carried over into the new Chamorro government. The president, her top advisers, and nearly all cabinet ministers had no party affiliation whatsoever. The parties initiated efforts to build new social bases on the basis of their presence in the municipal governments and in the National Assembly.

The following list includes only those parties represented in the National Assembly as a result of the 1990 elections.[17] Although the seven parties which ran independent of UNO and the FSLN maintain a legal presence in the country, they have been largely marginalized since they have no parliamentary representation.[18] Also, at least three new parties were formed shortly after the elections, including the Nicaraguan Resistance Civic Organization, made up of ex-contras. (The information given below on these parties includes: whether or not the party belongs to UNO; who its principal leaders are; how many National Assembly seats were won in the 1990 elections; and when the party was formed.)

## Liberals

**Independent Liberal Party (PLI):** UNO; Virgilio Godoy; Five seats in the National Assembly. Formed in 1947 by dissidents from Somoza's Nationalist Liberal Party, the PLI belongs to the Liberal International and is officially recognized by the U.S. Democratic Party. In the immediate period after 1979 the PLI collaborated with the FSLN and Godoy served as Labor Minister under the Sandinistas until 1984. The PLI came in third in the 1984 elections with close to 10 percent of the vote. The PLI is probably the best-organized party within UNO.

**Neo-Liberal Party (PALI):** UNO; Jorge Ramírez and Andrés Zúñiga; Three seats in the National Assembly. Split from the PLI in 1986 and received legal status in 1989.

**Constitutionalist Liberal Party (PLC):** UNO and Nicaraguan Democratic Coordinating Committee (CDN); Ernesto Somarriba and Jaime Cuadra; Five seats in the National Assembly. The PLC split with Somoza's Nationalist Liberal Party in 1968. The PLC is harshly anticommunist. Managua's controversial Mayor Arnoldo Alemán belongs to the PLC.

## Conservatives

**Popular Conservative Alliance Party (PAPC):** UNO and CDN; Miriam Argüello; Six seats in the National Assembly. Split from the mainline Democratic Conservative Party (PCD) in 1984 and received legal status in 1989. Argüello, an ally of Virgilio Godoy, was elected president of the National Assembly in 1990.

**National Conservative Party (PNC):** UNO and CDN; Silviano Matamoros and Mario Rappaccioli; Five seats in the National Assembly. Split from the PCD in 1984 and received legal status in 1989. The PNC represents Nicaragua's traditional oligarchy, and of the country's four conservative party factions, it is the one party officially recognized by the Conservative International.

## Social Democrats

**Social Democratic Party (PSD):** UNO and CDN; Guillermo Potoy and Alfredo César; Five seats in the National Assembly. The PSD was formed mostly by ex-conservatives shortly after the 1979 Sandinista victory. Starting in 1981 its membership declined sharply as several leaders left to join the contras (including Alfredo César, Pedro Joaquín Chamorro, and Fernando Chamorro). During the 1980s the PSD enjoyed close ties to the Catholic church hierarchy and to *La Prensa*. It is linked to the Confederation of Trade Union Unity (CUS) federation. With Violeta Chamorro's victory it is now well positioned around the presidency. Many observers predict that social democrats, led by the PSD, will begin to displace the traditionally dominant liberal and conservative tendencies during the 1990s. César, a close adviser to President Chamorro and a key player within UNO, is widely believed to be positioning himself for a run for the presidency in the next general elections.

**Nicaraguan Democratic Movement (MDN):** UNO; Alfonso Robelo; Three seats in the National Assembly. The MDN, formed in 1978, transferred en masse to the counterrevolutionary forces in the early 1980s and returned to the country to register for the elections in 1989. Robelo was named Nicaraguan ambassador to Costa Rica by Chamorro.

## Social Christians

**Popular Social Christian Party (PPSC):** UNO; Luís Humberto Guzmán; Two seats in the National Assembly. The PPSC won 5.6 percent of the votes in the 1984 elections. In September 1989 the PPSC formally withdrew from UNO, but two of its representatives who stayed with the alliance won seats in the elections as part of the UNO slate.

**National Democratic Confidence Party (PDCN):** UNO; Agustín Jarquín and Adán Fletes; Five seats in the National Assembly. Split from the mainline Social Christian Party (PSC) in 1986 and received legal recognition in 1989. The PDCN has strong ties to the autonomous Nicaraguan Workers Federation (CTN-A) led by Carlos Huembes.

**National Action Party (PAN):** UNO; Eduardo Rivas Gasteazoro; Three seats in the National Assembly. Split from the PSC in 1985 and received legal status in 1989.

## Others

**Nicaraguan Socialist Party (PSN):** UNO; Gustavo Tablada and Luís Sánchez; Three seats in the National Assembly. Nicaragua's traditional communist party, formed in 1944, the PSN steadily moved toward the right after the mid-1980s. The PSN has a well-organized national structure, and is tied to the Independent General Labor Federation (CGT-I). Tablada serves as UNO's agrarian-reform minister and Sánchez, a key Chamorro ally, is the National Assembly's first vice president.

**Communist Party of Nicaragua (PC de N):** UNO; Elí Altamirano and Roberto Moreno; Three seats in the National Assembly. Split from the PSN in 1970. The Communist Party's labor wing is the Trade Union Action and Unity Confederation (CAUS). Altamirano has become a close ally of Godoy.

**Central American Integrationist Party (PIAC):** UNO; One seat in the National Assembly. The PIAC formally belongs to UNO, although the party was not granted legal status in time for the 1990 elections. The PIAC is a splinter party originating with the Central American Unionist Party (PUCA), which ran independent of UNO in the 1990 elections.

**Conservative National Action (ANC):** UNO; Two seats in the National Assembly. Like the PIAC, the ANC did not receive legal status before the 1990 elections.

**Social Christian Party (PSC):** The PSC ran independently of UNO in the 1990 elections with Erick Ramírez as its presidential candidate. An electoral alliance was formed between the PSC and the PPSC, and another with the Miskito Indian organization Yatama. Yatama broke its alliance with the PSC, switching to UNO before the elections, but it was too late to have the ballot changed. The PSC-Yatama candidate won a seat representing the North Atlantic Autonomous Region (RAAN). In practice, the representative has voted with UNO on all legislative initiatives.

**Revolutionary Unity Movement (MUR):** Francisco Samper and Moisés Hassán; One seat in the National Assembly. Formed in 1988 by ex-members of several leftist parties, including the FSLN, the MUR was awarded a seat in the National Assembly for having won more than one percent of the vote for president. The seat went to Hassán, a former Sandinista leader, who was expelled from the MUR in July 1990 for having consistently voted with the UNO bloc in the legislature and for public statements in support of controversial government initiatives, both of which the party leadership opposed.

**Sandinista National Liberation Front (FSLN):** Party leadership is in the hands of an eight-member National Directorate led by Daniel Ortega.[19] The FSLN has 38 elected representatives in the National Assembly, plus an additional seat which went to Daniel Ortega as the losing presidential candidate. Founded in 1961 by Tomás Borge, Carlos Fonseca, and Silvio Mayorga. During the course of the armed struggle against

Somoza, the FSLN split into three tendencies over differences regarding alliances and the strategy for confronting the dictatorship. A year and a half before the 1979 victory, the tendencies were reunited and throughout the 1980s the party remained united, although several high-level individual desertions did occur. Ideologically the FSLN is a hybrid. Among the leadership and base can be found marxists, socialists, social democrats, and Catholic priests as well as evangelical pastors. The party is rooted in nationalist and anti-imperialist traditions.[20] The Sandinista Workers Federation (CST) has served the labor wing of the FSLN. As the governing party, it also had affiliated mass organizations among youth, women, rural workers, and the peasantry.

## Coalitions and Elections

In 1980 the provisional government announced that national elections would be held in 1985. The decision was harshly criticized by the right wing and by Washington, both of which called for elections to be held immediately. The governing junta argued that holding elections at such an early date would represent a major diversion of energies and resources at a time when the top national priority should be economic reconstruction. Given that elections in Nicaragua had historically been used as an instrument to legitimize those already in power—even the Somozas occasionally held "elections"—many in the revolutionary government also questioned the validity of holding elections under the conditions prevailing during the early 1980s. For starters, more than half the population was illiterate. Prior to 1979 legitimate political organizing activity, outside of the clandestine activities of the left, had been practically nonexistent. With the mass insurrection still a fresh memory, and popular enthusiasm for the goals of national reconstruction running high, even unsympathetic observers conceded that the FSLN would have won an overwhelming majority of votes at this stage.

In the absence of a single opposition party or leader who could act as a magnet to attract popular support, anti-Sandinista forces—with the United States providing funding, guidance, and logistical support—engaged in intense efforts beginning in 1983 to build broad opposition coalitions. The Nicaraguan Democratic Coordinator (CDN) was consolidated in 1983 with a view toward presenting a united rightwing opposition front and a single presidential candidate in the elections, by that time scheduled for November 1984. The CDN, which would later go on to form the core of UNO, was dominated by far-right politicians and COSEP, although other groups had formal representation in the alliance.

The bulk of the country's more independent-minded center and center-right parties maintained their distance from the CDN.

Urged on by the Reagan administration, the CDN's political parties eventually boycotted the 1984 elections. After months of internal squabbling, Arturo Cruz, a banker and one-time member of the provisional government junta, was named CDN presidential candidate only to withdraw from the contest after a four-day campaign. Despite the fact that the Sandinistas brought the CDN into the process of negotiating the electoral ground rules, and later made additional concessions in an effort to assure their participation, the CDN refused to reverse its position. According to senior Reagan administration officials, "[We] never contemplated letting Cruz stay in the race, because then the Sandinistas could justifiably claim that the elections were legitimate."[21] At the time, U.S. strategy was centered around military support for the contras, and the pro-U.S. internal political opposition was largely relegated to an adjunct role. By 1990 these positions would be inverted.

Despite Washington's attempts to bolster support for the contra project through the electoral boycott and contra military efforts to impede voters from going to the polls, the balloting was held according to schedule without the CDN. On November 4, 1984, 76 percent of registered voters cast their ballots. The FSLN won 67 percent of the vote and six opposition parties representing the right, center, and left split the remainder.[22] The Reagan White House denounced the elections as a "Soviet-style sham." In contrast, almost all of the more than 500 officially registered international observers and some 1,500 journalists on hand agreed to the integrity of the electoral process and results.[23] The White House's boycott largely succeeded in delegitimizing the elections in Washington, but it had much less success in Nicaragua, Latin America and Western Europe. Observers calculated that even had the CDN stayed in the race and obtained all of the votes of those who abstained plus 20 percent of the FSLN's votes, an optimistic scenario by any standards, the Sandinistas still would have won the elections.[24]

According to the constitution, the next general elections were to be held in November 1990. In the framework of the Esquipulas peace negotiations, however, the Sandinista government decided to move up the date for elections by ten months to February of 1990, reform the country's electoral legislation to conform with the opposition's main demands, pass a new media law, and open the entire electoral process up to extensive international observation. These and other initiatives were made in exchange for commitments by the other Central American countries to collaborate in disbanding the contras. By May 1989 Nicaragua had fulfilled its side of the bargain even though effective contra demobilization still was blocked by the intransigence of contra leaders and U.S. foot-dragging.

With the political space opened up in preparation for the elections, the United States – particularly through the National Endowment for Democracy (NED) – sent in millions of dollars and dozens of advisers and "party-building experts" to unite the scattered internal opposition into a cohesive anti-Sandinista force. Established in late 1983, NED is recognized by an act of Congress and functions as a quasi-private organization to channel U.S. Information Agency (USIA) and U.S. Agency for International Development (AID) monies to U.S. and foreign private organizations that support U.S. foreign-policy goals.[25]

Amidst the flurry of political activity in mid-1989 around party legalization for the 1990 elections, UNO ("one" in Spanish) was born. An eclectic grouping of 14 parties, their affiliated trade-union federations, and COSEP, UNO began hammering out an electoral strategy and building the support structures necessary to implement it. The formal party alliance was bolstered by NED-supported groups that worked to mobilize different sectors of Nicaraguan society: labor, women, the media, and youth. (See U.S. Economic Aid)

In the United States NED support was billed as backing nonpartisan democratic institutions and practices. In reality, however, the Nicaragua project focused exclusively on one sector of the anti-Sandinista opposition, UNO, marginalizing more centrist and less openly pro-U.S. sectors.[26]

The mainline parties of the center and center-right that had taken the lion's share of the opposition vote in the 1984 elections – the PDCN, the PPSC, the PLIUN, and the Social Christians who were with the CDN at that time – either chose to stay out of UNO, or withdrew or were expelled shortly after its formation.[27] In the end, seven opposition parties ran in the 1990 elections independently of UNO. A leader of one of them, the Social Christian Party, complained that NED funds had undercut the independent political parties: "The United States funded only those groups that would go along with what the United States wanted for Nicaragua."[28]

Once the centrist parties had been flushed out of UNO, the appearance of ideological diversity within the coalition was largely reduced to the continued presence of the Socialist and Communist parties. Although their inclusion was clearly significant, these forces were for the most part far outgunned by the coalition's conservative core, represented by the far-right parties which had belonged to the CDN and COSEP. Beyond the main factors of U.S. funding and pressures – assistance from

Washington was contingent upon unity—the disparate forces in UNO came together, and managed to stay together, out of pragmatic concerns. Frustrated from ten years of ineffectual opposition, and recognizing that going into the elections individually would tend to relegate them to the same position, the members came to see that only by subordinating their ideological and political differences to unity would they be able to take advantage of the electoral opening.

Despite this conviction, the lengthy and heated process of selecting a presidential candidate nearly tore the fragile alliance apart. In the end, unity was achieved around the compromise Chamorro-Godoy ticket. Even so, the divisions which opened up at that time—the three basic poles consisted of Violeta Chamorro and her advisers, old-line politicians grouped around Godoy, and COSEP—would persist throughout the campaign and grow sharper still during UNO's first three months in office.

Throughout the campaign UNO divided its energies between two contradictory sets of activities. On the one hand the coalition attempted to delegitimize the electoral process itself, repeatedly threatening to withdraw from the race and denounce it as fraudulent. On the other UNO made serious efforts to win as much support as possible among the electorate. In part, this schizophrenic electoral style reflected the belief among many within UNO that the FSLN would win the elections, but it also was a reflection of the very real divisions within the coalition. The rightwing sectors were more interested in toppling the Sandinistas by whatever means necessary, even if that meant withdrawing from the race, denouncing fraud, and calling for foreign intervention to remove the "illegitimate" government. Moderates, on the other hand, were more interested in sticking to the rules of the game, believing they could actually win or, if not, at least gain a substantial foothold as a legitimate opposition force.

Under the watchful eyes of more than 1,000 international observers—all sides agreed that this was the most closely scrutinized electoral process in history—Nicaraguans cast their votes on February 25, 1990. The upset victory gave UNO presidential candidate Violeta Chamorro 54.7 percent of the popular vote to Daniel Ortega's 40.8 percent for the FSLN. In terms of percentage, the UNO presidential victory was closely paralleled in races for the National Assembly, while UNO candidates swept 32 of the municipal races in large cities and towns to the FSLN's ten.[29] Although several voting locations had to close down due to contra activity, more than 86 percent of all registered voters went to the polls, up from 76 percent in the 1984 elections. The observer missions—headed by the United

Nations, the Organization of American States, and the Carter Center —
unanimously testified to the fairness and integrity of the polling process
and the vote count.[30]

Within days of the elections, dozens of theories had begun to circu-
late regarding the reasons behind the electoral results.[31] In many ways, it
was apparent that the vote was more a plebiscite-type rejection of the
FSLN's reelection bid than an expression of active support for the UNO
program or for the parties which belonged to the alliance. Many
Nicaraguans simply voted for a change. Four days before the elections,
Alfredo César, one of Chamorro's closest advisers, candidly admitted
that UNO was in fact aware that it did not need to persuade Nicaraguans
to vote for Chamorro or her program. All UNO needed to do was to "con-
vince them that their vote can change the country."[32]

Above all, "changing the country" boiled down to two things: ending
the war and reversing economic decline. During the campaign, UNO successfully portrayed itself as the only party that could bring peace — with
the contras and with the United States — to a populace which had been
devastated and exhausted by war. Likewise, the economic deterioration
suffered by the majority of Nicaraguans had become so acute that UNO's
promises of prosperity, and of the turnaround in relations with
Washington necessary to achieve it, were difficult to resist. President
Bush had promised to lift the economic embargo if Chamorro won, and
there was a general sensation that an UNO victory would result in a
generous flow of U.S. aid. Some evidence indicates that a significant portion of the electorate saw the United States as the prime factor behind
the war and the economic crisis and voted for UNO on the conviction that
it would get the United States off Nicaragua's back.[33]

When the FSLN agreed to move up the elections date as part of its
commitment to the Esquipulas peace process, it had anticipated entering
the campaign with contra demobilization an achieved fact and the
demilitarization process — including suspension of the draft and a reduction of the army — well underway. In fact, the contras not only avoided
demobilization, but during the electoral campaign succeeded in relaunch-
ing the war which had largely petered out over the previous two years.
The specter of continued war, together with the government's refusal to
suspend the draft, were by most accounts the primary factors influencing
voters' decisions.

In the economic terrain, harsh austerity measures sustained over a
two-year period, seen by the government as necessary for laying a foundation for economic recovery over the long term, exacted a heavy price.
"The Sandinistas' program of structural adjustment," wrote analyst Car-

los Vilas in evaluating the electoral defeat, "was no different from anyone else's: It favored the rich and hurt the poor. And it gave official confirmation that there was no legitimate room in the revolutionary economy for a good part of *sandinismo's* social underpinnings."[34] In this respect, the FSLN found itself in the same position as nearly all incumbent regimes in Latin America that had presided over periods of sharp economic decline during the 1980s.

Factors internal to the FSLN also played a role. Convinced from the outset of the inevitability of victory, the Sandinistas ran a campaign designed to secure and widen their victory margin, rather than actively win over the voters. In addition to the relative absence of substantive content in the FSLN campaign, the Sandinistas also failed to explain to the population what the real implications of an UNO victory might be. Those factors which contributed to weaknesses in the campaign were further aggravated by a series of public opinion polls which showed a solid and growing margin in favor of the FSLN.[35]

The Sandinistas' slick, high-profile campaign, seen as arrogant and lavish by many Nicaraguans, fueled a "protest vote" phenomenon. Many voters who had no affinity for UNO, and in some cases even identified with the Sandinista program and policies, decided to "punish" the FSLN by voting for UNO to reduce what they saw as its inevitably wide margin of victory.[36] Even victorious UNO legislative candidate Luís Humberto Guzmán declared just two days after the elections that "the vote wasn't a vote for UNO, but a vote to punish the FSLN."[37] The arrogant campaign crystallized widespread disaffection with the FSLN's leadership style which had been brewing for years. Factors such as the reliance on top-down chains of command, the lack of democratic procedures for selecting leaders within the party and mass organizations, and the tendency to close ranks behind long-standing party members who fell out of grace, often for good reasons, with the grassroots had eroded the FSLN's image among the population to a degree that the leadership never imagined.[38]

As a candidate Violeta Chamorro was often belittled as a poor public speaker, and indeed UNO's campaign rallies were generally quite small. Nonetheless, the FSLN seriously miscalculated the degree to which the symbolism behind Chamorro—portrayed as the heroic, self-sacrificing widow of one of the martyrs of the anti-Somoza struggle, a devout Catholic close to Cardinal Obando, and a mother who had managed to keep her family together despite fierce ideological differences among her four children—could persuade Nicaraguans to vote for UNO. The candidate's advisers were extremely successful at integrating the two most important traditional institutions in Nicaragua—church and family—into

Chamorro's campaign themes and images and at portraying the Sandinistas as irreconcilable enemies of these same institutions.

## A Difficult Transition

In the predawn hours of February 26, 1990 Daniel Ortega visited Violeta Chamorro in her home to congratulate the president-elect for her electoral victory. Embracing Ortega, Chamorro declared, "Here there are neither victors nor vanquished." Those on the left and the right who wrote the statement off as a publicity stunt and had begun the countdown for the eruption of an inevitable civil war were increasingly startled as the transition process unfolded. For practical and strategic reasons, Chamorro and her closest advisers agreed to break with the long-standing Nicaraguan tradition of decimating the losers. The structures, institutions, and constitutional order erected while the Sandinistas had been in power would be left in place, including the armed forces. The FSLN would assume the position of a legal opposition party, in effect moving into a political space that had been created by the Sandinista revolution itself.

High-level teams from the outgoing and incoming governments, led by Antonio Lacayo for UNO and Sandinista Army chief General Humberto Ortega for the FSLN, negotiated a seven-point Transition Protocol to guide the transfer of power from the FSLN to UNO.[39] The essence of the pact, signed on March 27th after a month of tense negotiations, was respect for the existing constitutional order, including the state apparatus and armed forces which had been built up since 1979.[40] The signing of the protocol was seen as a landmark event, both because it served to defuse the short-term threat of civil war and because it constituted the foundation for the first democratic transfer of government in Nicaragua's history.

The right wing within UNO had a radically different vision of what the transition should look like. Its members launched a barrage of criticism against the agreement and labeled Chamorro's advisers as traitors for having negotiated with the FSLN. They argued that UNO's election victory gave them the mandate to impose their program regardless of the consequences and of the FSLN's demands for the security of its supporters. Antonio Lacayo's response, however, was categorical: "What happened in Nicaragua [on February 25] was not a social revolution, but an election victory within the legal order."[41]

The Chamorro group clearly recognized that in the absence of minimal guarantees for security and stability, the transfer of power itself would be jeopardized. But the transition protocol also reflected the deeper motivation among Chamorro's inner circle—their sharp ideological differences with the FSLN notwithstanding—to break the syndrome of victors and vanquished.[42] During the transition talks, Lacayo recalled how throughout Nicaraguan history, the winning political force "would throw the losers out the back door....We must break that cycle."[43] Breaking that cycle was seen not as a concession to the Sandinistas but as the only practical way to move toward the political and social stability necessary for implementing UNO's program of economic recovery and development.

The Chamorro government's first 100 days in office highlighted the contradictions which the spirit behind the transition protocol would have to confront in practice. First, that spirit was widely repudiated by important sectors in and around UNO, sectors whose collaboration Chamorro would need in order to govern. The far right within UNO, sectors of the Catholic church hierarchy, and COSEP left little room for doubt that the number one item on their agenda was the rapid elimination of *sandinismo* by any means necessary. Second, talk of reconciliation, pluralist democracy, and peaceful coexistence were increasingly undermined in practice as the government moved to dismantle the key institutions engendered by the revolutionary process. Third, although the Chamorro group was willing to act pragmatically in reaching substantive agreements with the FSLN in order to assure a modicum of stability, it was at the same time working hard on many fronts toward the more long-range goal of politically marginalizing its chief adversary, the Sandinista opposition. Many came to feel that "throwing the losers out the back door" had simply been exchanged for more gracefully and slowly escorting them out.

## UNO in Government

By the end of UNO's first 100 days in office the coalition's diverse factions had jelled into two distinct groupings. One sector, led by President Chamorro, was characterized by a moderate and tempered approach to resolving the country's pressing problems. The second sector, more ideological and extremist in vision, was headed by Vice President Virgilio Godoy and included the group of far-right political parties from UNO. The leadership of COSEP had, for the most part, thrown its weight behind the Godoy faction. Although differences existed over a wide array of issues, the most important factors separating the two factions were their stances vis-a-vis the Sandinista opposition and the scope and pace of change needed to roll back the social and economic transformations undertaken after 1979.

Although both factions shared an anti-Sandinista outlook and agreed on the need to isolate and weaken the FSLN, major differences emerged over how to achieve these goals. The pragmatists believed that to govern and implement the UNO program, Chamorro would have to assure a minimum of stability by working through peaceful means and within the bounds of certain national realities. The fact that the FSLN represented more than 40 percent of a highly politicized and well-organized population constituted the foremost of those realities. Essentially the Chamorro group felt that in the short run the government could tolerate a legitimate Sandinista opposition and that the best way to neutralize *sandinismo* was through a protracted campaign waged principally in the ideological terrain aimed at coopting, dividing, and domesticating the FSLN. The Godoy faction and COSEP, by and large, shared the radically different view that implementing UNO's program required the swift and total elimination of *sandinismo*, through violent means if need be.

But the divisions within UNO had begun long before Chamorro donned the presidential sash. During the electoral campaign, parallel structures and power centers within the coalition had become evident. Major decisions and the tone of the campaign itself were increasingly in the hands of candidate Chamorro and her "inner circle" of personal advisers. The coalition structures grouped around the UNO Political Council — formally the alliance's highest decision-making body, comprising one representative from each of the 14 political parties — were often left watching from the sidelines. After a brief honeymoon in the wake of the February 25 victory, the delicate negotiations with the FSLN on the transfer of power brought the divisions out into the open as the "inner circle" took exclusive responsibility for managing the transition.

On April 26, 1990 when Chamorro's new cabinet reported for its first day of work, there was no room left for speculation: not a single representative from the Political Council or from COSEP occupied a ministerial post.[44] Vice President Godoy was given no specific functions within the government and was even denied an office in the presidential office complex. The overwhelming majority of ministerial positions were given to professionals and technocrats with little prior experience in politics and no party affiliation whatsoever. The three most delicate assignments, the Ministries of Defense, Presidency, and Interior, went respectively to Chamorro herself, to her son-in-law and closest adviser Antonio Lacayo, and to Carlos Hurtado, Chamorro's cousin and a close associate of her number-two adviser Alfredo César. Much of the rest of the cabinet came from the Commission for the Reconstruction and Development of Nicaragua (CORDENIC), a "group of experts" to which Chamorro had repeatedly consulted during the campaign.[45]

Inspired by the Esquipulas II Peace Accords, CORDENIC was formed in 1988 as a think tank which sought to facilitate debate on policy alternatives for the eventual peacetime reconstruction of the Nicaraguan economy.[46] CORDENIC founding members in Chamorro's cabinet included Foreign Minister Enrique Dreyfus (CORDENIC's founder and President); Minister of the Presidency Antonio Lacayo; Central Bank President Francisco Mayorga (CORDENIC General Secretary); and Labor Minister Francisco Rosales. Agriculture Minister Roberto Rondón and Minister of Economy and Development Silvio de Franco are also affiliated with CORDENIC. CORDENIC Vice President Felipe Mántica, a prominent Nicaraguan businessman and member of the charismatic Catholic group City of God, is also a personal adviser to Chamorro as is his brother Carlos, who is the founder of City of God.[47] (See Religion)

Prior to the electoral campaign, CORDENIC's main activity consisted of sponsoring a series of seminars on economic strategy held under the auspices of the Harvard-linked Central American Institute of Business Administration (INCAE).[48] In Nicaragua's highly charged political atmosphere, where the opposition's discourse on Sandinista economic policy was dominated by the extremist positions of COSEP, CORDENIC stood out for its attempts to substitute technical and professional criteria for ideological ones in debates on the economy.[49] In the emerging division, COSEP was seen as the conservative old guard, mainly representing traditional sectors of Nicaraguan capital in agroexports. CORDENIC, whose younger technocrats had studied engineering, business, or financial administration in places such as Harvard, MIT, and the Sorbonne, was more closely linked to modernizing factions in agroindustry.

Monopoly control over the cabinet gave the Chamorro group the upper hand in the central government apparatus and the executive branch. A shuffling of the Supreme Court in late July 1990 served to bring the judicial branch under effective control of the presidency as well.[50] But in the National Assembly, the municipal councils, and at the grassroots level, UNO's rightwing parties – bitter opponents of Chamorro's handling of a long list of major issues – clearly had the upper hand. On at least two occasions during Chamorro's first five months in office, the right's most prominent leader, Vice President Godoy, was involved in what the government interpreted as incipient movements toward a coup d'etat.[51] "In any part of the civilized world," complained Chamorro ally Alfredo César, "the vice president of the Republic owes loyalty to the president.... Only in Nicaragua can you see cases in which the vice president, who accepted this role subordinate to the president, promotes actions against the will of the government."[52]

The new municipal governments were seen as a major power base for the Godoy faction, which reportedly counted on the sympathies of some 70 percent of all UNO-controlled municipal councils, including Managua which was led by Mayor Arnoldo Alemán. The UNO-controlled councils were seen as key institutions to be used in the process of constructing and mobilizing a grassroots social base to support the UNO program and in confronting Sandinista institutions and initiatives at the local level.[53]

The most graphic example of the threat posed by UNO's right flank came during the heat of the July 1990 general strike. Criticizing the government's hesitation to employ force in confronting striking workers and barricade builders, Godoy went public with the formation of a National Salvation Commission, under the direction of a handful of UNO's better-known hardliners.[54] Chamorro publicly denounced the commission as "extra-governmental" on the same day it was formed. Within weeks, however, Godoy announced that the commission was working on the formation of a network of National Salvation Committees at the town and village level. Godoy asserted that the salvation committees were to be used in the eventuality of a future social confrontation on the scale of the July strike. Some saw in them the makings of paramilitary death squads, while others were convinced they formed part of a larger plan aimed at bringing down the Chamorro government, to pave the way for the rise of the far right.[55]

COSEP, by any standards a major power bloc within UNO, was in a unique position. Having largely spearheaded political opposition to the Sandinistas during the 1980s, COSEP shared the resentment of the Political Council's party leaders at having been brushed aside in Chamorro's cabinet appointments. The organization's bitter feuds with Chamorro's advisers actually stretched back to the formative days of the UNO alliance. COSEP leaders felt they had been cheated and undermined by newcomers like Lacayo and César who managed to assure candidate Chamorro's nomination over the early favorite, COSEP nominee Enrique Bolaños. Their frustrations were only compounded when the UNO politicians edged Bolaños out of the vice presidential slot in favor of Godoy. Following the elections, COSEP's ideological instincts prevailed and, for the most part, the group sided with Godoy in denouncing President Chamorro's "conciliatory" gestures toward the Sandinistas.

But COSEP's stance toward the government was also motivated by concerns outside the realm of politics. As the country's main organization of capitalists, it had expected that the UNO electoral victory would result in the rapid privatization of the state sector of the economy, a process in which most of the spoils would be divided up among COSEP members. The government's cautious and methodological posture regarding privatization proved to be a major disappointment. (See State of the Economy) Similarly, although it shared the basic framework regarding economic policy employed by the government, COSEP was more closely wedded to classic neoliberal recipes than the INCAE-based technocrats who predominated in Chamorro's economic cabinet.

The Chamorro group's tenuous hold on power was further complicated by the ambiguous posture adopted by the Catholic church hierarchy and by the United States. Although for different reasons and at different times, both had largely embraced a strategy of alternately playing the Chamorro and Godoy factions off against each other, and at other times of throwing their support to both.

## The FSLN: Challenges for the 1990s

After more than a decade at the head of the government, preceded by more than 20 years leading the armed struggle against the Somoza dictatorship, the February 1990 elections threw the Sandinistas into the ranks of the political opposition. It was a role that the FSLN never expected and for which it was ill-prepared. The electoral defeat obliged the FSLN to enter into a process of identifying and correcting the errors which contributed to its stunning loss at the polls, redefining its identity as a party, and devising a new program and strategy capable of simultaneously defending the revolutionary gains of the 1980s and paving the way for retaking the reigns of government through elections, scheduled for 1996.

While the need to define new programs, platforms, and tasks for the party became a pressing priority after the Chamorro government's inauguration in April, the deeper challenge consisted of striking a new Sandinista identity. Given the dramatic changes which took place in the international order during 1989-1990, and the reality of a conservative U.S.-backed government installed through elections in Managua, the very definition of a revolutionary perspective in Nicaragua needed to be reformulated. Furthermore, the FSLN's 1969 Historic Program, which had largely served as the platform for guiding the revolutionary changes of the 1980s, had been for the most part exhausted by the time of the electoral defeat. A new platform needed to be agreed upon in accordance with the new conditions.

Both in terms of rectifying the mistakes which led to its electoral defeat and in hopes of moving forward, there was an emerging consensus within the FSLN over the need to democratize internal party structures and institute mechanisms to ensure closer connections with the party's base. The initial critiques of the reasons behind the electoral results pointed to a long list of factors.[56] Some were bound up directly or indirectly with the relentless siege imposed on the revolution since the arrival of the Reagan administration in 1981. Others emphasized political mistakes made by, and weaknesses within the FSLN itself. Reflecting on what many saw as the key dynamic of the 1990 electoral defeat, Sandinista leader Dionisio Marenco commented: "In ten years the Front adopted the psychology of a party in power. We lost our capacity to converse, to listen, to criticize ourselves, the capacity to measure."[57] The subsequent distancing from the majority of Nicaraguans who had once supported the Sandinistas was not only a major factor behind the electoral defeat itself, but also of the party's inability to have even foreseen such a possibility.

The FSLN's distancing from the masses did not occur overnight. Methods for decision-making and leadership styles within the party — which defined itself as the "vanguard of the Nicaraguan masses"[58] — had remained fundamentally unaltered over the course of three decades. The centralized leadership and vertical, top-down organizational methods which had been adopted in the 1960s and 1970s in order to operate as a clandestine movement against Somoza were maintained and reinforced during the 1980s in the face of U.S.-sponsored aggression against the revolutionary process. Outside of the nine-member National Directorate, and its adjunct Sandinista Assembly — a consultative body comprised of 105 leading party militants — there was little room for direct, grassroots participation in the definition of the strategic issues and tasks confronting the FSLN. While there was hardly a shortage of debate and discussion among the party's estimated 12,000 members,[59] once the National Directorate handed down its position on a given issue the entire party was expected to close ranks. Unity within the party was seen not just as an important goal, but as a prerequisite for survival. The FSLN also lacked democratic electoral procedures for selecting personnel for internal posts, and leaders at all levels of the party and affiliated mass organizations were appointed by those in the corresponding sector of the Sandinista hierarchy.

Within weeks of the electoral defeat most of the FSLN leadership and base had agreed on the need for thoroughgoing democratization and for an overhaul of the party's internal organization. These tasks had been postponed for years as, in typical Sandinista fashion, the leadership insisted on "waiting for better times." Significant differences did emerge, however, with respect to how far and how fast such changes should go and what priority they should be given in relation to the other pressing tasks facing the party.

Parallel to the efforts to democratize the party and to analyze the errors committed during the 1980s, the FSLN was engaged in a reevaluation of the ideological foundations of *sandinismo* — including the character of anti-imperialist struggles and the viability of socialist models in the 1990s — as well as a search for a new definition of the party itself. In both cases, several different tendencies existed within both the leadership and the base. Regarding the nature of the party, a few different options were being explored. One was to move toward the framework of a more traditional party oriented along social-democratic lines. While in power, the FSLN maintained observer status in the Socialist International (SI). After the electoral defeat, the SI invited the FSLN to become a member, a proposition which some sectors in the party were willing to consider and which others rejected outright.

Another option was to convert the FSLN into a mass membership party. In the months leading up to the elections, the party had already taken initial steps in this direction. Alternatively, the FSLN might retain the form it originally had taken: a vanguard party led by a small group of cadre. Some were proposing that the Sandinistas should attempt to move toward a synthesis of these two poles, becoming a "party of cadre and masses."

The task of redefining the strategic contours of the FSLN took place side by side with the more immediate imperatives imposed by the Chamorro government's aggressive posture during its first 100 days in office. The FSLN attempted to walk the fine line between its commitment to its supporters to "govern from below" — understood as defending key revolutionary gains and taking the side of the masses in their struggles against anti-popular measures imposed by the government — and its stated objective of playing the role of a constructive, legal opposition force.

The latter position, seen as opportunist by many within the rank and file, was motivated by a series of factors. First and foremost was the impulse to contribute to the government's stability in the face of threats posed by the far right, spearheaded by Godoy. Second, the FSLN needed to buy time in order to rebuild its base. It sought to accomplish this feat by helping to strengthen institutional protections for opposition political activity. It also hoped to contribute to the country's economic recovery in order to ensure the stability necessary to launch an effective electoral challenge in 1996.

These tensions were highlighted during the July 1990 general strike. The strikers and their supporters among the population criticized the FSLN leadership's lukewarm support for the strike, some accusing the Sandinistas of having undermined the unions by negotiating behind their backs and entering into a "co-government" with Chamorro. Rightwing politicians from UNO and some members of the Chamorro government, meanwhile, insisted that the strike was part of a Sandinista plot to topple the government. They labeled the FSLN leaders terrorists and called for their arrest.

Efforts to portray the FSLN as a corrupt band of delinquents had been initiated long before the July 1990 strike. The highlight of this campaign was the accusation, launched in multiple incarnations through the mass media, that the Sandinistas had pilfered the State apparatus between their electoral defeat in February and the transfer of power in April. *La Prensa* readers were treated to an almost daily fare of stories about the lame-duck Sandinistas' *piñata* (giveaway): cars sold to party faithfuls at bargain-basement prices, government offices stripped of equipment and furniture, and even funds sent from Central Bank coffers to foreign accounts. The FSLN, while accusing the government of grossly distorting the issue for political purposes, openly admitted that it had adopted a deliberate policy of compensating key government officials for the years of service they had put in working for low salaries. There also was a last-minute "handout" program which distributed property titles to residents of urban squatter settlements and peasants who had been occupying public lands, in many cases for several years.

During the FSLN's June 1990 assembly the leadership recognized that abuses and excesses had been committed in the process, and an "ethics commission" was formed to investigate specific charges and recommend sanctions. Despite these initiatives and attempts to provide evidence refuting some of the Chamorro government's wilder accusations, the fact that public goods had been dispensed in an arbitrary fashion was a source of bitterness among much of the population. People were able to understand some of the cases, but many others were seen as unjustifiable for a party ostensibly based on revolutionary morals and some of the actions were seen as downright scandalous.

The electoral defeat and intense events during Chamorro's initial period in office threatened not only to weaken the FSLN but to divide it. Efforts by the revolution's adversaries during the 1980s to force cleavages within Sandinista ranks reappeared with a vengeance. Major differences of opinion among Sandinistas, which before would have been handled within party circles, were now aired openly on the pages of the country's newspapers and on the radio.

Some of the speculation over divisions within the party focused on the resurfacing of the FSLN's three pre-insurrection tendencies. Prior to the formation of the National Directorate in 1979, the Sandinistas were divided into the proletarian tendency (led by Jaime Wheelock, Luís Carrión, and Carlos Núñez), the prolonged popular war tendency (Tomás Borge, Henry Ruíz, and Bayardo Arce), and the third way or insurrectional tendency (Daniel Ortega, Humberto Ortega, and Víctor Tirado López). The division of labor within the revolutionary state of the 1980s served to keep some elements of the earlier divisions alive. And although post-electoral differences between FSLN "hardliners" and "moderates" clearly revived some of the old animosities, the new situation was largely shaped by differences regarding questions largely removed from those of the 1970s. Similarly, while the three tendencies continued to hold sway among part of the historic party leadership, a new generation of grassroots activists, forged in the struggles of the 1980s, was pushing for a renovation of the FSLN leadership which cast the issues in different terms.

Through Chamorro's first 100 days in office, Sandinista ranks were full of effervescent debate on how to revitalize the party. During this period no formal divisions appeared, but conditions clearly existed for a serious bifurcation in the future. More than the question of historic tendencies or differences over interpreting the electoral defeat, the main issues of dispute centered on where the party should head in the immediate future. One pole felt that the future of *sandinismo* lay in rebuilding a broad popular consensus with a view toward capturing a majority in the 1996 elections. Adherents to this perspective believed that tactics and alliances should be subordinated to the prevailing conditions of the country. Such a viewpoint implied occasional support for the Chamorro government—for example in its efforts to isolate the UNO right wing. It also meant that the FSLN might advance political projects that appealed to those broad sectors of the electorate which had seen UNO as a centrist alternative.

Other members of the FSLN, including many of those close to the trade-union movement, were inclined to a more orthodox revolutionary perspective. These militants wanted the Sandinistas to place themselves at the head of the most radicalized sectors of the masses in their struggles to resist the anti-popular policies of the government.

Rather than a neat lining up of Sandinista forces behind two alternative approaches, differences of opinion among both the leadership and the base brought about a more fluid situation in which individuals staked out their positions in regard to a series of key issues:

* The need for maintaining the current party leadership versus the importance of a thoroughgoing modernization of the party, including the emergence of new leaders.[60] The latter position called for the "historic" Sandinista leadership, including at least some members of the current National Directorate, to step down to advisory positions.[61] In June 1990 it was decided that all party leadership positions, including the National Directorate, would be filled by secret ballot elections.[62]

* New social alliances for rebuilding the FSLN. Some Sandinistas called for rebuilding the worker-peasant alliance by reaching out to all forces — including ex-contras and UNO supporters — negatively affected by government policy.[63]

* The FSLN's place on the political spectrum and its international profile and alliances. This new identity was to include a definition of the anti-imperialist struggle appropriate to the 1990s.

* The type of economic model to advocate. Possible options included state-centered versus decentralized alternatives, orthodox stabilization versus a basic needs approach, and so on.

While many of these delicate issues would have to be resolved in practice as the FSLN found itself forced to take a stance in face of the daily struggles being waged in the country, the party was attempting to carry out the process of redefinition and reorganization in the most orderly fashion circumstances would allow. The June 1990 assembly of FSLN militants agreed to sponsor the first-ever party congress which will be held in July 1991. Preparatory discussions for the congress would take place at the grassroots level, and local assemblies would be responsible for electing delegates. The congress itself was to be a public event open to all Nicaraguans.

# Foreign Policy

On April 25, 1990 the U.S. delegation to President Chamorro's inauguration touched down at Managua's Sandino Airport. Vice President Dan Quayle, leading a 95-member delegation which included long-standing contra supporters like Jeane Kirkpatrick, Jeb Bush, and Bernard Aronson, was no doubt pleased to see the U.S. flag flying alongside the Nicaraguan one. The tribute was not repeated for any of the other visiting delegations.[64]

Quayle and others in his entourage surely had visions of an updated version of the type of U.S.-Nicaragua relations which existed before 1979. As a key U.S. ally, the Somoza dictatorship's foreign policy was largely a reflection of U.S. interests in the region. But the legacy of 11 years of Sandinista rule, plus the fact that the regional and international political map was radically different in 1990 than in 1979, made such visions all but impossible in practice. Despite the fact that Chamorro was largely in debt to Washington for her electoral victory, and that many of the key players in UNO enjoyed close ties to the United States, Nicaraguan foreign policy in the 1990s promised to be dictated more by pragmatic concerns than by ideological ones. After all, "diversified dependence" – including aid and trade relations with Japan, Western Europe, and the Soviet Union – was just as advantageous to Chamorro as it had been to the Sandinistas. With Nicaragua for the most part dropped off the list of U.S. foreign-policy priorities – a fact driven home by foot-dragging over approval of a $300 million aid package for the new government – it could hardly be otherwise.

Thus in many ways, Chamorro's foreign policy would be based more on a continuation of that followed by the Sandinistas than on a radical break with the past. Nonetheless, a few key distinctions stood out. Where relations with the United States during the 1980s had been adversarial, the UNO government would attempt to make them cordial without falling into submission.[65] The militancy and activism which characterized the Sandinistas' nonaligned diplomacy would be abandoned in favor of a greater concentration by the foreign ministry on matters of economic assistance and cooperation.[66]

Symbolically, this shift in priorities could be seen by the difference in who sat at the top. The chief of Sandinista diplomacy, for example, was Maryknoll priest Father Miguel D'Escoto, an eloquent and forceful speaker who took up as a crusade the defense of Nicaraguan sovereignty in international forums. In contrast, Chamorro's foreign minister, Enrique Dreyfus, is one of the country's key representatives of private enterprise. Dreyfus, who enjoys extensive contacts in international trade and financial circles, was the key architect behind the formation of CORDENIC in 1988. (See Political Parties)

Under the Sandinista government, Nicaragua's foreign policy was framed by the concepts and practices of nonalignment. The Sandinista leadership's early decision to pursue a course of nonalignment was based on the conviction that only through diversification of trade and aid relations could the country break its historic dependence on the United States. Toward this end, Nicaragua in 1979 became the eighth nation in the hemisphere to join the Non-Aligned Movement (NAM). Deeper ideological considerations also came into play in these early foreign-policy decisions, including the lofty goal of constructing a new national identity from the rubble of *somocismo.*[67]

In the diplomatic realm, authentic nonalignment was achieved with relatively few problems. The bottom line was to accept relations with any country that respected Nicaragua's right to self-determination. Diplomatic and trade relations were maintained throughout the 1980s with dozens of countries in Asia, the Middle East, Africa, and Eastern Europe.

The Sandinistas' efforts to diversify trading partners and aid sources brought more mixed results. By 1987 Western Europe had become Nicaragua's leading trade partner, receiving almost half of all Nicaragua's exports and providing more than a third of all imports.[68] But after 1985, in part due to the U.S. trade embargo and pressures on international lending institutions, Nicaragua became heavily dependent on external credits, and the shortfall in foreign aid for development or economic-stabilization measures became a major problem.[69]

In the area of military assistance, diversification proved all but impossible. From 1979 through 1981 the young Sandinista government made concerted efforts to secure military assistance from Western countries, mainly the United States, but to no avail.[70] With the advent of an openly hostile Republican administration in Washington, Nicaragua accepted armaments donations from the Soviet Union and several Council for Mutual Economic Assistance (COMECOM) countries. Throughout the years of the contra war, these countries continued to act as Nicaragua's principal source of arms.

Foreign Minister Dreyfus has publicly asserted that his government plans to continue as a member of the Non-Aligned Movement. Out of practical necessity, the Chamorro government declared its intention to push for the maintenance of Soviet aid levels, a position which was openly backed by Washington. UNO had placed high hopes on a close relationship with conservative governments in Western Europe and with Japan, but thse hopes were only partially realized as foreign donors found other priorities, like Eastern Europe, for their economic aid.

## Relations with the United States

As U.S.-sponsored aggression developed in the early 1980s an increasingly important aspect of Sandinista diplomacy was its effort to ward off a potential U.S. invasion. Nicaragua worked to build international opposition to the diverse forms of U.S. destabilization, while actively seeking peace.

The high point in this campaign began in 1984 when Nicaragua opened a lawsuit against the United States in the International Court of Justice. Nicaragua accused the United States of violating the UN Charter, the OAS Charter, the longstanding Treaty of Friendship, Commerce, and Navigation between Nicaragua and the United States, customary law, and other international juridical commitments. In June 1986 the Court handed down its verdict, declaring the United States—which refused to accept the Court's jurisdiction over the case—the aggressor country. It ordered a cessation of all hostilities and reparations for damages to Nicaragua. The verdict gave credence to Nicaragua's claim to the moral and legal high ground of the conflict, giving Managua greater leverage in its diplomatic efforts to isolate U.S. war policy. Following the verdict, Nicaragua formally petitioned the court to demand $17 billion in reparations. With the Chamorro government in office, the U.S. Embassy moved quickly to pressure Managua to drop the World Court case. In response, Chamorro declared that she would not withdraw the case, but rather would seek a negotiated extrajudicial solution with the United States. "We're trying to ensure," commented Antonio Lacayo, "that the United States looks at Nicaragua as a friend."[71]

On many occasions the Sandinista government tried a conciliatory approach, launching several initiatives to resolve its differences with the United States through bilateral channels and negotiations.[72] Despite Nicaragua's efforts, in late 1984, after several rounds of talks held in Manzanillo, Mexico, Washington abandoned the bilateral negotiations with its Sandinista adversaries. By 1985, in the wake of the U.S. declaration of the trade embargo when diplomatic relations began to deteriorate irreversibly, Managua already had presented Washington with more than 30 peace initiatives.[73] Sandinista peace offers proposed the withdrawal of all foreign military advisers from Nicaragua, El Salvador, and Honduras. They called for a regionwide inventory of troops and weapons, with a view toward achieving regional balance, along with concrete mechanisms for verification. At the time the Reagan administration turned a deaf ear to the proposals, but their substance was later incorporated into the Contadora Group negotiations process, and finally adopted in the Esquipulas II Peace Accords. In retrospect, it appears that even had the Sandinistas won the elections in 1990 and continued down the path of accommodating certain demands from Washington, the Bush administration would not have moved seriously toward coexistence with the revolutionary government.

# Peace Process

On June 27, 1990, during an emotional ceremony held in the small Nicaraguan town of San Pedro de Lovago, President Violeta Chamorro officially declared that the war was over in Nicaragua.[74] On that day, top contra Israel Galeano symbolically handed his weapon to Chamorro, following the lead of the rest of the Nicaraguan Resistance General Staff and more than 19,000 contra foot soldiers and supporters who had demobilized since early May. The Central American peace process, which had begun three years earlier in Esquipulas, Guatemala, reached a conclusion of sorts in Nicaragua, bringing to a close nearly a decade of war. Ironically, the Chamorro government was thus poised to reap an enormous "peace dividend" which in large part had been earned by the Sandinistas.

## A Double-Edged Sword

The emergence of *sandinismo* as a powerful political and military force was a key factor in redefining Latin America's relations with the United States in the 1980s. From the June 1979 rejection of President Carter's request for an OAS "peacekeeping force" to the dramatic signing by the Central American presidents of the Esquipulas II Peace Accords in August 1987, Washington faced an uphill battle in attempting to secure Latin American support for its military efforts to roll back revolution in Nicaragua. As the U.S.-sponsored war escalated under the aggressive Reagan policy of the mid-1980s, the Sandinista government came to rely increasingly on regional diplomatic initiatives. The government worked first through Contadora and later the Esquipulas II Peace Accords to isolate the U.S. policy of aggression and to shift the focus of conflict from the military to the political terrain.

Regional negotiations were always limited by the fact that a major party to the conflict – the U.S. government – refused to be a party to the process or to the agreements. This meant that any regional accord, no matter how viable on its own terms, ran the risk of being undermined by a decision from Washington and the contras not to comply. After the signing of the Esquipulas accords, the peace process was further hampered by the extent to which the parties involved shifted their interpretations of both the spirit and the letter of the accords.

Broad regional consensus around the goals of avoiding direct U.S. intervention and the outbreak of regional war had given birth to the peace process in the first place. This soon gave way to a more complex situation

(continued on page 42)

## Nicaraguan Compliance

* August 1987: Within weeks of the signing of the Esquipulas II Peace Accords, Nicaragua became the first country to establish a **National Reconciliation Commission** (CRN). Cardinal Obando y Bravo, a staunch opponent of *sandinismo*, was appointed as head of the CRN. The government lifted all prior censorship of the press and authorized the reopening of *La Prensa* and Radio Católica, as well as the return of expelled priests Pablo Vega, Bismarck Carballo, and Benito Pitito.

* September: Reception centers were opened in the countryside for all contras seeking **amnesty.**[75] Between the initial amnesty program of 1983 and January 1989, more than 5,000 Nicaraguans received amnesty.

* October: The Sandinista Army declared a 30-day unilateral **suspension of offensive military operations**. The first working meeting of a resumed **National Dialogue** took place with the participation of 11 opposition parties.

* November: Nicaragua took initial steps toward **cease-fire negotiations** with the contras. Some 985 **prisoners** jailed for their participation in counterrevolutionary activities were released.

* December: In the Dominican Republic, government and contra representatives held their first indirect meeting, under the mediation of Obando.

* January 1988: Daniel Ortega announced the decision to enter direct negotiations with the contras, lifted the State of Emergency, in effect since 1982, and declared that an Amnesty Law already approved by the National Assembly would go into effect as soon as a cease-fire agreement was reached.

* March: Direct negotiations in Sapoá, Nicaragua between the government and contras resulted in the signing of a preliminary **cease-fire accord**.

* June: Contras suspended cease-fire negotiations with the government and refused to endorse a joint suspension of offensive military actions.

* November: Costa Rica and Nicaragua established mechanisms to facilitate the return of Nicaraguan refugees.

## with Peace Plan

* February 1989: Daniel Ortega announced the moving up of the date for **general elections** from November to February of 1990. The elections, for president and vice president, National Assembly, municipalities, and Atlantic coast autonomous governments, were to be supervised by international observers, including representatives from the OAS and United Nations.

* March: The National Assembly granted **pardons** for 1,894 former Somoza National Guardsmen in prison since the Sandinista victory in 1979.

* April: In accordance with accords reached in February at Tesoro Beach, the National Assembly passed new Electoral and Media Laws, and a new five-member board was chosen for the Supreme Electoral Council.

* August: The government and opposition parties signed accords granting new concessions for the elections and calling on the Central American presidents to approve contra demobilization. At a regional summit held in Tela, Honduras, Nicaragua agreed to more concessions in exchange for a commitment by the Central American presidents to push for contra demobilization by December.

* December: The electoral campaign began with a total of nine parties and the UNO coalition fielding candidates for the executive and legislature.

* February 1990: A total of 1,190 former National Guardsmen and contras were pardoned and released from prison. The **elections** were held without incident and the observer missions certified the cleanness and integrity of the results which gave an upset victory to the UNO coalition.

* April: Violeta Chamorro was sworn in as President marking the first peaceful **transfer of power** from government to opposition in Nicaragua's history.

* June: Contra **demobilization** was completed.

Sources: "Nicaragua: Contra Policy after Esquipulas II," Central America Bulletin, June 1988, pp.8-9; and "1988 in Review," Barricada Internacional, December 22, 1988.

in which the protagonists viewed the process as a forum for advancing their own, separate agendas. All five Central American presidents supported regional negotiations to the extent that they brought increased legitimacy at home, for themselves, their parties, and the political projects which they represented. This was particularly the case in Guatemala and Costa Rica. Similarly President Azcona of Honduras used Esquipulas as a crafty mechanism to give at least the appearance of resolving one of the country's most pressing problems: how to rid national territory of the contras. Costa Rican President Oscar Arias, awarded the Nobel Peace Prize for his leadership role in the process, saw in Esquipulas a means to end military conflicts in the region and simultaneously get rid of the Sandinistas. Essentially, Arias staked out his terrain, often in the face of open hostility from the White House, firmly grounded in the conviction that the incumbent Sandinista administration, running for reelection in the midst of a grinding economic crisis, had little chance of prevailing in the elections.

What initially had been billed as a framework for moving toward peace, national reconciliation, economic recovery, and democratization in all five Central American countries was largely reduced over time to a practical mechanism to exchange guns for ballots in Nicaragua. Increasingly, a blind eye was turned toward the widespread lack of compliance by the other four countries. This was graphically demonstrated during the first regional summit meeting attended by newly installed President Chamorro. Despite the continued existence of major political-military conflicts in El Salvador and Guatemala, the agenda dealt almost exclusively with topics related to economic recovery.

For those in the region and among the Nicaraguan right wing who felt that the Sandinista government had essentially brought the war upon itself by provoking an unnecessary conflict with the United States, the peace process could only come to fruition with the FSLN's ouster from power. On the other hand, for those who saw Nicaragua as the victim of a U.S. policy of aggression, Sandinista accommodation under the framework of the peace process was the only practical alternative to perpetual war.

Ultimately, the Sandinista government's decision to negotiate in good faith and to comply unilaterally with the accords' stipulations contributed to their defeat in the 1990 elections. Some criticize the concessions as reflecting the FSLN's overconfidence in popular support and naivete regarding the strategy being pursued by the United States and its regional allies.[76] Above all, the Sandinista government's decision to make concessions in the framework of the Esquipulas negotiations was based on two strategic considerations. First, the revolution's social project of improving living standards for the poor majority had largely stalled, with few options for recovery outside of addressing the economic crisis which was being fueled by the defense effort. In short, until definitive peace with the contras and with the United States was achieved, the transformations which were the essence of the revolution itself would remain on ice.[77] Second, with the contra forces largely defeated on the battlefield, it was felt that a relatively quick demobilization process, accompanied by even minimal improvements in relations with the United States, would pave the way for the FSLN to enter the electoral campaign as the party of peace and reconciliation.

As it unfolded in practice, however, the peace process became something very different. While the FSLN accepted the "ballots," the contras never did give up their "bullets." The Bush administration too stuck to its guns. Backed by the congressional "Bipartisan Accord," the administration boycotted contra demobilization plans approved by the Central American presidents and used the contras as an integral part of the electoral strategy to defeat the Sandinistas.[78]

# Human Rights

After nearly a decade of wartime restrictions on civil liberties and human rights abuses perpetrated by the contras and government security forces in the zones of military conflict, the Nicaraguan people entered the 1990s eager for a respite. The peaceful transfer of power from the Sandinistas to the Chamorro administration, and above all the definitive disbanding of the contra army, were promising signs that the harsh realities of the previous decade had passed.

The transition, however, was not without its difficulties. In Nicaragua, unlike its Central American neighbors to the north, even the post-electoral political context did not favor the appearance of death squads operating with the tacit approval of the police or security forces. Nonetheless, some forces on the far right interpreted the UNO electoral victory as a mandate for a "war to the death" against *sandinismo*. The ambivalence of the Chamorro government toward these factions plus an openly hostile climate in which Sandinistas were publicly described as "terrorists" and "delinquents," were ominous signs, particularly in light of the fact that 40 percent of the population had voted for the FSLN in the elections.

As promised in the campaign, one of the Chamorro government's first acts after taking office was the approval of an unconditional general am-

nesty covering all Nicaraguans accused of political violations and common crime linked to political conflicts, whether in or out of prison. In
practice, the move was largely symbolic since, by virtue of the post-
Esquipulas political opening and a similar amnesty law passed by the
lame-duck Sandinista administration, there were virtually no political
prisoners left in Nicaragua.[79]

During Chamorro's first 100 days in office, reports of human rights
abuses were largely confined to the murder of several FSLN activists at
the hands of former contras and UNO extremists, and allegations of
police misconduct against both FSLN and UNO supporters during the
tense strike-related events of May and July 1990. The government, for its
part, strove to credit itself after settlement of the July strike — which
paralyzed the capital and brought the country to the brink of chaos — for
having defused the conflict without a single death or torture having occurred at the hands of government forces.

One lingering human rights problem which the Chamorro government
refused to resolve was the fate of contra kidnap victims, the Nicaraguan
equivalent of the "disappeared." An organization formed in mid-1988
comprised of family members of the kidnapped presented the National
Commission for the Promotion and Protection of Human Rights
(CNPPDH) with a list of 863 names of kidnap victims, including details
of when and where they were taken.[80] The contras have consistently
denied any responsibility, arguing that all members of the Nicaraguan
Resistance joined voluntarily, a position which was echoed by Cardinal
Obando on the repeated occasions that the victims' family members
solicited his assistance. Having spent years exhausting all avenues, in mid-
1990 the families of the kidnapped resolved to seek assistance and
authorization to visit the locations used as contra camps in Honduras to
search for their relatives' remains in burial sites.

## Human Rights and the Revolution

Many international observers feared a bloodbath in the wake of the
July 1979 Sandinista victory, expecting Nicaraguans to take revenge
against the National Guardsmen who had relied on brute force and
repression to prop up the Somoza dictatorship. Despite widespread sentiment that those former Guardsmen convicted of the most heinous
crimes should face a firing squad, one of the new government's first acts
was to abolish the death penalty. Captured Guardsmen were tried and
most sentenced to the legal maximum of 30 years in prison.[81] After serving less than one-third of their terms, all but a handful were pardoned and

released from jail in 1989, even though many of their former comrades-in-arms continued to wage war against the country.

The treatment of the ex-Guardsmen was powerful testimony to the Sandinistas' commitment to respect human rights. In sharp contrast to its northern neighbors, government-sponsored or -condoned death squad activity and the disappearance or assassination of opposition political leaders were conspicuously absent under the Sandinistas. In equally sharp contrast, the Sandinista government systematically investigated reports of human rights abuses and punished those members of its security forces found guilty of misconduct.[82]

Despite the Sandinista government's policy of respect for human rights and its attempts to put the policy into practice, the Reagan administration and its allies inside Nicaragua repeatedly fabricated stories of Sandinista strong-arm tactics and repression of the opposition. Dozens of issues were taken up in the effort to portray Nicaragua as, in Reagan's words, a "totalitarian dungeon." However, the sweeping accusations did not hold up under examination by international human rights organizations.

One such case occurred in 1989 with denunciations of the existence of several thousand political prisoners and dozens of "clandestine jails." Americas Watch sent a high-level delegation to visit Nicaraguan prisons and inspect all locations cited by the opposition as detention centers. They found that a list of "clandestine jails" which had been published by La Prensa included many facilities which were officially and openly used for detentions, while others, including private homes, a horse stable, and a Red Cross warehouse, were apparently not used to hold prisoners at all. Likewise, following its inspections, the group declared estimates made by the Bush administration, La Prensa, and the rightwing Permanent Commission on Human Rights of up to 7,000 political prisoners to be "patently false."[83]

It became clear that these attempted manipulations were as much aimed at diverting attention from human rights violations by the contras as they were at delegitimizing the Sandinista government. It was frequently forgotten or ignored that the contras not only engaged in systematic human rights abuses against the civilian population, but that such abuses were, in the words of Americas Watch, "endemic to their method of waging war."[84]

This is not to say, however, that the Sandinista government and its security forces were blameless. Wartime conditions took a heavy toll, and organizations like Amnesty International and Americas Watch reported incidents of maltreatment of prisoners, violations of international laws of wartime conduct, arbitrary detentions, and police brutality.[85] Individual abuses were particularly prevalent in the remote war-torn areas of the countryside and on the Atlantic coast where, according to one report, "from 1987 through the early part of 1989, Nicaraguan military and security forces engaged in a pattern of killings of contra supporters and contra collaborators..."[86]

As peace began to emerge toward the end of the 1980s, those who had charged the Sandinistas with using the war as a convenient excuse to crush political dissent were left with few arguments. Shortly after the August 1987 signing of the Esquipulas II Peace Accords, censorship of the press was suspended and both *La Prensa* and Radio Católica were allowed to reopen. The January 1988 lifting of the State of Emergency restored *habeas corpus*, eliminated the special tribunal system set up to try ex-Guardsmen and those accused of counterrevolutionary activities, and established strict time limits on incommunicado and pre-trial detentions. Later that year, 985 contra collaborators were released from prison. In March 1989 the National Assembly granted a pardon for 1,894 ex-Guardsmen who had been imprisoned since 1979. In preparation for the 1990 elections, the few remaining restrictions on opposition organizing and demonstrations were liberalized or eliminated.

## The Organizations

In mid-1990 the newly formed Nicaraguan Human Rights Center (CENIDH) became the Nicaraguan affiliate of the regional umbrella group, Commission for the Defense of Human Rights in Central America (CODEHUCA), a regional body whose affiliates are structured along guidelines laid down by the United Nations. CENIDH replaced the National Commission for the Promotion and Protection of Human Rights, a governmental organization active in human rights advocacy during the 1980s. Although CENIDH maintains no formal links with the FSLN, its general orientation has remained pro-revolutionary. CENIDH follows the lead of CODEHUCA in adopting broad definitions of human rights and governmental responsibility, including concepts such as the social and economic rights of peoples.

The Permanent Commission on Human Rights (CPDH) was founded in 1977.[87] The group's board of directors are either members of, or are closely linked to, the far-right parties of the UNO coalition. Frequently cited in U.S. State Department reports on human rights violations by the Sandinistas, the NED-backed CPDH often relied on questionable sources and distorted its conclusions to conform with the guidelines of the broader anti-Sandinista campaign.[88] Aware of the risks of appearing too pro-government, under the UNO administration the CPDH dedicated new energies to building an image of independence.

The contra factions which comprised the Nicaraguan Resistance (RN) had their own human rights agency, the Nicaraguan Human Rights Association (ANPDH). The ANPDH received more than $5 million in U.S. funds as its share of contra-aid packages.[89] With the installation of the Chamorro government, the ANPDH moved its operations to Managua and, like the CPDH, was slated to receive new U.S. government funding. In addition to these nongovernmental organizations, the National Assembly also has its own human rights commission.

## Chapter 2

# Military

## Security Forces

In the highly charged atmosphere surrounding the transfer of power from the Sandinistas to UNO, many of Violeta Chamorro's decisions elicited harsh criticisms from diverse quarters. The move which drew the most heat was the agreement to leave the Sandinista People's Army (EPS)[1] intact, with FSLN leader General Humberto Ortega at its head. Citing the decision to keep Ortega on, two COSEP leaders named to cabinet posts opted to decline their nominations. Emissaries from the Bush administration warned Chamorro that future U.S. aid could be jeopardized by her decision to retain General Ortega. Vice President Virgilio Godoy and other UNO hardliners began referring openly to key Chamorro advisers as "traitors."

The decision to respect the EPS as an institution was denounced as an unnecessary "concession" to the defeated Sandinistas. Some in UNO went so far as to warn that the Sandinistas would take advantage of the first opportunity which presented itself to have the EPS launch a coup d'etat.

Chamorro countered that her decision was based on the Transition Protocol worked out in March by high-level FSLN and UNO negotiating teams. Both the protocol and statements by Sandinista leaders made it clear that a peaceful and orderly transition required guaranteeing the security of all Nicaraguans as well as the institutional integrity of the existing state and governmental apparatus. The Chamorro group recognized that any attempt to dismantle the security forces — particularly since the defiant contra army was resisting demobilization and rightwing political forces within UNO were speaking out with vengeance about the need to *ajustar cuentas* (settle scores) — could well trigger civil conflict and threaten the transfer of power.

The Chamorro group's decision reflected a tempered and realistic approach based on its keen understanding of the compromises necessary to assure a peaceful transfer of power and modicum of stability beyond. In response to her critics, Chamorro explained that the very constitutional framework which proscribed the wholesale dismantling of the EPS also required that the security forces defend the constitutional order, pay allegiance to the government and not to a party, and that the institution be brought under civilian control. Indeed, more far-sighted observers commented that the decision was crucial in strengthening the hand of the new government by demonstrating its independence, moderation, and dedication to reconciliation at a critical moment when it faced potential challenges from the contras and from the right wing within UNO.

The decision to retain Ortega and work with the EPS was successful in terms of avoiding short-term problems. But for the long term Chamorro would have to come to grips with a dilemma faced by governments throughout Latin America. Imposing harsh economic austerity measures and social and agrarian policies which tended to reverse the reforms of the 1980s necessitated at least the credible threat of using armed force against those who would protest and resist. To the extent that the EPS and police could not or would not fulfill this function, changes would have to be made.

Thus, with short-term stability assured, the Chamorro government turned its attention to policies and strategies designed to bring about a gradual, albeit radical, transformation of those same forces. This would be achieved through reductions, institutional modifications, leadership changes, and perhaps most important, changes in the composition of the rank and file through cooptation of some existing members and replacement of others with pro-UNO recruits and ex-contras.

## The Formation of a People's Army

As an institution, Somoza's hated National Guard—which had been installed by the U.S. Marines before they abandoned Nicaragua in 1933—virtually disintegrated following the 1979 Sandinista victory.[2] When the dictator fled the country, his faithful soldiers disbanded. Some 7,000 were captured and imprisoned, an estimated 3,000 managed to cross the border into Honduras, and a few officers sought asylum in local embassies. Thanks to the assistance of President Jimmy Carter's diplomatic delegation, a lucky few from the top brass even managed to be flown out of the country in planes disguised with Red Cross markings. Washington's attempts to preserve the Guard intact, however, proved a bitter failure.

With the Guard so closely linked to the dictatorship and to the United States, the FSLN never entertained notions of institutional reform or of incorporating the Guardsmen into new ranks. A new army had to be built from scratch. In this case, it meant building a professional army from the ragtag guerrilla columns which had fought the revolutionary war and led the popular insurrection.

The FSLN's original plan was to build a small, well-trained standing army, the EPS, backed by a larger, mass-based militia, the Sandinista People's Militia (MPS). Formation of the initial army units began immediately, while the militias were officially inaugurated in February 1980. By the first anniversary of the revolution the MPS counted on some 100,000 volunteers, mainly workers and peasants, ranging in age from 16 to 60.

The military doctrine of the EPS, originally devised with a view toward defending the country and the revolution from a foreign invasion, was based on two key principles. First, the army and its weaponry were defensive in nature; their only purpose was to defend national territory from external aggression. Consequently, Nicaragua's armed forces never developed an offensive capacity able to operate beyond the country's borders.[3] Second, during the 1980s defense was ultimately seen as a mass-based activity. As a small country, Nicaragua could never hope to defend itself from a U.S. invasion with a professional army alone, no matter how large or well-trained. Its only hope would lie in broader defense structures, such as the militias, which could incorporate larger portions of the population into the defense effort.[4]

With the advent of the aggressive Reagan government in 1981, the EPS accelerated preparations for resisting a possible invasion, largely through a quantitative expansion of the militias. With the first large-scale incursions of the U.S.-backed contras, the militias were sent into action. As the contra army grew in size and began to employ irregular warfare tactics, the EPS was forced to defend the country and population against the ongoing contra attacks while simultaneously preparing for the possibility of a full-scale invasion. To meet this challenge, the armed forces were expanded, upgraded with better weaponry, and given a pursuit-oriented capacity to launch offensive operations to root out the contras.

In mid-1983, with contra aggressions on the rise, a draft, known as the Patriotic Military Service (SMP) was instituted. The draft called for obligatory military service for males between the ages of 17 and 25 and voluntary service for women. Between 1984 and 1990 more than 150,000 youths were drafted for two-year tours of duty.[5] In an effort to spread the defense burden as equally as possible across the population, there were no exemption categories (although exceptions were made on a case-by-case basis for religious, family, and scholastic reasons). Unlike most countries in the region, even sons of the wealthy had to serve. The regular draft was backed up by the Reserves (SMP-R) starting in 1985. More than 450,000 adults enlisted in the reserves, 175,000 of whom were actually mobilized.[6]

The draft was the key element in the strategic military defeat of the contra forces during 1986 and 1987, thus paving the way for the peace process. Enabling the EPS to employ more sophisticated weaponry and wage large-scale offensives against the contra forces, the draft successfully confronted contra attempts to expand operations to new areas of the countryside and defused the military threat which they posed to the revolutionary government.

Nonetheless, the draft had an enormously high social cost, with consequent political repercussions that fell upon the FSLN. Unpopular from the beginning, the draft became a rallying cry for the opposition, a cry which struck a responsive chord in many Nicaraguan homes. As is often the case in a protracted war, the most challenging phase turned out to be the end. As peace drew nearer in 1988 and 1989, the population grew increasingly resentful of the draft and the continued need for sacrifices. Overconfident of its chances for victory at the polls, the FSLN resisted suspending the draft until the promised contra demobilization became a reality. As expected, President Chamorro suspended the draft immediately upon taking office.

As Chamorro took office the EPS and militias constituted Nicaragua's land-based army. Security forces under the authority of the Defense Ministry also included the Air Force and Navy. The small air force had no jets, relying for the most part on its fleet of Soviet-supplied helicopters, a vital asset used for ferrying troops and supplies into isolated regions during the contra war. The navy essentially functioned as a coast guard force, and counted on about a dozen patrol boats. With no mine-sweepers at the time, the navy had to rely on fishing vessels and tug-boats dragging nets to remove mines following the 1984 U.S. mining of Nicaragua's harbors. Nicaragua later received light mine-sweepers from North Korea.

In late 1989, with the initial round of peacetime reductions of the security forces already completed, the total number of permanent troops in the Army was 74,000, while the Air Force had 3,500 men and women and the Navy 2,500. At that time, there were an estimated 120,000 reservists and militia members.[7]

## The EPS Under Chamorro

From the outset, the rightwing sectors in UNO, the contras, and the United States advocated the elimination of the EPS as an institution, replacing it with a new force under a different mandate with its ranks comprised principally of ex-contras.[8] The accord worked out by the FSLN and Chamorro transition teams bore no resemblance to the rightwing demands. In exchange for respecting the integrity of the EPS and the Ministry of the Interior — which in practice meant leaving intact the command structure and internal rules of the institutions — Chamorro received three things. First, the security forces would be "depoliticized": no member of the armed forces would be allowed to hold a leadership position in a political party and all parties would be free to proselytize among the rank and file. Second, the government would have exclusive authority for naming the Ministers of Defense and Interior, thus bringing these institutions under civilian control. Third, the EPS would be significantly reduced in size.

In the context of the Esquipulas II Peace Accords, Nicaragua had committed itself since 1988 to a reduction in the size of its armed forces and weapons stock, to a mutually agreeable Central American standard. (See Peace Process) By September 1989 the size of the permanent army had already been reduced by 30 percent and Nicaraguan officials spoke of plans to move toward a model similar to that of neutral countries like Switzerland, with a small full-time force backed up by ongoing compulsory reserve service.[9] But plans to cancel the draft and for further reductions among the standing army and reserves were put on ice in the face of the contras' boycott of the demobilization accords and their continued refusal to accept a cease-fire.

On June 11, 1990, the day after contra demobilization officially closed, General Humberto Ortega delivered to President Chamorro a new plan for EPS troop reductions. Ortega's plan, as well as the Esquipulas-inspired reasonable balance-of-forces argument upon which it was based, was accepted by the Chamorro government. "The total number remaining in the army at the end of this stage of restructuring will depend partially on the future of the Central American region. A peaceful, democratic Central America, in which all conflict is resolved by means of dialogue, will not need armies, either large or small," said Chamorro.[10]

The plan consisted of two major elements: a quantitative reduction in troop levels — from 82,000 down to 41,000, roughly on par with El Salvador and Guatemala, including cuts in the 10,000-strong officer corps — and a restructuring of the military institution which would affect several hundred high-ranking officers. The first stage was to be applied in gradual phases, culminating in December 1990.[11]

For both the EPS and the government, the planned reductions entailed benefits and risks. Chamorro needed the reductions to free up revenues for spending in other areas of the economy. In the 1988-1990 period, 40-60 percent of the national budget went to defense; the government estimated that anticipated reductions in the Army would save the country $12-15 million annually.[12] But at the same time it would have to deal with the problem of some 40,000 former soldiers being thrown into an economy which already suffered from a 40 percent unemployment rate. Predictably, social tensions would be aggravated to the extent that those demobilized from the EPS received little or no assistance from the state, while demobilized contras benefited from more than $50 million in aid approved by the U.S. Congress and other assistance channeled to the development poles. (See Guerrilla Opposition)

Within the EPS itself, some clearly saw demilitarization as healthy for the nation and personally welcomed the opportunity to return to civilian life. One EPS colonel expressed the view that there would not be much resistance to reductions in the officer corps: "Many of us did not see the army as a career. We saw it as a necessity to defend the country. The Sandinista army is not a power bloc as in Guatemala or El Salvador."[13]

Others had a less sanguine view of the process. By July 1990, with the reductions plan already underway, rumors began circulating in Managua over alleged divisions within the armed forces high command and rank and file. Few doubted that serious differences of opinion existed over the nature, scope, and pace of the reductions which would be carried out, and over the general role which the security forces should play in relation to the new government. But there was little agreement over how such divisions might play themselves out.

Some saw the army divided between those commanders and troops who had spent the better part of the previous eight years in the mountains fighting the contras, and that part of the officer corps which had directed the bureaucratic and institutional aspects of the EPS from Managua. Others felt that the schisms tended to reflect social and class differences within the EPS, placing the well-educated officers who came from elite families on one side, and the less educated troops and officers who came from a background of poverty on the other. A third argument focused more on political differences, pitting those who accepted the army's new role and saw institutional loyalty to the command structure as paramount against others who wanted to act more independently in the face of what they saw as violations of the army's mandate and historic role as defender of the revolutionary order.

Likewise, there were several views within the Chamorro administration regarding future plans for the EPS once the reductions were accomplished. Some members of the economic cabinet, particularly Central Bank President Francisco Mayorga, talked of plans to use the army in public works and economic-reactivation projects. One such project, contemplated in UNO's economic recovery plan, consisted of employing the army in a logging and reforestation scheme in the remote northeastern tropical forests. Other members of UNO were anxious to send the army into the streets to confront popular protests, labor conflicts, and land disputes.

Hardline members of the ruling coalition criticized the degree to which the EPS had become an autonomous institution, questioning what authority Chamorro, as Defense Minister, actually had. In particular, they cited a controversial decree, issued before Chamorro took office, granting broad powers to the army commander. These included the authority to make military promotions, procure and produce arms, deploy forces, build bases, and authorize the use of foreign troops in Nicaragua.[14] UNO legislators promised to overturn the statutes.

## National Police

Transformations in the country's police forces under the Chamorro government closely paralleled those of the EPS. First came the cosmetic changes. The Ministry of the Interior, responsible for the regular police force, transit police, and immigration, was renamed Ministry of Government, and the Sandinista Police became the National Police. New uniforms were issued, and the bold letters over the main entrance to the Ministry's office complex— "Sentinels of the People's Happiness" — were painted over. Newly appointed Minister Carlos Hurtado banned the use of the words *compañero* and *compañera* in the Ministry. Officials would now address each other according to military rank, while standard forms of address such as "Dr.," "Mr.," and "Mrs." would be used for civilian employees and the public. Before long, however, the superficial changes gave way to more profound transformations.

Police units decked out in riot-control gear, used rarely under the Sandinistas, became a familiar sight on the streets of the capital. The first major test of police loyalty under the new UNO leadership came with the eruption of a public-sector strike in May 1990. On several occasions the police reluctantly followed orders to launch tear gas against striking workers, but larger confrontations were avoided.

During the course of the 1980s the Sandinista Police earned a reputation as an honest, professional and well-disciplined force. Bribery, torture and abuse of authority, endemic to police forces throughout Latin America, were virtually unknown. The unique character of the Sandinista Police was built on two elements. First, their rigorous training routine was designed to create a mentality among the police as public servants in defense of popular interests. Second, salaries were kept at or below those of the average worker as part of the effort to reinforce bonds of class solidarity between the population and the police.

Having been put to the test on numerous occasions during Chamorro's first three months in office, the National Police had, for the most part, succeeded in walking the fine line: they neither openly failed to disobey orders handed down by superiors, nor did they alienate the population through the use of excessive force. Faced with the tense clashes between scabs and UNO-extremists and striking workers and their supporters during the May and July 1990 strikes, the police generally assumed the task of physically placing themselves between the conflictive sides to prevent further deterioration of the situation. In the July strike, both the police and the army followed orders to remove barricades erected by strike supporters. The extreme right within UNO sharply criticized the government for not sending in the police to evict strikers forcibly from the workplaces they were occupying. The Chamorro administration, for its part, congratulated itself for having defused an explosive conflict without a single case of imprisonment, torture, or killing at the hands of the police. In a clear admonishment to those who had insisted on using force to confront the strikers, Minister of the Presidency Antonio Lacayo commented: "If the failure to use force is a sign of a vacuum of power, then we should welcome a vacuum of power with open arms."[15]

While the Chamorro team thus managed to put a good face on these early standoffs, its long-range goals clearly sought the creation of greater loyalties within the ranks of the police. In anticipation of future conflicts which would be provoked by the economic plan—an explosion in the crime rate due to growing unemployment, drops in real wages, and the elimination of social services; land conflicts in the countryside through bank foreclosures and farm occupations by landless *campesinos*; the eventual need to evict urban squatters; and similar social collisions— various approaches were being employed to slowly transform the nature of the police.

One was to simply sit back and wait, letting attrition within the ranks run its course. Due to ideological conflicts and discontent with low salaries in the face of suddenly rocketing prices, some 2,000 police resigned during the first few months of the Chamorro administration, bringing the total number of police forces down to 5,000. In June, Hurtado announced plans to expand the force to 10,000, citing the need to combat the growing crime wave. Despite the talk of "depoliticizing" the security forces, it was obvious that the first in line for the new jobs would be UNO sympathizers. New police instructors—trained by Israel's Mossad[16]—had arrived in May from Venezuela and by August, the first new recruits had already been turned out of the training academy. An agreement also was signed with Spain for the provision of training and equipment for the police.

The contras' rural police force, the Internal Order Police— Nicaraguan Resistance (POI-RN), assigned to patrol the development poles promised by the government, also fall under Ministry og Government's authority. (See Guerrilla Opposition) Although the initial accord calls for the POI-RN not to exceed 150 members, many fear that this force composed of ex-contras will become the embryo of a parallel body to rival the national security forces.

# Guerrilla Opposition

Over the course of nine intense years the amalgamation of forces engaged in military struggle against the Nicaraguan government, known as the *contrarevolucionarios* or contras, went through powerful changes.[17] They began as a few roving bands of former National Guard members who had fled Nicaragua in 1979. Initial covert CIA support for the formation of an "arms-interdiction contingent"—supposedly to block Sandinista arms shipments to El Salvador's FMLN guerrillas—gave way to increasingly firm and public backing from the Reagan administration. By 1984 the contras were an army of 15,000, complete with an air force, naval detachments, and a diplomatic wing.[18] At the decade's end, after military defeat at the hands of the EPS and political uncertainty in the wake of the Central American peace process, those contras who had not given up altogether were sitting in limbo as unwelcome guests in southern Honduras.

Given a new lease on life by virtue of the UNO electoral victory, the contras were able to wring a series of major concessions in exchange for demobilization. In effect, the deal negotiated with the Chamorro government allowed the defeated contra army to transform itself from an armed movement with a political wing into a political party with an armed wing. It also gave them something which they had been unable to achieve through a decade of war: a piece of Nicaraguan territory, now known as the "development poles."

## From Expeditionary Force to Peasant Army

At least until the serious military setbacks in 1986-1987, the bulk of those who joined the contras over the years never harbored any illusions about their goal. They sought to overthrow the Nicaraguan government militarily and eliminate all traces of *sandinismo* and the revolution from the country. "The FDN is a military organization under the command of [former Somoza National Guard Colonel] Enrique Bermúdez, whose sole interest is reviving the National Guard, his 'glorious' National Guard," commented former contra leader Edgar Chamorro in 1985. "They have no political alternatives, no democratic program. [Their victory] would mean a rightist dictatorship...it would be like returning to one of the worst chapters in Nicaraguan history. They only want to recover what they lost, their properties and privileges. They are programmed to kill, to destroy *sandinismo*, with the sole mentality of annihilating anything associated with it."[19]

In the initial period, 1981-1982, the contras were dominated by former Guardsmen.[20] From their bases in Honduras, small groups of contras launched incursions into the northern border regions aimed at destroying key infrastructure targets and terrorizing rural communities thought to be sympathetic to the Sandinistas. In 1983 a reorganized and expanded contra army took the initiative, launching three large-scale offensives spanning hundreds of kilometers in the northern and southern border regions, the central highlands, and the Atlantic coast. The following year brought more of the same, this time with greater direct participation by U.S. forces, particularly in sabotage operations along the coasts and in the mining of Nicaragua's harbors.

The Nicaraguan army and militias kept the contras from achieving their main goals of seizing a piece of territory, bringing the war to the cities, and creating conditions for a mass insurrection led by the right wing. But the aggression did succeed in inflicting a heavy toll in both human and economic terms. Between 1980 and the end of 1986 direct economic losses from contra attacks had climbed to more than $1.1 billion, while indirect effects were valued at more than twice that amount. The contras were notorious for sowing terror among the population and avoiding clashes with the army as a matter of policy. More than one-third of the nearly 60,000 casualties in the contra war were civilians.[21]

During the mid-1980s the initial contra strategy of seeking the military defeat of the Sandinistas gradually gave way to a new formula, framed within the precepts of low intensity warfare which were rapidly gaining adherents in the Pentagon and CIA at the time. The contras concentrated increasingly on waging a grinding war of attrition whose aim — in concert with diplomatic, ideological, and economic aggressions sponsored by Washington — was to erode support for *sandinismo* among the population and ultimately make the revolution cave in on itself.[22]

The new approach proved to be much more effective than its predecessor. As the military conflict dragged on and the economic crisis worsened, the FSLN began to lose legitimacy among the population as

| Costs of the U.S. War 1980 - 1988 | |
|---|---|
| **Human Costs[*]** | |
| Dead | 29,270 |
| Wounded | 18,012 |
| Kidnapped/captured | 10,449 |
| **Total victims** | **57,731** |
| **Economic Costs[**]** | |
| Direct Damage | |
| Material damage and lost production | $1,997,900,000 |
| Excess defense costs | 1,933,000,000 |
| Credit embargo | 642,600,000 |
| Trade embargo | 458,900,000 |
| Indirect Effects | |
| Lost production | 2,584,300,000 |
| Credit embargo | 837,900,000 |
| Trade embargo | 633,100,000 |
| **Total economic costs** | **$9,087,700,000** |

Source: Official government figures from the Ministry of the Presidency, cited in "Instituto Nacional de Estadísticas y Census, Diez Años en Cifras," July 1989.

[*] These figures include troops from the EPS and contras as well as civilians, the latter accounting for more than one-third of all victims.

[**] In its case against the United States at the International Court of Justice, Nicaragua presented claims for $17.8 billion in damages. This figure comes from the $9 billion here, plus damages to development and sovereignty, compensation for the dead and wounded, and "moral damages."

key initiatives boomeranged. The draft, for example, which had been implemented in order to end the war through superior military power, wound up prolonging it by alienating thousands of peasants who then became combatants or part of a social base for the contras. Likewise, the Sandinistas' attempts to bring Cardinal Obando y Bravo into cease-fire negotiations with the contras in hopes of furthering the peace process actually strengthened the hand of the contras, giving added legitimacy to their demands, and ultimately postponing the real possibilities of achieving peace.

Other factors, including major mistakes committed by the Sandinistas, had been contributing to support for the contras in the countryside since even earlier in the war. Throughout the different stages of agrarian reform, certain sectors in the rural areas were favored, often to the detriment of others, fueling open resentment. (See Agriculture) For example, the early prioritization of state farms and cooperatives engendered opposition from thousands of landless *campesinos*. Policies aimed at defending the living standards of urban workers, such as government-fixed prices for basic-grains purchases, had a strong negative impact on *campesino* producers. Particularly in the remote war zones of the north, the government's security forces alienated rural communities with their strong-arm tactics and cases of arbitrary abuses were reported. In the face of growing polarization, many *campesinos* blamed the Sandinistas for their inability to remain neutral in the conflict, and when push came to shove, they opted to join family members already fighting with the contras.

Despite these advances in the political terrain, the military situation for the contras was increasingly bleak. The strategic military defeat inflicted by the EPS in 1986-1987 left the contras with few possibilities for retaking the initiative through military means. Under the auspices of the Esquipulas peace plan, the Sandinista government and contras entered into negotiations aimed at establishing a cease-fire and eventually a definitive end to the hostilities. While many contras were anxious to put an end to the war through the negotiations process and several contra leaders signed a preliminary cease-fire with the Nicaraguan authorities at Sapoá in March 1988, the top contra leader Colonel Enrique Bermúdez received full backing from the United States to oppose the negotiation process. The ensuing conflicts threatened to bring about the disintegration of the contra movement itself. Thousands of contras simply gave up and returned to civilian life in Nicaragua or joined the ranks of the undocumented in the United States and Central America. Many formed "dissident" contra groups opposed to Bermúdez' uncompromising positions while others, including several top leaders, decided to join the electoral battle inside Nicaragua.

By the time the electoral campaign got underway in late 1989, the most intransigent sectors of the contra leadership, including Bermúdez, had been displaced, their places taken by a younger generation of contra field commanders who had risen through the ranks during the 1980s. Like the majority of the contra troops, the new leaders, under the command of Israel Galeano, were mostly of *campesino* origin.[23]

In preparation for the 1990 elections, the bulk of the contra forces were sent from their bases in Honduras into the Nicaraguan countryside. Their mission was to intimidate FSLN supporters and to campaign for the UNO ticket among the peasantry, while simultaneously rekindling the embers of war. In response, the government – with a view toward defending against the military attacks and safeguarding the electoral process – canceled the unilateral cease-fire it had maintained since the signing of the Sapoá Accords a year and a half earlier. Then, in a strategic public-relations coup, UNO capitalized on the FSLN's decision by campaigning as "the party of peace."[24]

## Demobilization: The Last Goodbye?

The timetable worked out by the Central American presidents under the auspices of the Esquipulas peace plan initially called on the contras to finalize the process of demobilization by December 1989, nearly three months before the scheduled general elections. With firm U.S. backing, the contras effectively resisted all pressures to disband, brandishing the argument that their continued existence was the only guarantee that the Sandinistas would hold fair elections and respect the results. Within days of UNO's upset victory, however, it became clear that the contra leadership had more ambitious goals.

Representatives of President-elect Chamorro, the Nicaraguan Catholic church hierarchy, the army, and the UN and OAS-sponsored groups responsible for overseeing the demobilization – the United Nations Observer Group in Central America (ONUCA) and the International Commission for Support and Verification (CIAV) – entered into a lengthy and complex process of negotiations with the Nicaraguan Resistance (RN) contras. Playing on Chamorro's campaign promises of national reconciliation and the need to establish peace and stability as a prerequisite for launching UNO's sweeping economic program, the RN effectively used the threat of restarting the war to extract a series of hefty concessions from the government. Four months after the first agreements had been signed, ONUCA officially declared the process complete. They reported that a total of 19,256 contras had been demobilized.[25]

The heart of the payoff designated for the contras consisted of the right to form several semi-autonomous "development poles" in remote areas of central and southeastern Nicaragua.[26] According to the May 30, 1990 agreement the contra leadership signed with the Chamorro government, the poles could be placed in 23 locations totaling 3,280 square miles of Nicaraguan territory. The poles will be patrolled by the new security force, the contra-based POI-RN. The POI-RN is slated to receive training from Spanish and Venezuelan security teams.

Contras who decide to relocate to the poles will be granted direct representation in local governments. They also may send delegates to act as high level advisers in the central government ministries whose work involves the poles (Construction, Health, Labor, Agrarian Reform, and Repatriation). In addition to the government's commitment to prioritize social and development projects and job-creating investments in the poles, $47 million in aid from the $300 million package approved by Congress is earmarked specifically for demobilized contras and their family members who repatriate from Honduras. Contra widows and families will receive pension benefits.

The notion of the poles and the rural police caused widespread apprehension among Nicaraguans. Visions of the contra army reanimated in the form of the "rural police" and of a huge, autonomous contra colony, bolstered by amounts of aid from the United States unavailable to the general population, raised hackles in many quarters. Many were perplexed as to how such a project could contribute to the Chamorro government's professed goal of reconciliation when in fact it seemed destined to heighten animosities and concretize existing divisions.

Faced with widespread public criticism, some government leaders tried to play down the magnitude of the poles and their broader impact on Nicaraguan society. For example, Minister of Agrarian Reform Gustavo Tablada, one of the negotiators of the accords which granted the poles, insisted that there would only be three or four poles, that each contra family would be given between 5 and 8.5 acres of land, and that the rural police would not exceed 250 members.[27]

In practice, the poles got off to a slow start. By September 1990 many contras waiting in the three locations where the first poles would be built — El Almendro, El Coral, and Nueva Guinea — were furious that the much-touted aid had not arrived. Blame was alternately placed on bureaucracy in the U.S. Agency for International Development (AID) and in the OAS and UN commissions charged with distributing the aid, on Chamorro for not fulfilling her promises, or on the Sandinistas for having provoked chaos with the July general strike. One U.S. correspondent who visited what was to become the main development pole in El Almendro described the scene this way: "The ragtag remnants of what was once the contra army wander the unpaved streets of this fetid little town in a listless daze, remote from the rush of events in Managua and bitter about their fate."[28]

The ultimate fate of the contras remains uncertain. In the immediate aftermath of demobilization, individual contras went in several different directions. Most were eager to return to their families and farms. About one in ten chose to remain at the sites where the development poles were to be established. Others began work with the new contra political party, the Nicaraguan Resistance Civic Organization.[29] Several former contra leaders participated in discussions with the National Union of Farmers and Ranchers (UNAG), a pro-Sandinista organization of farmers and peasants. The talks were aimed at uniting peasants irrespective of their political or ideological leanings and past affiliations in the face of growing landlessness and negative fallout from Chamorro's agrarian policies.

Some ex-contras took advantage of the tensions unleashed during the July 1990 general strike to take up paramilitary activity in support of the extreme right within the UNO coalition. Ex-contras quickly turned up in the ranks of the National Salvation Committees which Vice President Virgilio Godoy was busy organizing. According to press reports, some 2,000 armed contras remained in the Honduran department of Olancho, not far from the border with Nicaragua.[30] Despite these ominous signs there were few indications that the contras had any chance of fully reviving themselves as an organized force, or of seriously threatening to relaunch the war.

Chapter 3

# Economy

## The State of the Economy

In the daily lives of most Nicaraguans, the state of the economy occupies center stage. The Sandinistas' inability to provide a minimally acceptable standard of living for the poor majority and the widely held perception that they were incapable of managing the economy were major factors behind their electoral defeat in 1990. In the face of a desperate economic situation, many Nicaraguans were easily convinced that the possibility of change offered by UNO was a better gamble than the probability of more of the same under a new Sandinista administration. At a minimum, voters felt that with an UNO government the hundreds of millions of dollars spent by Washington to destroy the country would instead flow in to rebuild it.

On the other hand, the Chamorro government's chances for converting its electoral victory into support for an alternative to the Sandinistas' program of revolutionary transformations are constrained by competing priorities and economic interests. The success of the new government will depend in large measure on its ability to resolve these contradictory impulses. Thus – in a task reminiscent of the challenges which confronted the Sandinistas – UNO must revive production and correct macroeconomic distortions, while at the same time attempting to fulfill the popular sectors' expectations of improvements in living standards.

### The Economy: Sandinismo's Achilles Heel

The mixed-economy model of the Sandinista government envisioned ownership in industry and agriculture divided between the state, small producers (including cooperatives), and a capitalist sector. Within a context of popular hegemony, the mixed economy would guarantee a place for all, regardless of ideological or political preferences, as long as a commitment to production was maintained.[1] According to the plan, the government would effect a redistribution of income and property while expanding consumption levels for the popular sectors. Agrarian reform and a state-controlled banking system and foreign-trade apparatus were established to facilitate the redistribution.

The prevailing view in the early stage was that ambitious state investment projects would provide the accumulated income needed to fund development and social projects. Some Sandinista leaders also saw the investment projects as essential in building a proletariat which would move the economy toward socialism. Others, while they shared the goal of striving for socialism, saw the mixed economy as a more permanent phenomenon, in part because of the country's highly skewed class structure.[2] The cities are dominated by an informal sector which dwarfs the tiny industrial working class, while in the rural areas there is a relatively even division between the proletariat and a stratified peasantry, with a tiny agrarian bourgeoisie.[3]

In their efforts to transform the economy the Sandinistas did not start with a blank slate. Destruction from the war of liberation against Somoza had left much of the country's productive infrastructure in ruins. The treasury was empty because Somoza and his associates looted the Central Bank vaults before fleeing.[4] Even before the onset of the war and U.S. financial aggression, the web of economic constraints meant that, according to the World Bank, "per capita income levels of 1977 will not be attained, in the best of circumstances, until the late 1980s."[5]

Between 1980 and 1984, blessed with relatively generous levels of international economic assistance (the cutoff in U.S. aid notwithstanding) and widespread popular enthusiasm and participation in the new revolutionary programs and institutions, economic performance was quite positive. Government investment for reconstruction averaged 20 percent of GDP, far above the Central American average, and many areas of the economy were successfully reactivated.[6] Significant gains were registered in consumption levels and in the extension of basic social services such as education and health care. Agrarian reform, along with flexible credit and technical-assistance policies, benefited thousands of formerly landless farmers and agricultural workers and helped the country move toward its goal of self-sufficiency in basic-grain production.[7]

But parallel to these positive developments, troublesome signs were also emerging. A web of interrelated factors, some tied to internal contradictions and mistakes committed by the Sandinistas, others related to external factors beyond their control, was increasingly forcing the hand of economic policymakers. While some within the government began to sound the alarm, no one envisioned the magnitude of the economic crisis which would emerge a few years down the road.

First, the costs and stresses of the reconstruction period demonstrated the limits of trying to apply economic planning in a mixed economy dominated by small and medium private producers and the commercial sector. Changes in the government's alliance strategy, made in order to satisfy the demands of diverse economic actors, often produced counterproductive results. For example, price and marketing policies aimed at strengthening the purchasing power of salaried workers had an adverse effect on much of the peasantry. (See Agriculture) Similarly, state-provided incentives intended to coax a reluctant private sector into cooperation increased the economic burden on the popular sectors.

Second, Nicaragua's ambitious efforts to transform the economy took place at a time when international conditions were wreaking havoc throughout the third world. Contracting markets, deterioration in the terms of trade, dwindling sources of external financing, and a mounting foreign debt were problems from which Nicaragua was hardly immune.

Third, and most important in terms of constricting the government's maneuvering room, was the war and U.S. financial aggression. Ongoing destruction caused by contra attacks and sabotage, and by U.S. economic warfare including a trade embargo, loan cutoffs,[8] and the 1984 mining of Nicaragua's ports, extracted a high price. (See Guerrilla Opposition) At its peak, the national defense effort involved a full 20 percent of the economically active population, 40 percent of the Gross National Product, and 60 percent of the national budget.

In the face of these adverse circumstances, the government's response essentially boiled down to implementing a series of stopgap measures while postponing the difficult choices in an effort to buy time.[9] An increasingly unmanageable budget deficit was sustained year after year, covered through the printing of unbacked currency notes. The cost was a growing chain of macroeconomic distortions, a skyrocketing debt, uncontrollable hyperinflation, and, most important politically, a precipitous decline in living standards for the country's already poor majority.

The government's attempts to confront the imbalances behind the economic crisis brought mixed results. In 1985, the year the U.S. trade embargo was declared, the Sandinistas placed the country on a war footing and instituted a "survival economy." Defense spending jumped from 30 percent of the national budget in 1984 to 50 percent in 1985. The economic-adjustment program included the first devaluation since 1979. Specific measures aimed at stimulating production and at correcting some of the economic distortions included spending cuts (investments, credit, and subsidies), wage and price adjustments, and a crackdown on the black market.

Although trade and budget deficits were reduced somewhat, the general economic decline continued. Inflation, for example, climbed from 220 percent in 1985 to 912 percent in 1987. The relative inability of the 1985 measures to arrest economic decline underlined the degree to which economic stability and heavy defense spending were irreconcilable. Although there was increasing recognition among Sandinista leaders that harsher economic measures were needed in order to bring the economy under control, it was agreed that implementing such a package would have to be postponed until the contra military threat was eliminated.

It was in this context that in 1988 the government launched its "shock" package, which in many ways resembled plans adopted in other countries at the behest of the International Monetary Fund (IMF). Aside from the immediate goal of reducing inflation, the thrust of the 1988 adjustment package, executed in two phases, was to create a framework and context in which the economy could recuperate over the long run. Spearheaded by a 3,000 percent monetary devaluation and a currency swap, the new package of reforms included the virtual elimination of subsidies, reductions in the government budget (including defense, health, and education) and the curtailment of new investments in strategic development projects. Other measures were a tightening of credit conditions, indexing of interest and exchange rates to adjust them to inflation, additional restrictions on imports, and a near total elimination of wage and price controls which further strengthened the market orientation of the economy.

Structural-adjustment policies like the 1988 package in Nicaragua inevitably entail a political cost for the governments which impose them. Countries working with IMF-approved plans usually have access to external financing which is used to back up the measures and provide a cushion to those sectors of the population hardest hit by austerity measures. Despite some promises of postwar financing from Western European countries and from the United Nations, foreign-exchange backing for the Sandinistas' economic reform fell far short of what the government had projected. As a result, the plan was the equivalent of surgery without anesthesia. Furthermore, the plan itself was dealt a severe blow by the devastating economic impact of Hurricane Joan at the end of 1988.[10]

The austerity package brought unprecedented hardships to an already poverty-stricken population. Real per capita income fell to levels of the 1940s. Although some Nicaraguans saw the war and U.S. aggression as the ultimate causes of the economic crisis, the predominant sentiment by

1990 was one of exasperation. Survival strategies began to take precedence over political loyalties or ideological convictions. After the first few weeks of analyzing its electoral defeat, many in the FSLN came to the conclusion that the most striking thing was not that they had lost, but that under such adverse conditions 40 percent of the population still voted for them.

For its part, the Chamorro government stepped into a situation where most of the toughest measures involved in instituting structural-adjustment plans had already been taken. The measures adopted by the Sandinistas, although their immediate impact on the popular sectors had been harsh, had at least partly succeeded in addressing some of the macroeconomic distortions which had brought on the crisis in the first place. By the end of 1989 both hyperinflation and the fiscal deficit had been substantially reduced, and export levels had begun to recuperate. Although problems still abounded, UNO inherited an economy which was ripe for recovery.

## UNO's Program:
## "Recovery, Reconstruction, and Prosperity"

The economic program unveiled by UNO shortly before its electoral victory was based on dismantling the state sector of the economy and establishing the private sector and agroexports as the driving force of economic recovery and expansion.[11] Ultimately, the Sandinistas' mixed-economy model was to be transformed into a "social market economy." The plan's principal architect, Yale-educated Central Bank President Francisco Mayorga, promised to eliminate inflation within 100 days of Chamorro's inauguration, and to achieve a 10 percent economic growth rate within the first year, a rate which was to be sustained through 1996.

The program consisted of three phases: I) Emergency Reactivation; II) Recovery and Reconstruction; and III) Modernization and Prosperity. Phase I, which in part overlapped with what became known as the "100-day plan," aimed to completely eradicate inflation through harsh austerity measures and the introduction of a new, freely convertible currency, the *córdoba oro*, pegged to the dollar. This phase also contemplated major budget and tax reforms as well as the privatization of state enterprises. Beyond the initial "emergency aid" — which essentially boiled down to some $330 million in U.S. aid — economic planners calculated they would need $500-600 million per year in foreign assistance to back the measures. Economic reactivation in this initial phase was to be stimulated by bringing idle state farmland into production, rejuvenating the country's deteriorated transportation network, and providing incentives to encourage the return of exiled professionals and entrepreneurs.

Phase II aimed to recover production levels of the late 1970s through the large-scale reduction of the state apparatus, the privatization of all state-owned businesses, and the gradual privatization of the banking system. The economic transformation sought in this phase was to be implemented through various measures. Resources and manpower from the armed forces were to be transferred into productive activities, with ex-combatants given priority in land assignments, technical training, and for new jobs. Reconstruction of the nation's infrastructure, with major investments in electric, water, and telecommunications networks, was another priority. Finally, special programs to promote the formation of new small businesses in industry and agriculture also were planned.

The long-term projects laid out for Phase III were somewhat more ambitious. The aim of this phase was to modernize the nation's productive capacity, in part through the promotion of unrestricted foreign investments. The plan called for modernization of agroindustry, industrial conversion of the existing manufacturing base, promotion of nontraditional exports, and establishment of duty-free zones, all dependent upon capital from foreign investments.

### The First 100 Days: A Honeymoon Goes Sour

The newly installed government opted immediately to push full steam ahead with the most confrontational aspects of the "Mayorga Plan," judging that the FSLN and the pro-Sandinista union movement, still reeling from the electoral defeat, were weak and divided and that Chamorro's own popularity was at its "honeymoon" peak. The offensive was multipronged: twice-weekly currency devaluations; massive public-sector layoffs; elimination of subsidies; and initiatives aimed at turning state farms over to private producers.

The quick reaction of Nicaragua's organized labor movement and popular sectors took the government by surprise. The first showdown came in May, with a strike by public-sector employees, and was followed by a nationwide general strike in July. (See Labor) The government's ambiguous posture in both strikes—initially confrontational responses, followed by conciliatory gestures and negotiated settlements, and then systematic violation of those settlements—fueled resentment among the unions and their supporters. The chief union demands were for job stability and workers' inclusion in the process of defining how economic policy would be implemented. Over time the unions became increasingly convinced that the government would not, or could not, negotiate in good faith. While continuing to push for a national dialogue on economic policy, union representatives increasingly expressed the view that the only demands the government would take seriously were those backed by militant actions.

In raising their demands the unions were careful to point out that they were not out to sabotage the economic plan and that it was as much in their interests as anyone's that cooperation be achieved in order to facilitate economic recovery. In fact, the basic thrust of Mayorga's economic stabilization measures was very similar to that which had prevailed in the last two years of the Sandinista government, with two major distinctions. First, the Sandinistas had attempted to include the unions, as well as the private sector, in negotiations over how economic policy would be implemented. UNO, however, had simply imposed its measures, with no attempt at consultations or even explanation to the population and in apparent disregard of the social cost. Second, although the Sandinistas' stabilization package implied harsh conditions for the population, the measures were implemented with a degree of flexibility and with certain "cushions" left in to attenuate the impact on the poorest sectors, aspects which were conspicuously absent from UNO's program.

The government's handling of the strikes and their aftermath also produced resentment among UNO's political and economic right wing, represented respectively by Vice President Virgilio Godoy and COSEP. Representatives from both sectors chastised Chamorro as "weak and indecisive" for having caved in to worker demands and for failing to confront the strikers with the police or army. Godoy's political maneuvering during the July strike was described by some in Chamorro's camp as an attempted "technical coup d'etat," raising to new heights the divisions which had been festering within UNO since the elections campaign. The conservative producer organizations, already apprehensive over the slow pace of a privatization process in which they had expected to become the primary beneficiaries, began to speak openly of an inadequate "climate" for the private investments needed for economic recovery.

The strikes were at once fueled by and aggravated the poor economic performance which characterized Chamorro's first 100 days in office. A popular Nicaraguan saying declares that *entre lo dicho y lo hecho, hay mucho trecho* — between what is said and what is done, there lies a large gap. A more fitting phrase for the economic performance of the "100-day plan" could not be found. By August 1990 — amid skyrocketing inflation, a dizzying spiral of currency devaluations and price hikes, and growing unemployment — the glittering campaign promises of prosperity had vanished and the population's confidence in the government's ability to address the economic crisis had seriously eroded.[12] Mayorga had become the object of ridicule in the streets, and rumor had it that several top government officials were actively pushing for his resignation.

Inflation, which Mayorga had repeatedly insisted would be eliminated, in fact had averaged 83 percent per month between May and July, far above the 10-20 percent per month achieved in the last year of Sandinista economic reforms. The policy of devaluations — which sought to stabilize the currency, unify the official and parallel exchange rates, eliminate the black market, and increase the competitiveness of agroexports — saw the *córdoba*/dollar ratio jump from 53,800:1 when Chamorro took office to 560,000:1 three months later. Mayorga's goal to spearhead a revival of economic production through a doubling of cotton exports fell far short of the mark as estimates of acreage actually planted fell some 50 percent short of the target.

Although prices for consumer goods and public services, as well as interest rates on agricultural credits, were all being calculated in dollar terms, the highly proclaimed *córdoba oro* — which Mayorga insisted would "never" devalue from its position of parity with the dollar — had still not been brought into circulation by the end of the 100 days. This meant that while the population's daily expenses, such as bus fares, food, utility bills, and gasoline, were charged at, or in some cases above, the equivalent of international prices, their income was still being received in a currency which was literally worth less with each passing day. Household shoppers, who had complained bitterly about the long lines and rationing of basic goods under the Sandinistas, were now confronted with a different problem: market stalls and supermarket shelves overflowed with products, including essentials such as rice and beans, which few could afford to buy.

In the social sphere, signs were hardly less dramatic. The crime rate began to soar as a "what have I got to lose" mentality began to take root among the most destitute. Diseases which had been practically eliminated during the 1980s, such as measles, reached epidemic proportions.

The causes for the gulf which separated Mayorga's lofty promises and projections from the reality of the first 100 days were manifold. Above all, the goals themselves had been grossly unrealistic, far out of line with the material conditions prevailing in the country. Even under ideal circumstances, Mayorga's projections would have been difficult to achieve. Beyond that, several unforeseen factors came into play:

* Foreign exchange shortfalls: Mayorga had devised his plan on the assumption that substantial levels of foreign aid would begin flowing into the country before, or shortly after, Chamorro's inauguration.

In reality, much less aid than anticipated was received, and that which did come arrived far later than had been planned and with strings attached. Delays in the arrival of the U.S. aid package, and the lack of funds necessary to clear arrears with the international financial institutions in order to free up credit, led to liquidity problems. (See Industry and Finance) Among other detrimental effects, this shortfall spurred inflation and forced a postponement in the introduction of the new currency, which could only achieve stability if sufficient amounts of foreign reserves were available to back it up. By the time the first new bills were introduced in August 1990, confidence had dropped to the point where thousands of workers rushed to the banks to convert their paychecks into dollars.

* Last-minute wage demands and economic distortions: Although the Sandinistas' stabilization and adjustment measures in 1988-1989 had met with some success, during the electoral campaign and lame-duck period (March-April 1990) fiscal and financial austerity measures were relaxed and government spending expanded. This led to an accumulation of macroeconomic distortions in terms of the exchange-rate differential, interest rates, and relative prices. Also, in anticipation of an FSLN victory in the elections, pro-Sandinista unions had held back on calls for salary increases, thus leaving the new government to deal with the problem of pent-up wage demands. Added to these factors was the cost of the Sandinistas' "giveaway" of state goods before leaving office. (See Political Parties and Elections)

* Budget deficit: Factors such as the strikes, exorbitant new salaries for top government functionaries, and big credit outlays aimed at stimulating agroexport production combined to keep the budget deficit at unmanageably high levels.

* Speculative activities: Excessive amounts of money in circulation, consumer price levels higher than the Central American average, and the population's growing lack of confidence in the economic plan, spurred speculative activities including a thriving black market in dollars and contraband imports of consumer products from neighboring countries.

Wherever the blame lay, the 100 days' balance was not good for Mayorga. The social polarization and production losses resulting from the stabilization measures and strikes set back by many months the timetable for economic recovery. Other factors, such as the faltering confidence of the private sector and potential investors in the plan's inherent viability, also threatened to undermine essential elements of the plan itself.

By mid-August, amidst rumors of new strikes in the works, signs began to appear indicating that the government was moving toward modifying key aspects of the economic plan. In fact, Mayorga himself had ceded the role as spokesperson for economic policy to other members of the cabinet.

The extended transition period highlighted a series of broader dilemmas which UNO's economic policies are likely to face in the future. Any economic-recovery program will require minimum levels of social peace and the cooperation of the existing union movement, something which all of Chamorro's economic policymakers have acknowledged. Another confrontation on the scale of the July strike, for example, could easily plunge the country into chaos and civil strife.

On the other hand, the very concessions which could create an atmosphere of cooperation with workers would likely alienate important elements of the private sector. Perhaps more importantly, such policy decisions would almost certainly prove unacceptable to the International Monetary Fund, whose approval Nicaragua needs in order to have access to the credits and loans necessary for reconstruction.

Despite these obstacles, a fragile consensus was emerging within the government around the idea that the only way to maneuver around these and other dilemmas bound up with economic policy was through a broad process of national dialogue, incorporating the government, private enterprise, the unions, and the FSLN opposition. The first round of meetings was scheduled for September 1990. Although most observers saw the move toward dialogue as positive, widespread doubts remained as to whether the Chamorro government had the will or the power to reach substantive accords and have them respected in practice.

## Privatization

One of the most controversial aspects of the Chamorro government's economic policies, and the one which most forcefully signifies a rupture with the Sandinista past, has been privatization. Regarding the scope and speed of privatization all the key actors — the U.S. embassy, the economic cabinet, COSEP and exiled Nicaraguan businessmen, the FSLN, and labor — have somewhat different views. The delicate nature of the task, and the difficulty of reaching minimal consensus among the various sectors obstructed implementation of the projected policies. As a consequence, during Chamorro's first four months in office, privatization — defined as the selling off of state enterprises — failed to proceed beyond the planning stages.

By August 1990 the nationalized sector of the Nicaraguan economy, known as the Area of People's Property (APP), comprised more than 400 companies, grouped into 25 corporations, which together accounted for more than 40 percent of Gross Domestic Product (GDP).[13] APP companies spanned a wide array of activities: international transport (air and shipping lines); public transportation services; international trading companies; national retail store chains; textile factories; chemical processing and pharmaceutical plants; mining complexes; fishing boats; hotels and restaurants; food processing and metallurgic factories; an important share of the construction industry; and large coffee, cotton, sugar, and cattle estates.

Under the Sandinistas, the APP companies were attached to the corresponding government ministries (agricultural production and trading enterprises, for example, were under the Ministry of Agriculture and Agrarian Reform). The UNO government opted to concentrate all of the companies in a single entity, the National Corporation of the Public Sector (CORNAP) placed under the jurisdiction of Minister of the Presidency Antonio Lacayo. Lacayo's Vice Minister Ervin Krügger was named as CORNAP president and chairman of the General Committee of Corporations, the entity charged with overseeing the privatization process.

In practice, implementing privatization in Nicaragua required navigating a minefield of contradictions. Many of the potential Nicaraguan investors already had profitable businesses in other Central American countries and would have to find other motives to invest in risky Nicaragua. Likewise, foreign investors seeking profit margins through access to cheap labor could easily find opportunities in other countries of the region with less militant union movements and more stable political situations. Many sectors of the APP, for example the manufacturing enterprises and the mining sector, were in need of large investments for the modernization or conversion of the existing plant just to break even. For the government, selling off the most profitable companies quickly would mean forfeiting the revenues generated by them, while closing down the unprofitable state companies to reduce the budget deficit would aggravate an already serious unemployment problem, estimated at between — 35 and 45 percent of the economically active population.

The views of the different actors involved in the privatization process varied predictably. The FSLN — which created the APP in large measure through confiscating Somoza's properties — agreed that unprofitable and poorly administered state enterprises should be sold off. However, believing that in a small, underdeveloped economy like Nicaragua's, certain strategic areas of the economy should serve national interests as opposed to private, profit-making ones, the FSLN maintained that even the UNO government could find plenty of good reasons to hold on to the competitive enterprises such as some of the sugar-processing plants and the state coffee farms. COSEP — comprised of representatives of the business sector — insisted that the state exists to govern and should not be involved in

## COSEP: Where Business

From the end of the Somoza period, through the years of Sandinista rule, and into the initial period of the Chamorro administration, political opposition to the governing regime has always found a major center in the Supreme Council of Private Enterprise (COSEP). The umbrella organization was founded in 1978 — the outgrowth of a similar body, COSIP, which had been formed in 1972 — to coordinate the activities of the following six private business associations:

* Nicaraguan Development Institute (INDE): Founded in 1963 as the "social arm" of the private sector, INDE was closely linked to the "Banamerica" financial group of modernizing interests in the Conservative Party.

* Chamber of Commerce (CCN): The oldest COSEP member, the CCN was founded in 1928 to represent large import-export interests and industrialists. Today the CCN includes 17 departmental chambers and 10 associations of distributors, transportation firms, and specialized merchants.

* Chamber of Industry (CADIN): In 1957, Nicaraguan industrialists separated from the CCN to form CADIN. This group of manufacturing and agroprocessing industry representatives was substantially reduced through expropriations and confiscations carried out under the Sandinista government. Two of its leading representatives, Enrique Dreyfus and Antonio Lacayo, were founding members of CORDENIC and occupy ministerial positions in the Chamorro government.

* Chamber of Construction (CNC): Formed in 1967, most of the big construction companies belonging to the CNC were expropriated in the 1980s.

production at all. Its members called for the swift privatization of the APP in its entirety.[14] AID adopted a similar position and conditioned its economic assistance to the Chamorro government on progress toward privatization.[15]

Krügger's views, at least as stated publicly, differed substantially from those of COSEP. "Privatization is a very delicate issue," he said. "Those who are pushing for an irrational privatization and adopting ideological

---

### and Politics Mix

* Union of Agricultural Producers (UPANIC): Founded in 1979, UPANIC brings together eight agricultural producer associations in the cotton, coffee, beef, sorghum, dairy, rice, banana, and sugar sectors. UPANIC's 5,717 associated producers control an estimated one-fourth of the country's agricultural land and one-third of cattle lands.

* National Confederation of Professionals (CONAPRO): Founded in 1979, CONAPRO includes 14 associations ranging from architects and engineers to economists, lawyers, and pharmacists.

COSEP's opposition to Somoza stemmed largely from the dictatorship's "unfair competition" with fiscal policies and allocation of resources designed to bolster the family empire rather than the capitalist class as a whole. After the Sandinista victory, COSEP became the first major national institution to become embittered over the definition of the revolution as subject to "popular hegemony." Throughout the 1980s COSEP was the strongest and most staunch source of opposition to the FSLN inside the country.

Given the relative weakness of the opposition parties, COSEP was seen as the strongest single domestic source behind the 1989 formation of UNO. Resentful over its marginalization from the presidential ticket and during the UNO campaign, and subsequent exclusion from the Chamorro cabinet, COSEP has once again taken an opposition stance. It has called for a much more radical neoliberal economic plan than that being pursued by the Chamorro government. COSEP also has urged the immediate privatization of the state sector of the economy and a more confrontational posture towards the Sandinistas.

---

Source: Envío, July 1990, pp.22-23.

positions should realize the seriousness of this problem and the need for a proper technical analysis to make the recommendations which best suit the country." Krügger left open the possibility that part of the APP might remain in state hands and spoke of a slow, deliberative process of consultations and evaluations, hinting that privatization might take years.[16] It remained to be seen, however, whether such positions could withstand the pressures from AID and the IMF to accelerate privatization.

# Agriculture

Nicaragua is primarily an agrarian country. Agricultural production generates roughly 70 percent of the country's export earnings, and during the 1980s Nicaragua approached self-sufficiency in basic-grains production for domestic consumption. Despite a growing trend of migration to the urban areas, more than 40 percent of the economically active population has remained in agriculture.[17] Owing to its strategic importance in the economy and the fact that the countryside under Somoza was characterized by extreme inequalities and widespread poverty,[18] the agricultural sector was at the heart of revolutionary transformations undertaken by the Sandinistas.[19] By 1990 the agrarian reform had affected more than half of the country's arable land, benefiting some 60 percent of all rural families.[20] Many, although not all, of the big agroexport *haciendas* were broken up, and by 1990 the majority of farms were in the hands of small and medium-sized producers, some 88,000 of whom were organized into cooperatives.

Although by far the most comprehensive agrarian reform ever undertaken in Central America, the Nicaraguan experiment had serious shortcomings. The Sandinistas' goal of redistributing land and wealth in the countryside without alienating large private producers proved elusive as agroexporters tended to reinvest generous state credits in speculative operations or bank accounts in Miami, effectively boycotting production. Meanwhile, political and ideological mistakes and contradictions in the Sandinista policy of alliances — during the different phases of economic policy specific measures alternately favored or "punished" the state sector, urban salaried workers, *campesinos*, or big private producers — created conditions which allowed the contras to build a significant social base among the peasantry and the UNO coalition to sweep broad expanses of the countryside in the 1990 elections.

A very different process of transformation in agriculture, dubbed "agrarian counterreform" by pro-Sandinista *campesino* groups, was a fundamental component of the Chamorro government's plans for economic recovery. Forces linked to UNO in and out of the government immediately began dismantling the state and cooperative sectors and creating the conditions necessary for a rejuvenation of key agroexports like cotton, sugar, and beef. Publicly, the government spoke of its intention to respect land titles given out under the Sandinista agrarian reform as long as the farms remained productive. Despite such assurances, many feared a process of reconcentration of land in large holdings through the return of properties confiscated during the revolution to their former owners and through the market-based elimination of "inefficient" small producers and cooperatives.

## Land to Those Who Work It

For the Sandinistas, applying the mixed-economy model meant trying to meet the varied needs of small and large private farms, cooperatives, and state-owned farms.[21] The Nicaraguan Agrarian Reform Law, promulgated in 1981 and then broadened in January 1986, was designed to meet the needs of the rural poor and increase production of food and export crops simultaneously. The law explicitly protected private farmers and ranchers, no matter how large their landholdings, provided they continued to farm productively and efficiently. Those who left their land idle, however, were subject to expropriation with compensation.

By 1984, the year when the effects of contra activity in the countryside began to be felt in earnest, the reform sector incorporated more than four million acres, benefiting thousands of rural families. Production levels for most major crops climbed steadily. In 1983 overall agricultural production grew by 15 percent, the highest growth rate in Latin America that year.[22]

Despite these auspicious beginnings, contra advances in their efforts to create a social base among sectors of the peasantry in the northern war zones pointed to a glaring weakness in the character and pace of the agrarian-reform process. While many of the broader goals of agricultural policy were indeed being met, important sectors of the landless peasantry, a key part of the revolution's historic support base, had benefited little or not at all. The bias toward cooperatives virtually required *campesinos* to join a cooperative in order to receive land and largely excluded those who were reluctant to farm collectively.[23] Recognition of this weakness led to a sharp policy shift beginning in mid-1985.

The changes, mainly channeled through the National Union of Farmers and Ranchers (UNAG), ushered in a period of massive land distribution to individual *campesinos*, particularly in the war-torn northern mountains where some 70 percent of corn and bean crops originate. At

the same time, the government stepped up the process of granting legal
titles to lands occupied for years by small and medium producers.[24] This
redistribution was largely achieved by distributing land owned by state
farms and through government purchases of private land. The decision
to draw from the state farms was made not only to protect the
government's alliance with the big growers — whose cooperation was seen
as essential for arresting the economic decline and for promoting national unity in the face of U.S. aggression — but was also based on a critical
reevaluation of the state's overall role in agriculture. It had become clear
that the cooperatives and private farmers were in many cases more efficient producers than the state farms. By 1989 the state sector had distributed nearly a third of the land that it had acquired between 1979 and
1984.[25]

The economic and political clout of the small private producers expanded considerably after 1985. By 1989 it was estimated that this sector,
together with the cooperatives, was responsible for 47 percent of all
agricultural production (and nearly 100 percent of corn, bean, and
vegetable production for the domestic market). Medium-sized private
producers accounted for 14 percent; the big private producers, 17 percent; and the state sector, 22 percent. The small private producers and
cooperatives were the only sectors willing to invest and expand production during the harsh years of war and economic crisis. Between 1985
(when the total area planted in the country hit bottom) and the 1988-1989
agricultural cycle, these sectors brought an additional 170,000 acres under
cultivation, while state administrators and the big private producers
either maintained or reduced their areas planted.[26] The *campesino* sector was also a key beneficiary of the state's expansion of support services,
including easy credit terms, technical assistance, tractor and transportation services, as well as crop-storage and processing facilities.[27]

## Mistakes and Shortcomings of Agrarian Reform

Despite a series of advances which benefited the Nicaraguan
peasantry and rural workers, the Sandinista agrarian reform suffered
from several key policy mistakes. Many of the difficulties encountered
during the 1980s could be traced back to a long-standing debate among
those responsible for defining agrarian policy. Conflicts between those
who saw the big agroindustrial projects and the APP as the strategic
centerpiece of economic transformations and others who favored a
strengthening of the *campesino* sector often resulted in the adoption of
contradictory policies.

Most Sandinista policymakers later recognized that in the first years of the revolution, there had been an overemphasis on modernizing state farms, new large-scale investment projects, and on the promotion of cooperatives as the only acceptable form of *campesino* organization. Although these policies were modified over the years, the initial phase of agrarian reform left a bitterness among many *campesinos* which was never fully overcome and which played into the hands of contra efforts to develop a social base.

Prior to 1986, when prices for basic grains were liberalized, artificially low prices fixed by the state constituted a major factor in alienating sectors of the peasantry. The aim of the policy was to stimulate a supply of affordable foodstuffs for the urban population. While official consumer prices for the most part remained low, the net effect of the policy was to stimulate a thriving black market, a drop in area planted by *campesino* producers of basic grains, and most importantly, widespread disaffection in the countryside with the government . By the time price controls were lifted, resentment had already taken root.

Confiscations and the nature of the land titles given out under the agrarian reform caused further difficulties. In some parts of the countryside, the contras successfully manipulated the land question and won over *campesinos* on this basis. Underlying such efforts was the Sandinista policy of giving *campesinos* "use" titles to their land as opposed to outright property titles. The use titles allowed beneficiaries to pass their land on to children or to trade it for land elsewhere in the country, but not to sell it outright. The Sandinistas argued that such a step was necessary to avoid a future reconcentration of land in the hands of big private growers through the selling off their property during hard times by desperate *campesinos*. Nonetheless, the contras' insistence that the use titles were worthless, and UNO's campaign promise to exchange them for "real" titles, had a significant impact among the peasantry.

## UNO's Agrarian Counterreform

Formally, the Chamorro administration was committed to respecting the land-tenure transformations undertaken by the Sandinista agrarian reform. Some government leaders—including Gustavo Tablada, the Socialist Party leader appointed to direct the Agrarian Reform Institute (INRA)—spoke not only of respecting *campesino* land titles and the cooperatives, but of deepening the agrarian-reform process.[28]

In practice, things looked very different. On May 11, 1990 Chamorro announced two executive decrees which set the process of counterreform in motion. Decree 11-90 called for the installation of a five-person commission charged with reviewing land confiscations carried out by the previous government. The former landowners would have six months to present petitions soliciting the return of their farms. Decree 10-90 — seen as a temporary bridge for those who would have to wait for resolution of their cases under 11-90 and as a short-term incentive to expand cotton production for the 1990 cycle — empowered the state to lease lands which had been affected by the agrarian reform to private individuals. Decree 10-90 explicitly excluded lands which had been confiscated from Somoza. By the end of June the government had approved requests by 57 former landowners to rent some 86,000 acres of land on state farms. As the former owners — for the most part businessmen who had returned from exile in Miami — began showing up at the farms, many faced the active resistance of the workers. As the conflicts spread throughout the countryside, growing numbers of state farms were seized by the workers. It was this momentum which led to the July general strike.

Topping the list of the National Workers Federation's (FNT) demands in the July strike was the repeal of decrees 10-90 and 11-90. In the accord negotiated between the FNT and representatives of the Chamorro administration, the government assured that decree 10-90 had already fulfilled its purpose and that no more land would be rented under its provisions. The FNT heralded this as a victory for the strikers, and an important sign that the government would not be able to reverse the gains of the revolution at will. But by late August, the FNT cited the government's flagrant violation of the accords and increases in the pace of new land rentals under decree 10-90 as one of the reasons it would refuse to participate in *concertación* (national dialogue) meetings scheduled for September.[29]

Dismantling the APP is seen as a top priority by UNO and its U.S. backers for several reasons. Many of the 70,000 workers on the state farms are affiliated to the pro-Sandinista Rural Workers Association (ATC) and the APP generally is seen as a key FSLN power base. At the same time, while the cooperatives and individual *campesino* beneficiaries of the agrarian reform received land from a variety of sources, the state farms came almost exclusively from confiscations and expropriations. Politically, UNO needs the allegiance of some of these former owners, and feels it can be won by returning their land. Economically, some sectors in the government are wedded to the principle that the state should not be involved in production at all and are convinced that private ownership will bring greater efficiency and increased production levels.

The Sandinistas recognized that many state farms were poorly administered and that underexploited lands exist in the APP which could be put to better use. For these reasons, most land given out by the agrarian reform to *campesinos* after 1985 came from holdings in the APP rather than from expropriations of private lands. But there were also state farms that were well run and maintained high yields. Greater "efficiency" achieved by some capitalist producers was largely due to the fact that they were not obliged to provide social benefits to their workers. Many workers in the APP have all too fresh in their memory the days when they worked for subsistence wages under miserable living conditions for the same former owners who today wish to reclaim their land. Gains such as a minimum wage for agricultural work, worker participation in the management of state farms, and decent housing, child care centers, schools, and health clinics built with profits generated on the state farms will not be easily relinquished. Because many of these benefits serve both the workers on the state farms and *campesinos* and agricultural workers from the surrounding areas, there is likely to be broad community opposition to plans for returning lands to exploitative owners.

The cooperative movement also found itself embroiled in various altercations after the arrival of the new government. The Chamorro administration's role in this instance has been less one of taking the initiative in dismembering the cooperatives set up under the Sandinistas than remaining passive in the face of illegal takeovers of cooperatives by ex-contras and by forces aligned with the hardline sector in UNO. In dozens of takeovers around the countryside, the government, fearful of provoking a backlash from the right wing, has failed to act on its promise to defend the rule of law and the integrity of the cooperative movement.[30]

For the APP and the cooperatives, equally as ominous as these short-term threats is the possibility of a more gradual whittling away of the two sectors and their absorption into private hands. "The fear is not so much of violent eviction," explained Sinforiano Cáceres, founder of a cooperative in Chinandega department, "but of the slow economic strangulation of the sector."[31] Economic policy, including access to credit, is clearly designed to favor the big private growers producing export crops. The cooperatives are likely to come out on the short end of price and credit policies. Banks and private lenders will be able to foreclose on those cooperatives which cannot pay their debts; cooperative members will be tempted to sell off at least part of their properties in order to finance their operations; and the government could expropriate cooperative land which is not under active production.

The unstable situation on the APP farms and cooperatives is aggravated by the persistent problem of landless *campesinos*. By 1989 the Sandinista government was already facing serious pressure from the landless. Unwilling to antagonize the private sector, it was forced to take a public stance against a spate of land invasions which had occurred in the central and northwestern parts of the country. During the electoral campaign both the FSLN and UNO promised to address the needs of an estimated 40,000 landless families. While to date the Chamorro administration has not unveiled a plan to meet this promise, the ranks of

---

### The Cooperatives

Along with the state-owned farms, agricultural cooperatives have become a central focus of the land struggle under the Chamorro government.[32] The cooperative movement, marginalized under Somoza and a major target of contra attacks during the war,[33] had grown by 1990 to incorporate more than 88,000 members in 3,533 cooperatives. Of these, about one-third—the Sandinista Agricultural Cooperatives (CAS)—were based on collective ownership of land and resources while the other two-thirds consisted of farmers who continued to own and farm individual plots but shared credit and machinery—the Credit and Service Cooperatives (CCS).[34]

Cooperatives play a strategic role in the economy. They are responsible for 78 percent of all corn production; 59 percent of beans; 73 percent of sesame; and 47 percent of the national coffee harvest. In all, 73 percent of the nation's domestic food supply is produced by cooperatives.

Shortly after the 1990 elections, fearful that they would become a prime target of the Chamorro government's efforts to roll back the Sandinista agrarian reform, cooperative members banded together to form the Nicaraguan Federation of Agricultural Cooperatives (FENICOOP). Previously, cooperative members had been represented together with private producers in the National Union of Farmers and Ranchers. FENICOOP aims to provide cooperative members with an organizational base which will assist in their efforts to survive economically. The organization plans to establish training programs, supply companies, and services which cater to the cooperative sector. Most financing will come from the contribution of 1 percent of the gross sales of each member cooperative, but as a nongovernmental organization FENICOOP also will be able to seek foreign assistance.

the landless are growing rapidly as a result of contra demobilization, reductions in the army, and repatriation of refugees.

Meanwhile, uncertainty in the countryside provoked by the government's failure to clearly define its agrarian strategy, combined with high interest rates and a general apprehensiveness over the economy, have resulted in serious shortfalls in most planting targets. In particular, *campesino* producers of basic grains for the domestic market, both private owners and cooperative members, have for the most part decided not to risk planting anything beyond what is necessary for their subsistence needs.

## The Agroexport Economy

Historically, the overwhelming majority of Nicaragua's foreign-exchange earnings has come from the export of a few key products: coffee, cotton, beef, and sugar. Secondary exports like bananas, seafood, tobacco, and sesame trail far behind the "big four."

From the outset the Sandinista model of agrarian transformations envisioned moving away from this chronic dependence on primary agroexport products. The initial long-range goal was to have a series of large-scale, modern agroindustrial and processing plants, for the most part owned by the state, play the central role in the economy. But within a few years the combination of increasing difficulties in obtaining investment capital abroad and rethinking of the Sandinistas' alliance with the peasantry ushered in a gradual deprioritization of these big investment projects. Instead, resources were channeled toward *campesino* producers of basic grains, with a view toward achieving national self-sufficiency in foodstuffs, and toward new experimental projects in nontraditional agroexports. This shift also responded to the growing debate among policymakers over the question of class alliances in the countryside. Differences between those who supported rural workers as the priority sector, and those who favored benefiting land-owning *campesinos*, often resulted in ambivalent and contradictory policies.

The second half of the 1980s witnessed still another shift in the government's agrarian strategies. Under the combined weight of the U.S. trade embargo, cutoffs in loans and development funds from the IMF and World Bank, and the economic destruction wrought by the contra war, the Sandinistas prioritized support for big private producers growing traditional crops like cotton in efforts to generate desperately needed foreign exchange. If reliance on agroexports and the private sector was an undesired necessity largely forced on the Sandinistas, they have, on the contrary, been wholeheartedly embraced by Chamorro's economic planners as the key to economic recovery in the short run, and a cornerstone of development for the future.

During the 1980s coffee production was the agricultural sector's single most important source of employment and accounted for roughly half of the country's total export revenues, outdistancing cotton, bananas, and sugar combined. In marked contrast to the other big export crops, coffee requires relatively few costly imported inputs. More than half of all coffee production in Nicaragua is in the hands of small and medium individual production units, whereas cotton and sugar are concentrated on large holdings. Although this provides an important source of employment, the traditional, low-tech methods used have meant that the country has the lowest yields per acre in Central America. Coffee production is projected to increase under the UNO administration, in part due to the end of the war. An estimated 51,000 acres of prime coffee lands in the mountainous north were abandoned or could not be harvested due to the contra presence.

Although less important than coffee in terms of export earnings, beef production was similarly affected adversely by the war and is now poised for a significant recovery. Several factors contributed to a decline in meat export earnings during the 1980s. The country's cattle herd, which by 1979 had already been significantly reduced owing to the war against Somoza, dropped more than 20 percent between 1980 and 1987 as a result of contra activity and indiscriminate slaughter for quick sale abroad. In neighboring Costa Rica and Honduras, ranchers could get 8 times as much for their calves as in Nicaragua. Exports also were cut back as greater quantities of meat were sold on the local market and traditional markets in the United States were lost after the 1985 trade embargo.

UNO's economic planners set ambitious targets for increases in beef exports. Like coffee and sesame, the ratio of foreign exchange generated versus required imported inputs is generally favorable in the case of beef production thus facilitating the sector's recovery. Recuperation of markets in the United States also was expected to stimulate production. As a further boost, UNO counted on support from the country's big cattle ranchers most of whom come from the conservative south central lowlands which voted overwhelmingly in favor of UNO in the 1990 elections.

Cotton and sugar were the country's least efficient agroexports during the 1980s, requiring extraordinary amounts of costly imported inputs to keep them going. Cotton reached the point where it became a net drain on foreign exchange. Production in both was hit hard by the chronic shortage of foreign exchange for essential inputs, and earnings suffered from falling prices on the world market. The COSEP-affiliated large private producers, who were often as interested in undermining the government's economic plans as they were in turning a profit on their farms, controlled nearly half of cotton production. The rest was equally divided between state farms, small and medium producers, and cooperatives.

Cotton was at the center of UNO's economic-reactivation plan for 1990. But the broad package of incentives offered was largely unsuccessful in overcoming a series of obstacles and by August 1990 the area planted was less than half what had been targeted in the economic plan. Producers cited several different reasons for the shortfall: disruptions caused by the July general strike, excessive interest rates and high production costs due to hyperinflation, and a lack of confidence in the government due to differences over economic policy and concessions to the FSLN and the unions.

Throughout the 1980s banana plantations on the country's Pacific coast provided steady employment for about 5,000 agricultural workers. After 1982, when Standard Fruit unilaterally broke its contractual obligations and suspended operations in Nicaragua, the country became the first to produce and sell bananas successfully without multinational control. Nicaragua first worked out agreements with importers in the traditional U.S. market, but following the U.S. trade embargo, banana exports were reoriented to European markets. Production levels and export revenues fluctuated over the course of the decade, hitting their lowest points after the plantations were devastated by Hurricane Joan in 1988. Production for 1990 is expected to be the highest since 1978 with 5.9 million boxes.[35] After Chamorro's inauguration, representatives from Standard Fruit toured the banana plantations and discussed possible buy-out and investment plans with government authorities.[36]

The category of nontraditional exports is one of the few areas in agriculture where continuity can be seen in the policies adopted by the Sandinistas and those of the UNO government. Several new export crops were being developed on an experimental basis under the Sandinistas, including pineapple, melons, star fruit, ginger, and peanuts. These and other new products will receive fresh backing under Chamorro's program of tax incentives for producers investing in nontraditional goods for export. Within weeks of the Chamorro inauguration, a group of entrepreneurs formed the Nicaraguan Association of Producers and Exporters of Nontraditional Products. The group will assist in securing and channeling foreign assistance to provide training in administrative and marketing techniques for those interested in investing in nontraditionals.[37] As in the rest of the region, nontraditionals were expected to become a focus of the U.S. assistance program.

# Industry and Finance

The industrial sector, which was never very large or developed in Nicaragua, has had a sad fate over the last two decades.[38] Dependent upon exports to the Central American Common Market (CACM), Nicaraguan industry was severely wounded by the virtual collapse of the market in the 1970s. In the mid-1980s the Sandinista government's economic policy increasingly prioritized agricultural production, often to the detriment of industry. By 1988 industrial exports only amounted to about $20 million, down from a peak of $110 million in 1976.[39]

Approximately 30 percent of the manufacturing sector was nationalized after 1979, with the remainder in the hands of a private sector reluctant to make new investments. Both state and private industry suffered from the contractions of the national market owing to the economic crisis and the acute shortage of foreign exchange necessary for purchase of required inputs such as imported machinery, spare parts, and raw materials. The larger, traditional manufacturing subsectors — textiles, clothing, shoes, and furniture — reduced their operations and laid off workers. By 1989 the industrial sector accounted for only 10 percent of country's workforce.[40]

UNO's economic program promised a major rejuvenation of the manufacturing sector based on the modernization and conversion of existing industrial plants, privatization of state factories, and procurement of foreign and national investments for the opening of new ones. The Chamorro government also planned to offer attractive conditions for investors at a duty-free industrial park built under Somoza.

## State Controls Financial Levers

The Sandinistas' mixed-economy model sought to provide space and incentives for private capital in terms of ownership of farms and factories. The state, however, maintained control over the chief levers for regulating the economy, stimulating productive activities in all sectors, and distributing profits generated in the state's productive enterprises to the nation as a whole. In part, this was achieved through the nationalization of the national financial system and banks, insurance, and foreign trade enterprises. The philosophy underlying this strategy held that part of the profits gained through commercial transactions and international trade should be reinvested according to criteria mandated by the national development model and in accordance with the needs of all Nicaraguans. The nationalized banking and foreign trade systems thus were seen as essential in effecting a redistribution of resources in favor of the poor majority, and ultimately, in allowing the country to move toward a socialist economy.

The state's national financial system was the main source of credit for both the public and private sectors. The Sandinista government made substantial modifications in the distribution of credit, attempting to stimulate production and rural development through extensive loan programs for small farmers and food producers.[41] The Chamorro government immediately modified credit policies, raising the prevailing interest rates and removing flexibilities which had existed under the previous system. With small farmers, traders, and artisans forced to put up their property as collateral, many foresaw a tendency toward ownership concentration through foreclosures and buy-outs.

UNO's plans for the banking system contemplated privatization through the establishment of new financial institutions which would gradually replace the nationalized banks. While some cabinet members spoke of selling off shares in the existing state foreign trade companies, others appeared more interested in keeping such services within the state.

Efforts by the Central Bank to increase tax revenues had several main thrusts. Levels were raised on "sin taxes" — alcoholic beverages, cigarettes, and petroleum products — and direct taxes were lowered. In addition, payment and processing schemes were simplified in an effort to eliminate the widespread problem of tax evasion which existed under the Sandinistas and to create more favorable conditions for investment.

Major reforms also were planned on the foreign investment law. The law promulgated by the Sandinistas in 1987 contained virtually no restrictions, leaving most conditions and terms to be dealt with on a case by case basis with the Ministry of Foreign Cooperation. The new law would offer tax rebates and other incentives for enterprises exporting nontraditional products. The proposal, similar to the regulations existing in the other Central American countries, also included import-duty waivers for raw materials.[42]

## The Burden of Debt

A major problem inherited by the Chamorro government was the massive external debt which had accumulated over the course of the 1980s. By the time the Sandinistas left office in 1990, the debt had mushroomed to $9.6 billion, a dramatic increase over the $1.6 billion debt which existed in 1979.[43] The key factor behind the growth of the debt was the government's need to finance the trade deficit which averaged $400 to $600 million per year after 1982.

Although the size of the foreign debt is staggering, one of the highest per capita in Latin America, Chamorro's economic policymakers will have two elements working in their favor when they sit down to renegotiate the debt with the banks, lending institutions, and governments involved. First, compared to other countries, the structure of Nicaragua's debt is advantageous: 59 percent is owed to governments (more than half of that is owed to the socialist and formerly socialist countries); 13.6 percent to commercial banks; 10.5 percent to multilateral organizations; others, including interest, cover the remaining 16.9 percent. In contrast, in 1979 more than 75 percent of the debt was owed to multilateral organizations and commercial banks, which do not offer the flexibility that governments do in terms of renegotiating the debt. Second, much of the international community, and in particular the governments to which the bulk of the debt is owed, recognize that Nicaragua's debt was incurred under unique circumstances—war and a U.S. trade and financial embargo—and have expressed a willingness to treat it as a special case.

For Nicaragua, the biggest burden in the foreign debt is the question of arrears with the international financial institutions. The outstanding debt owed to the Interamerican Development Bank (IDB) is $396 million and to the World Bank $160 million, with overdue back payments totaling $180 million and $50 million respectively. Until these arrears are cleared, the country cannot solicit fresh financing from these institutions. In mid-1990 a special consulting group—comprised of representatives from the International Monetary Fund, the IDB, and the World Bank— was set up to assist Nicaragua in its search for financing to clear its arrears. The government's aim was to have the back debts paid up by early 1991, the same date which was being proposed for the implementation of an IMF-approved economic-stabilization program.[44]

## Chapter 4

# Society and Environment

## Popular Organizing

When the victorious FSLN guerrillas marched into Managua on July 19, 1979 they enjoyed widespread popular support. The strongest backing came from the peasants, students, and poor urban residents who had taken up arms or built barricades during the insurrection. But the campaign to oust the Somoza dictatorship also brought together the traditional political parties, business organizations, and the Catholic church. It was a highly unusual multiclass coalition whose common denominator was the hatred of the Somoza regime and its National Guard.

As widespread as the initial support for the revolution was, there existed no extensive infrastructure of experienced popular organizations on which the new government could base its radical political and economic agenda. Although enthusiastic in their support for the new government, the popular sectors were largely unorganized. The heroic struggle of the Sandinista guerrilla when combined with the desperate, defensive violence of the National Guard had sparked a popular uprising in Nicaragua. The rebellion was, however, more the product of decades of pent-up anger than of decades of careful popular organizing. Repression had made organizing by the popular sectors difficult and dangerous during the Somoza years.

Until the FSLN helped organize the clandestine Association of Rural Workers (ATC) in 1978, most rural organizing was linked to the popular education and social justice initiatives of the Catholic church. In the cities, only 10 percent of the workers were organized and the student associations were weak and repressed. In the urban *barrios* the Sandinistas sparked the creation of the Civilian Defense Committees (CDCs). Except for the outlawed Communist Party, the political parties were small elitist cliques with no links to the popular sectors.

## Organizations of the Masses

The Sandinista victory sparked a flourishing of popular organizations. During the last two months of the Sandinista offensive, the CDCs were the only functioning civilian structure in many areas. They played an equally critical role following the change in government. Renamed the Sandinista Defense Committees (CDSs), these *barrio* organizations, which were highly regarded by their communities, coordinated relief operations as well as assuming vigilance and defense work for the new government.

One week after the July 1979 triumph, the FSLN reaffirmed the class nature of its government, declaring: "The key to our victory and also the bridge from which we will move toward defending and deepening the revolution is the unity of the Sandinista vanguard with the entire population but particularly with its most exploited sectors."[1] The ATC was charged with the task of organizing farmworkers and farmers with the expropriated estates of the Somocistas as the immediate focus. With the creation of the Sandinista Workers Confederation (CST), there was an explosion of union organizing. By 1983 at least 40 percent of the country's workforce had become union members, rising to 56 percent by 1986.[2] The two other major "mass organizations" associated with the new revolutionary government were the Nicaraguan Women's Association (AMNLAE) and the Sandinista Youth (JS).

The mass organizations were established with the dual function of serving as instruments of the revolutionary state and representing the sectoral interests of their own constituencies. During the first couple years of the Sandinista government they performed both functions well. With the assistance of the organized popular sectors, massive health and literacy programs were launched and new state structures were put into place. The mass organizations also proved critically important in propagating revolutionary analysis. Although the leaders of these organizations were FSLN militants, they were also strong advocates of the special interests of their respective organizations.

By 1981 the FSLN government began to face the often contradictory nature of its revolutionary experiment. While still wedded to its historic commitment to defend the interests of the workers and the peasants, the Sandinista leadership also recognized the necessity to increase foreign exchange earnings and keep the capitalist sector producing. The successful blending of the mixed economy and the politics of national unity with the capitalist sectors was seen as essential in the pursuit of the overall revolutionary model, but at least in the short term it meant putting the brakes on worker and peasant vindications. As sociologist Luís Serra observed in 1988: "The mixed character of the economy weighted heavily toward the bourgeoisie and small entrepreneurs, and with the corresponding program of national unity and pluralism, set the limits to the demands of the popular sectors for a more just distribution of national income."[3]

The government's economic project has been described as "development with redistribution."[4] During the first years of the Sandinista government that is exactly what happened: consumption levels increased for the poor and the economy was recovering from the war. At the same time the popular sectors were largely enthusiastic about the popular organizations. But as inflationary pressures mounted and production levels stagnated, the government began to intervene to defuse class-based confrontations. Marking the end of an era of aggressive popular organizing, the government issued the Social and Economic Emergency Law in September 1981. Strikes, lockouts, and spontaneous takeovers of private property were banned.[5]

No longer was the ATC encouraged to expropriate the estates of "unpatriotic" landowners, no longer did the government applaud when CST unions targeted factories for occupations and strikes. The government, concerned about the stagnating economy, sought to avoid aggravating class conflicts in the interests of increasing production. With the escalation of the contra war, national defense became an even more powerful justification for clamping down on economic disruptions. Although there was some opposition, the priorities of economic stability and defense were largely accepted by the mass organizations as corresponding to their fundamental interests. Increasingly, the focus of popular mobilizing became the military effort to defeat the counterrevolution.

The sacrifices demanded in the name of production and defense were not the only reasons the mass organizations lost their initial vitality. The lifeblood of the popular organizations also was sapped by the institutionalization of the revolutionary state. As the state bureaucracy expanded it took over tasks formerly coordinated by the CDSs and other voluntary groups. The formation of the Territorial Militias in 1983 also undermined the defense functions of the CDSs.

But it was the dual-purpose nature of the mass organizations that eventually proved to be their major weakness. Defining itself as the vanguard party, the FSLN expected the popular organizations to accept its formulation of priorities for revolutionary stability and progress. Since the directors of the mass organizations were themselves Sandinista militants, the particular needs and demands of the organizations they led were increasingly pushed to the side by the FSLN's own priorities. Confusion and contradictions developed because of the double role and dual responsibility. Since the party's hierarchy and discipline was superior to that of the popular organizations, the interests of the popular sectors often got lost.[6]

Instead of actively representing the special interests of their constituents, the leadership of the mass organizations regarded the overall defense of the revolution and the FSLN government as being the best way to guarantee the welfare of their constituents. While often appearing as mere auxiliaries of the FSLN, the mass organizations for the most part agreed with the government's analysis that the stability of the revolution and the war against the contras were the leading priorities.

At first, FSLN control over the mass organizations raised few questions. It was, after all, the FSLN which had created these organizations, and it was the FSLN that had sparked the explosion of popular organizing in Nicaragua. It also seemed that the mass organizations and the government were moving in parallel and complementary directions, and the members of the popular organizations often made the decision to defend the revolution despite the personal hardships.

As the FSLN government became institutionalized, however, the mass organizations lost their direction and their active membership dwindled. This decline in popular mobilization also represented a regression to a common condition of social noninvolvement in Nicaraguan society where griping and apathy prevail over social activism.

But emerging conflicts between the government and the popular sectors also contributed to the mass organizations' loss of dynamism. In the interests of boosting exports and building alliances with the "patriotic" business sectors, the government channeled credits and subsidies to large producers while ignoring the credit and technical needs of small basic-grains farmers and discouraging farmworker organizing. Similarly, the Nicaraguan Women's Association (AMNLAE) was discouraged from expanding its organizing to gender-specific issues like abortion and sexual abuse and instead was directed to concentrate on organizing support committees of the mothers and wives of combatants.

From its earliest days the Sandinista revolution pledged to create a participatory democracy that included the popular sectors not only in national policymaking but also in the decision-making in factories, agricultural estates, and schools. Women, students, peasants, workers, and neighborhood activists did gain an extraordinary new prominence in Nicaragua as a result of the revolution. But the new model of participatory democracy was limited and in the end seriously compromised by the ever-present control of the FSLN—itself a vertical and highly centralized political organization. The top-down working style of the Sandinistas also was closely reflected in the operations of the mass organizations, further inhibiting popular participation and limiting these organizations to Sandinista sympathizers.

The early Sandinista model of participatory democracy included the representation of the mass organizations in the Council of State. But this direct role of the popular sectors in policymaking was eliminated with the 1984 elections and the creation of the National Assembly, where only political parties were represented. But even when the leaders of the mass organizations had their own place in the Council of State, the particular interests of the popular sectors they represented often were lost in the common effort to strengthen the revolution and support the FSLN's leadership.[7]

The most dynamic and strongest popular organization in the late 1980s was the National Union of Farmers and Ranchers (UNAG). Originally founded in 1981 to organize small and medium-sized private farmers and cooperatives to offset the weight of the large grower associations linked to the Superior Council of Private Enterprise (COSEP) business chamber, UNAG had broadened its base by 1984 to include large producers.[8] By 1989 UNAG members were raising a large part of the nation's foodstuffs, as well as half the coffee and cotton and 60 percent of the livestock.[9] Of the country's 280,000 *campesinos*, some 125,000 were affiliated with UNAG.[10] UNAG played an increasingly central role in shaping agricultural policy at the national level and overseeing its implementation on farms and cooperatives. In negotiations with the government, UNAG won fundamental modifications in the agrarian-reform process to favor the peasantry, cancellation of *campesino* debts with the national banking system, increases in producer prices, and generous credit terms.

## The Promise of Peace and the Economic Crisis

The strategic defeat of the contras in 1986 and the opening of the Esquipulas peace process in 1987 raised the hopes of the popular sectors that the priorities of the revolution would soon switch from defense to meeting popular demands for higher consumption levels and a deepening of participatory democracy. But years of inflationary spending, an oppressive foreign debt, and declining foreign aid compelled the government to impose a structural-adjustment program. The "shock" program was greeted enthusiastically by COSEP but smashed popular expectations that the end of the war would finally mean improving living standards. Particularly hard hit were the urban poor and salaried workers who saw the compensatory "social wage" significantly reduced.

With the lifting of the State of Emergency in January 1988, the internal political opposition began mobilizing, supported largely by U.S. government funding. In Masaya there was a demonstration of more than 10,000 people protesting Sandinista policies. Sharply critical of the FSLN's economic performance and calling for the repeal of the military draft, the internal opposition attracted increasing popular sympathy.

At the same time, the FSLN strove to inject new life into its own mass organizations, particularly the CDSs. Criticizing the CDS for its verticalism and lack of community organizing, the FSLN appointed the popular Omar Cabezas to rejuvenate the moribund committees. But expanding popular support and reviving the mass organizations were difficult tasks at a time when austerity measures were hitting hard. The inability of the government to end the war and its consequent unwillingness to call off the military draft also contributed to popular alienation from the government. Attempts to democratize and reform the mass organizations were seen by many Nicaraguans as simply more political "partyism."

Despite all of the weaknesses and contradictions of the revolution, the popular sectors fought to protect it. The organized workers and the peasants recognized that for the first time the revolution had given them a voice and a dignified place in their country. The mass organizations also saw the revolution as being in the best long-term interests of the popular sectors despite the immediate hardships. During the height of the contra war the FSLN erected billboards that carried the words of Augusto Sandino: "Only the workers and the peasants will go all the way." Indeed, the Nicaraguan workers and peasants did demonstrate an heroic commitment to defend the revolution and turn back the contras.

By 1990, however, the FSLN government could no longer count on the committed support of the Nicaraguan majority. There were no signs that U.S. aggression would end, the war dragged on, the economic crisis was hitting the poor the hardest, and the definition of the revolution had become less clear. The majority of Nicaraguans were ready for a change of government.

## The Grassroots Revolution

With the Sandinistas no longer in power after April 1990, the country's popular organizations took on the shape and direction of popular movements in other Central American countries. Suddenly, a large segment of the popular movement was no longer constrained by its ties to the government and was freer to organize and militate for its particular demands.

The revolutionary popular movement, long identified with the ruling party, largely moved into the opposition after April 1990.

Major differences exist, however, between the circumstances facing the newly constituted popular movement in Nicaragua and the situation elsewhere in the region. Most significant is the absence of a repressive police and army. The Nicaraguan popular movement also is distinguished by its association with the country's largest and best-organized political party. Like their counterparts throughout Central America, the popular sectors in Nicaragua have been caught up in the struggle to defend themselves against government-stabilization policies. But the Nicaraguan popular movement is alone in also fighting to defend gains made by a revolutionary government. Although overwhelmingly leftist and revolutionary in political orientation, the popular movement also includes a significant anti-Sandinista component that is tied to the right wing and to U.S. funding.

The election victory of the UNO slate raised popular expectations that the war would finally end and that U.S. dollars would flow into Managua. In fact, UNO promises that foreign aid would help reconstruct the economy largely explained the opposition coalition's impressive majority. With no war and the economic blockade lifted, the country's popular sectors felt that the new administration would address their needs and demands, postponed for so long as a result of the war and U.S. economic aggression. Instead, the country's popular sectors found themselves the victims of a new and still harsher economic-stabilization program.

UNO's program lacked some of the compensatory mechanisms that had been retained by the stabilization plan instituted by the FSLN government. The popular movement also recognized that the new government's emphasis on privatization and the relinquishing of state control over important policy levers such as foreign exchange and banking also signified an institutionalization of a shift in economic power.

Ironically, it was these adverse circumstances—the defeat of the FSLN and the government's anti-popular economic program—that sparked an explosion of popular organizing. The most dramatic evidence of this revival of the popular movement was the united peasant, worker, and student reaction to government attempts to roll back revolutionary gains and impose its stabilization program. Acting independently of the FSLN directorate, the ATC, CST, and other unions showed impressive mobilizing power during the first few months of the Chamorro administration. Integrating wage issues with demands addressing the broader social welfare and a determination to protect the gains of the revolution, the newly formed National Workers Federation (FNT) forged widespread popular support for the general strikes of May and July.

At first, the FSLN's election defeat shocked and immobilized most popular organizers. But inspired by the FSLN's own recovery, activists of the popular movement began to redefine their work. Women within the mass women's organization AMNLAE, for example, called for the organization to disassociate itself from the FSLN and to deepen its commitment to women's issues. This process of redefinition and restructuring of the popular movement also saw the birth of dozens of new nongovernmental organizations (NGOs), many of them established by former government officials. Another new dimension of the popular movement was a focus on municipal affairs and community development, with a special emphasis on those towns controlled by the FSLN.

Unable to count on the support of the central government, the Sandinista-linked popular organizations faced fresh challenges and threats. Using U.S. aid programs, the Chamorro administration and UNO municipal governments were attempting to undermine and coopt the more militant popular organizations. The recognition of parallel unions and rural associations also threatened the unity of the popular movement.

Essential to the dynamism of the popular movement will be a thorough democratization of its leadership and a reconception of its relationship with the FSLN. As a Managua research institute observed: "The advance in representative democracy through elections moved faster than the democratization of participation within the popular organizations or in their relations with the state and vanguard party."[11] Immediately after the February 1990 election, however, the self-criticism process that had been haltingly started in 1988 took hold in most popular organizations. As a result, new and often more militant leaders were being elected. Within the FSLN a similar democratization process took hold after the party's defeat.

Still in question is the nature of the relationship between the popular movement and the FSLN. Even before the election, steps had been taken to democratize the mass organizations by having their leaders elected by the membership rather than being appointed by the party. The loss of state power has made it impossible for the FSLN to maintain responsibility for the mass organizations even if it wanted to. The party is having a difficult enough time maintaining itself financially without having to worry about the financial and institutional stability of these popular organizations.

Up for debate is the vanguard status of the party, meaning that it is the party that sets the political and strategic direction for the entire progressive movement. The FSLN itself is discussing this question, but it is also a matter that has been the subject of criticism within the popular organizations. Some leftist critics have charged that the FSLN is moving into an alliance with the "modern" bourgeois fraction of government and giving its support to an economic-stabilization program contrary to the interests of the popular sectors. During the strikes following Chamorro's inauguration, there also was criticism that the FSLN incorrectly assumed that it could step in and negotiate on behalf of the popular organizations. With their greater autonomy and need to respond to the demands of their members, the popular organizations may be more reluctant now to accept the FSLN's vanguard status. At the same time, there is widespread recognition of the FSLN's historic commitment to the poor and its proven leadership capacities.

Addressing this question of the party's vanguard role, former Interior Minister Tomás Borge said, "Leaders should always interpret the will of the base and the people, while not forgetting that, with some frequency, immediate measures must be taken with an agreed-upon tactic linked to the spirit of correctly interpreting popular and partisan wishes."[12] Another aspect of this "dialectic" between the popular organizations and the party is, as former President Daniel Ortega has said, that often the popular organizations must go ahead of the party.[13]

The success of the FSLN's determination to "govern from below" and to regain political power in 1996 will be determined largely by its ability to represent the interests of the popular sectors. Likewise the growth and influence of the mass organizations will depend on their ability to unite all the popular sectors around common economic demands and political principles.

# Labor and Unions

Before World War II the country's small working class was mostly grouped around the foreign enclave sector of the economy—the gold mines, banana plantations, and lumber companies.[14] Following World War I anarcho-syndicalist labor activists sparked the first workplace organizing in the country. But attempts to form unions were brutally repressed, as in the massacre of the Cuyamel banana strikers in 1925. In the 1930s some of the country's organized workers, like those of the Braggman Bluff Lumber Company, joined Sandino's anti-imperialist guerrilla army. In 1931 the short-lived Nicaraguan Workers Party was organized by one of Sandino's lieutenants.

For the next 40 years the country's labor history was marked by repression and cooptation by the Somoza family dictatorship. As a result no more than 11 percent of the country's salaried workforce was organized, making the Nicaraguan labor movement one of the most underdeveloped in the region. The National Guard was repeatedly brought in to crush militant and socialist unions, while other more moderate labor leaders and unions were deftly manipulated by Somoza's Nationalist Liberal Party. With the opening of the Central American Common Market and incipient industrialization, a new urban workforce emerged in the 1960s. The boom in cotton production and the displacement of thousands of small peasant farmers created a large pool of seasonal wage laborers in the countryside.

Dominating the labor scene in the 1950s was the General Confederation of Workers (CGT), a corrupt and pro-Somoza federation. Dissident unions broke away from the CGT in the 1960s forming the CGT-Independent (CGT-I), which had close ties to the Nicaraguan Socialist Party (PSN). In the mid-1960s the Confederation of Trade Union Unity (CUS) was founded with the assistance of the U.S.-government funded American Institute for Free Labor Development (AIFLD). Another important confederation during the Somoza period was the Nicaraguan Workers Confederation (CTN), founded in 1972 as an outgrowth of an earlier confederation founded by middle-class Social Christians and reformist Conservatives. There were also two leftist confederations. Trade Union Action and Unity Confederation (CAUS) was a creation of the Nicaraguan Communist Party while the Workers Front (FO) was the offspring of the Marxist-Leninist Popular Action Movement (MAP-ML), an ultraleft splinter group expelled from the FSLN in the 1970s.

One of the first attempts to organize the peasant sector was the creation of the Evangelical Committee for Agrarian Promotion by the Jesuits in 1969. Repression by the National Guard radicalized many peasant leaders, pushing them closer to the FSLN's revolutionary project. In cooperation with the Delegates of the Word, the FSLN began organizing the Committees of Agricultural Workers in 1976, and in 1978 these local committees joined together to form the Rural Workers Association (ATC). The urban counterpart to the ATC were the Workers Struggle Committees (CLT), which after July 1979 became the base of the Sandinista Workers Central (CST).

By 1978 all the country's unions were calling for the removal of Somoza, but the FSLN and the leftist unions, particularly those affiliated with the CGT-I, were the ones that organized striking workers into more active popular resistance. CUS declined to join the FSLN-led United

People's Movement (MPU), which refused to bow to U.S. pressure to negotiate with Somoza.

## Labor Movement 1979-1990

Labor organizing flourished under the Sandinista government, particularly during the early 1980s. When the FSLN took power, there were 183 workplace unions, representing less than 10 percent of all workers.[15] In 1978 there were only three agricultural union locals in the countryside where the bulk of the population resides. By the end of the 1980s there were more than 2,000 workplace unions, more than a third of them in rural areas, with some 55 percent of the working population unionized.[16]

Although the union movement was larger than ever, the economic circumstances of the working class had barely improved. When the FSLN left office more than 25 percent of the population was unemployed and real per capita income levels had regressed almost 40 years – paralleling regressive trends in Guatemala and El Salvador. Workers and peasants could, however, point to some fundamental gains, such as the right to review company financial records and participate in decision-making at state enterprises. The provision of new health, education, and social welfare services – what the FSLN called the "social wage" – was also attributed to the government's basic commitment to assist the poor and working class. Along with the entire popular movement, the war and economic crisis hit the union movement hard, creating new division and tensions.

Because of their institutional ties to the FSLN and their commitment to the revolutionary process, the leading labor organizations during the FSLN government were the CST and the ATC. Nearly two-thirds of the country's organized workers were affiliated with either the ATC or CST. Other much smaller union confederations were found to the left and the right of the Sandinista unions.

From the outset the CAUS and the ultraleftist FO opposed the Sandinista revolution for having made too many concessions to the bourgeoisie. When the Sandinista Peoples Army was formed in 1979 the FO refused to disband its own armed militias. The following year, the government closed the FO's militant tabloid, *El Pueblo*, which was given permission to publish again in the late 1980s. The CAUS – which brings together 22 unions with some 10,000 members among textile, farm, and metal workers – also assumed a militant posture during the 1980s. In 1981 the government arrested PCN president Elí Altamirano, along with several CAUS leaders, for violating the strike ban. In 1987 CAUS joined the anti-Sandinista Permanent Workers Congress (CPT).

To the right of the ATC and CST stand CUS and CTN, both of which have received U.S. government funding funneled through the AIFLD. Only CUS, however, is organizationally linked to AIFLD. Although representing only about 3 percent of the country's workforce, the two unions had high international profiles during the 1980s.[17] Although it had shied away from the political struggle against Somoza CUS became virulently anti-Sandinista, organizing several opposition demonstrations in 1988 and 1989. Membership estimates have ranged from the 2,000 figure given by the Sandinista Ministry of Labor to the 35,000 members claimed by CUS itself. Although it has denied any formal relations with political parties, CUS has been very close to the Social Democratic Party (PSD) and was a strong backer of the UNO campaign.

The other pillar of the rightwing labor movement has been the CTN, which is affiliated with the Social Christian Party (PSC). It has some 20,000 members from 63 unions, ranging from metalworkers to bus drivers, *La Prensa* staff, and banana workers. A CTN split in 1982 gave rise to the CTN-A, which affiliated with the Popular Social Christian Party (PPSC).

The CGT-I, along with the Nicaraguan Socialist Party (PSN), was divided on an appropriate response to the FSLN government. Although generally supportive for most of the 1980s, the CGT-I strongly criticized the government's austerity program and in 1987 joined the opposition alliance CPT. Strong in the construction industry, the CGT-I organized important strikes during the last year of the FSLN government.

The CPT was formed in late 1987 as an umbrella organization of four confederations from left and right: CUS, CTN-A, CGT-I, and CAUS. With the initiation of the Esquipulas peace accords, negotiations with the contras, and the increased U.S. emphasis on building the internal opposition, there was more political space available for organizing within the anti-Sandinista labor movement. Like UNO itself, CPT was largely a product of U.S.-sponsored unification efforts and benefited from large doses of advice and financing from AIFLD, the U.S. Agency for International Development (AID), and the National Endowment for Democracy (NED). (See U.S. Economic Aid) Despite the ideological diversity which separated them, the CPT unions managed to remain united around a series of demands, including revision of the Labor Code, elimination of preferential treatment for pro-FSLN unions, and restoration of full trade-union freedoms.

Under the State of Emergency (in effect for most of the period from March 1982 to January 1988), some trade-union rights were restricted, including the right to strike. Despite the legal restriction, dozens of strikes and hundreds of temporary work stoppages took place during the 1980s, all of which were eventually resolved through dialogue with the Sandinista authorities.

As noted elsewhere, the improvement in wage and consumption levels that followed the Sandinista triumph soon gave way to austerity and inflation. Initially, the declining wage rates were compensated, at least in part, by the benefits of the "social wage." As the economic crisis set in, the government attempted to cushion workers from its most harsh effects through the provision of subsidized workplace food programs, child care, and general stores or commissaries. Also partially compensating for declining purchasing power were "payment in kind" programs whereby workers were given textiles, produce, and other goods. New austerity measures adopted in the late 1980s brought sharp reductions in the social wage while leaving salary levels abysmally low. Urban salaried workers suffered additional losses due to government programs that prioritized the farm sector after 1985.[18]

## The New Labor Battlefield

During the 11 years of FSLN government the Sandinista unions maintained that the best defense of the working class was the defense of the revolution, even if that stance meant compromising on their own demands. As the war faded, this argument carried less weight with rank and file members of the CST and the ATC, who were hit hard in 1988 by severe austerity measures. Even after the lifting of the State of Emergency in January 1988 the pro-FSLN unions were reluctant to mobilize against the government's structural-adjustment program for fear of destabilizing the revolution.

Not constrained by any similar commitment to the revolution, the CPT discovered that its anti-government program found new acceptance among the increasingly desperate popular sectors. The prominent support of the CPT for the UNO political coalition was instrumental in combating Sandinista charges that UNO was the political instrument of the traditional oligarchy.

The April 1990 inauguration of President Violeta Chamorro dramatically changed the configuration of the Nicaraguan labor movement. The political positions of the two contending union sectors were suddenly reversed. Subject to discrimination and a certain degree of repression during the 1980s, the anti-Sandinista unions counted on rapid growth after the FSLN government was voted out of office. No longer tied to defending the government, the CST and ATC moved easily into the opposition. Tired of being labeled the *voceros oficiales* or official spokespersons of the government, the unions were ready to defend the revolution — but this time from below. In contrast, the former opposition unions were thrust into the more difficult position of defending the new government whose interests were more aligned with the national bourgeoisie and Washington than with the popular sectors.

With the change in government, the Sandinista unions gained a new prominence. To confront the harsh economic plan of the Chamorro government, the Sandinista unions formed the National Workers Federation (FNT), which joined the CST, ATC, National Employees Union (UNE), Nicaraguan Journalists Union (UPN), National Confederation of Professionals (CONAPRO), Federation of Health Workers (FET-SALUD), and National Educators Association (ANDEN).[19]

While the role and direction of the FSLN remained unclear after the election, the challenge of defending the advances of the revolution and mobilizing the popular sectors was enthusiastically assumed by CST, ATC, and other pro-FSLN unions. The mobilizing strength of the Sandinista unions and their new militancy were made abundantly clear by the general strikes of May and July 1990. An important new dynamic which emerged in both strikes was the increasing autonomy of the FNT unions from the FSLN. The strikes were largely the product of decisions reached by individual union assemblies, rather than the result of FSLN directives. Although the FSLN leadership did eventually express support for the union demands and then play a key role in negotiating the strike settlements, there was a clear gap between the radicalized union bases and the FSLN leadership, which was concerned about safeguarding the party's role as a legal and legitimate opposition force.

Those strikes also highlighted the marginalized and reactionary character of the CPT. Rather than offering at least conditional support for FNT's demands, the CPT attempted to mobilize an active worker resistance to the strikes. Its efforts were unsuccessful even though there was widespread public condemnation of certain FNT activities, such as the building of barricades of paving stones to block travel through Managua's *barrios*. Elements of the CPT were instrumental, however, in organizing small groups, mostly of unemployed youth, to attack strike supporters in such UNO strongholds as Ciudad Jardín. The CPT joined the country's right wing in condemning the government's politics of conciliation and negotiation with the Sandinistas, with the most radical factions of the CTN and CAUS associating with fringe elements of Vice President Godoy's National Salvation Committees. The inability of the CPT unions to mobilize workers against the Sandinistas disheartened AIFLD and the

U.S. embassy, which had been counting on the confederation to edge out the Sandinista unions after the FSLN's electoral defeat.

During the 1980s most union federations, especially the CUS and the CTN, had stressed political activity over workplace organizing. Similarly, the CPT's agenda since 1987 has been set more by the associated political parties than by worker demands. No longer forming the opposition coalition, the CPT unions have been labeled by the Sandinistas as "official" and "pro-government" organizations – a description the CPT categorically rejects. Although part of the same anti-Sandinista coalition, the four unions that compose the CPT are not unified around one political line but reflect the internal divisions within UNO and the government. As economic and political tensions increase and define themselves it is likely that some CPT unions will break away, uniting with other unions around economic demands and distancing themselves from the government.[20]

The CPT unions, which had so strongly backed the UNO campaign, found themselves torn in several directions at the start of the Chamorro administration. On the one hand the CPT found itself in the same position formerly occupied by the Sandinista unions – defending the government against the political and economic challenges of the opposition. But on the other hand the CPT, like the U.S. embassy, was extremely uncomfortable with the independent political stance taken by the Chamorro administration in its first months in power. Like the rightwing political parties and business organizations, the CPT unions for the most part are ardently anti-Sandinista and would like to see all vestiges of *sandinismo* destroyed. They fear that the Chamorro government, unwittingly perhaps, has given the Sandinistas a new lease on life. Nonetheless, although some elements of the anti-Sandinista unions quickly moved to the right of the government, there were signs that other elements were moving to the government's left, joining with the Sandinista unions in making wage demands and cautioning against wholesale privatization.

To bolster their own positions, the CPT unions are seeking to move into workplaces long controlled by the Sandinista unions. Sandinista-sponsored revisions to the Labor Code, approved by the National Assembly in April 1990, opened up workplaces to more than one union. The FSLN advocated this change to protect its own associated unions from being displaced by unions installed by the UNO government, while the CPT unions also regarded this multi-union environment conducive to their growth. Member unions of CPT quickly moved to establish new anti-Sandinista unions in both the private and public sectors, while the FNT charged that the government was firing thousands of public-sector employees only to replace many of them with UNO sympathizers.

The FNT called these new parallel unions *fantasmas* or phantom unions because of their failure to attract more than a handful of members. Typically the founding meetings of these parallel unions are held, not at the workplace itself, but in luxury restaurants and bars favored by the contras and UNO political parties. Ties with the government and the private sector, as well as the essentially nonconfrontational approach of these new parallel unions, may attract many workers who have differences with the revolutionary politics of the Sandinista unions.

Standing outside the two major union coalitions — the FNT and the CPT — are the Nicaraguan Workers Confederation (CTN) which is linked to a Social Christian faction called the National Democratic Confidence Party (PDCN) and the Workers Front (FO). Shortly after Chamorro's inauguration, the CTN expressed its basic support for the new government while warning UNO against polarization. For its part, the FO criticized the alleged pact between UNO and the FSLN as being against the interests of the popular sectors.[21]

All the country's unions realize that their future strength will depend on their ability to respond to worker demands.[22] The CPT member unions, for example, were careful to express their opposition to the Chamorro government's unpopular program of devaluations and austerity measures. Nilo Salazar, leader of the CGT-I, asserted that, despite the union's overall support for the government, "we will maintain our class independence. We're going to support measures which benefit the workers and fight those which don't."[23] Issues on which all unions will have to take sides for or against the government include privatization of state enterprises, revisions in the Civil Service Law and Labor Code, the maintenance of social services, and the right to participate in the government's economic-policy discussions.

The electoral defeat of the Sandinistas pushed the Nicaraguan labor movement to the forefront of the country's new economic and political struggles. Nowhere else in the region is the labor movement so strong, and the absence of repressive security forces means that the Nicaraguan labor movement enjoys a degree of freedom unique in the region. Although the government favors the CPT unions, the organizing environment is still extremely competitive. Union struggles in Nicaragua are highly politicized, but the success of one or another of the factions will likely depend more on its stand on economic issues than on its political affiliations.

# Schools and Students

Any doubts about the priority the Chamorro government would place on transforming the national education system were removed during the president's inauguration.[24] It was not Violeta Chamorro who sounded the battle cry, but Cardinal Obando y Bravo. During his lengthy speech, criticized by even conservative diplomats in attendance as overly political, Obando lashed out at the changes which had taken place in the nation's schools over the last 11 years and pointed the way forward: "The education of young Nicaraguans has to be accomplished according to the Christian doctrine, oriented by the Second Vatican Council."[25]

The new Minister and Vice Minister of Education, Sofonías Cisneros and Humberto Belli—close associates of Obando and members of the City of God charismatic Catholic sect (See Religion)—quickly set about the task of "depoliticizing" the nation's schools.[26] "Under the pretext of secular education," said Belli, criticizing the orientation of education under the Sandinistas, "an atheist, humanist view of life is promoted by education. Ideas which deny God and the transcendental concept of man cannot be encouraged."[27] Addressing critics who point to the Nicaraguan constitution, which defines education as secular, Belli and Cisneros have insisted that religion will not be taught as a subject in the public schools, but rather that education as a whole will be "permeated with Christian-inspired values."

The changes being implemented in Nicaraguan schools seek to marginalize Sandinista influence and revolutionary ideology, replacing them with a traditionalist worldview more appropriate to the social and economic policies pursued by the UNO government. "What Cardinal Obando wants more than anything else is to spread conservative Catholic values," commented Mignone Vega, a Nicaraguan sociologist, "and education is the one tool that affects nearly every Nicaraguan."[28]

Implementation of the new project has already generated conflict. The pro-Sandinista teachers union ANDEN has a significant presence among the country's 30,000 teachers, many of whom are resisting efforts to make a radical break with the past. Many parents, particularly those who belong to Protestant churches, may do the same. A glimpse of the struggles to come was provided early on in the Chamorro administration when a major battle was fought over proposed textbook changes. Within weeks of the government's inauguration, thousands of new primary school readers—printed with funds furnished by AID—arrived in the country. The Ministry of Education's (MED) goal was to substitute the imported texts for the Nicaraguan-produced reader which had been used during the 1980s. Faced with an uproar from ANDEN, as well as from pedagogic experts who criticized the notion of changing books in mid-semester, the MED temporarily backed off.[29]

Other bones of contention have been the firing of school directors and their replacement with UNO partisans and MED-sponsored efforts to impose a parallel, pro-government teachers' union. The pro-Sandinista National Workers Federation (FNT) denounced that in the first four months of Chamorro's administration, some 420 teachers had been either arbitrarily dismissed or transferred to schools far away from their homes.[30] In dozens of schools throughout the country, such incidents have provoked opposition from parents' groups and teachers, and in several cases have resulted in boycotts and the physical occupation of school installations. ANDEN has fingered MED Vice Minister Hortensia Rivas as the key force behind the arbitrary firings and asked for her resignation.[31]

Popular reactions forced the UNO government to back off on another early initiative, the move to undermine university autonomy. The University Autonomy Law, passed by the outgoing Sandinista-dominated National Assembly, guarantees "academic, financial, organic and administrative autonomy" for four state and two private universities and two centers of higher education. The law also stipulates that each university will be responsible for electing its own rector, faculty council, and other governing bodies. In mid-May Chamorro handed the legislature a bill of reforms to the autonomy law. The bill called for the immediate suspension of the electoral process for university authorities, already well underway at the time, pending review of the entire law.

The executive's action provoked a quick and massive response by students, professors, and administrators, many of whom had struggled for years in favor of university autonomy. In the face of the backlash, Chamorro changed tacks, asking the National Assembly to send the bill to committee for further discussion there and with the university community. The committee introduced only minor reforms and the bill was then passed by an overwhelming majority in the National Assembly.

Many in the university community predict that the law will come up for reforms again as UNO moves forward in its goal of eliminating what it sees as a "Sandinista stronghold" in the universities. Meanwhile, Obando announced plans to counter progressive currents at Managua's Jesuit-run Central American University by constructing a new papally sanctioned university.

### Education: The Sandinista Legacy

Before 1979 Nicaraguans were among the least-educated in the hemisphere. More than half the population nationally and up to 90 percent in some rural areas was illiterate. Only 22 of every 100 children managed to complete primary school, a figure which dropped to just six of 100 in rural areas. Vocational training, other than a few privately owned business schools, was practically nonexistent.[32]

The provision of minimum educational opportunities, free of charge, to the Nicaraguan population constituted a central goal of the Sandinista government's project to extend social services to the majorities. Like access to adequate health care, education was seen as a basic human right for all citizens.

Efforts to extend educational opportunities to the population were initiated in earnest in 1980 with the launching of a National Literacy Crusade. The crusade, part of a larger project which aspired to provide 92 percent of the population with a functional literacy level by the year 2000, was billed as a "cultural insurrection," a sequel to the armed struggle against Somoza. The successful crusade served as an important early mechanism for mobilizing the population around a new set of national goals. In all, some 55,000 *brigadistas* (volunteer teachers — mostly urban high school students) were mobilized and sent to the countryside. Another 26,000 taught in the cities. In the space of five months, a total of 406,056 Nicaraguans learned how to read and write.[33] The follow-up to this literacy crusade was the establishment of a widespread program of adult basic education. By 1984 some 17,000 education collectives had been set up, providing basic education to nearly 200,000 Nicaraguans.[34]

The total pre-triumph student population of about 300,000 had mushroomed to more than one million by 1989.[35] Parallel to the greatly expanded public education system, Nicaragua had 247 private schools, mostly religious, 188 of which received partial financing from the Sandinista government until the onset of austerity measures in 1989.

While new educational opportunities were provided at all levels, and a host of new technical and vocational programs incorporated to better match education to the needs of Nicaraguan society, the quality of education during the 1980s was hit hard by the combination of rapid population growth, war, and economic crisis. For example, books and school supplies were chronically in short supply. The turnover rate among teachers reached a staggering 94 percent in 1988, mainly due to the government's inability to provide a decent salary. Teachers still receive the lowest salaries of all public employees.

After 1983 the education system as a whole suffered both from the diversion of national resources toward fighting the war and because schools and teachers were priority targets for the contras. By late 1987 the toll was substantial: 411 teachers killed and 66 kidnapped; 59 students kidnapped; 46 schools destroyed, 21 damaged, and 555 temporarily forced to close, leaving 45,000 students without classrooms.[36]

### Student and Youth Groups

Nicaragua has the distinction of being one of the "youngest" countries in the world, with more than half the population 16 years old or under. As a group, students and youth in general played a key role in the efforts to overthrow the dictatorship. With a legal voting age of 16, youth continue to be a politically important group. They constituted one of the key constituencies identified by the NED-funded advisers working on the Nicaraguan electoral project in 1989. Those efforts resulted in the formation of UNO's Youth Training Center (CEFOJ) movement.

Throughout the 1980s the largest and most influential youth group was the Sandinista Youth (JS). Founded in 1980, the JS, which operates as the youth wing of the FSLN, united several major student groups which had been active in the war of liberation and insurrection. In the early years of the revolution, the JS played an important role as a key organizer of the National Literacy Crusade and in mobilizing student brigades for volunteer coffee and cotton-picking as well as health campaigns. But undemocratic and vertical work styles, combined with an almost exclusive concentration on activities related to the military draft, contributed to eroding much of the organization's support among youth.

The independent Federation of Secondary School Students (FES) works with the high school-aged population. In July 1990 elections for the FES leadership resulted in victory for the JS candidate, María Esther Solís. The vote totals, 54 percent to 40 percent for the pro-UNO candidate, were the inverse of those in February's presidential election. Not surprisingly, Solís won in all of the public schools but in only three of the elite-oriented private schools. University students also have their own independent organization, the National Nicaraguan Student Union (UNEN).

# Communications Media

With the demobilization of the contras achieved shortly after the Chamorro government took office, military conflict in Nicaragua largely came to a close. But the clash between pro- and counter-revolutionary forces was far from over; it had simply moved into less lethal arenas. At least for the time being, the Nicaraguan right wing chose the ideological terrain as the preferred battleground to isolate and weaken *sandinismo* and to build broad national support for its political project. The two key institutions for this struggle were the media and the education system.[37] Support from the United States for these efforts took the form of continued assistance from the NED for those media outlets which it had assisted during UNO's electoral campaign.[38] (See U.S. Economic Aid)

But the ideological confrontation which accompanied the Chamorro government's transition was not entirely a product of the UNO electoral victory. The Nicaraguan media has long been a hotbed of polemics. Even during the 1980s, when censorship of opposition media was imposed on several occasions, the country's radio waves and newspapers were vociferous defenders of opposing political projects.[39] Even the harshly anti-Sandinista *New York Times* conceded in a March 1988 editorial that "there's more diversity of published and spoken opinion in Managua than in Guatemala, Honduras, and El Salvador."

Although the pro-revolutionary Nicaraguan Journalists Union (UPN) made some attempts to professionalize media discourse during the decade of Sandinista rule, more often than not polemics degenerated into bitter feuds. As one media analyst wrote in 1988, "the concept of objectivity or even fairness simply does not exist in Nicaragua; passion, partisanship, and personal attacks are the norm."[40] On several occasions during the 1989-1990 electoral campaign, the international observer missions expressed their concerns that mud-slinging in the media on both sides threatened to undermine an otherwise orderly and clean election.

At a deeper level, efforts throughout the 1980s to transform the country's media institutions constituted an integral part of the Sandinistas' project to empower the Nicaraguan masses. Such initiatives were based on a democratic model of media structure and access unique in Latin America. Its features included: 1) balance in the ownership of media outlets between public, private, and cooperative forms; 2) political and ideological pluralism in media content; and 3) the promotion of popular participation and horizontal communication through the mass media. The underlying philosophy was that the media, instead of serving the narrow interests of a wealthy elite, should become the vehicles for expression of the opinions of the broad majority of society, and that notions of social responsibility should guide the media's activities as opposed to narrowly defined profit motives. Many of the resulting experiments in participatory and community radio, popular access to state-owned television, and the birth of dozens of new print publications were cut short by war-related restrictions and economic constraints. Nonetheless, the media access gained by broad sectors of the population during the revolution is a major legacy which the Chamorro government will have to confront.[41]

Formally, the government is committed to absolute freedom of expression, and much of Chamorro's reputation is built around her image as a resolute defender of press freedom. During the UNO government's tense first four months in office, the battle for public opinion was intense. Electronic and print media, bolstered by the addition of dozens of new shows, newsletters, and magazines, quickly came to reflect an increasingly fractured and polarized society.

Danilo Lacayo, head of the Presidential Press Office, stated that for his government the plurality of opinion expressed through the media — often harshly critical of Chamorro from both the right and the left — constitutes "the essence of democracy."[42] Nonetheless, during the July 1990 general strike, Lacayo himself ordered the indefinite suspension of the pro-FSLN TV news program *Extravisión* for "inciting strikers." A few weeks later, the program was back on the air, but no official explanation was ever given.[43] In August, retreating from his earlier position that "the best media law is no law at all," Lacayo announced that a new bill regulating electronic media was under study. The draft bill reportedly included fines and sanctions for infractions, raising fears among journalists of a return to elements of the "Black Code" in effect under Somoza.[44]

## The New Media Lineup

Not surprisingly, the April 1990 change of government was accompanied by major shakeups in the ownership and content of many of the country's existing media outlets, as well as the creation of dozens of new ones. Radio and television stations and newspapers staked out their positions in alliance with the Chamorro government or with the broad array of opposition forces to the left and to the right. There was little room for "independent" media projects.[45]

*La Prensa* found itself confronted with a serious dilemma. For decades the paper's mystique had been built upon its image as the "bastion of opposition." In a political culture which thrives on criticism of those in power and opposition to anything associated with the government, the paper suddenly became the semi-official mouthpiece of the country's president.[46] At the same time, while knee-jerk *antisandinismo* provided a consistent and mutually agreeable editorial line throughout the 1980s — acceptable to the near entirety of the Nicaraguan political opposition, its own editorial staff and writers, its readership, and its U.S. sponsors – the paper was now forced to navigate through much murkier waters of conflicting political interests and shifting alliances.

Accordingly, during the conflict-ridden first three months of Chamorro's administration, the pages of *La Prensa* became a portrait of contrasts. Lofty calls to patience and reconciliation appeared side by side with the crudest forms of Sandinista-bashing. Articles citing Central Bank President Francisco Mayorga harping on the need for belt-tightening and austerity were laid out alongside splashy advertisements for new cars or luxury consumer goods. The Catholic church and Cardinal Obando y Bravo were displayed prominently both in the news coverage and through the regular column "La Voz del Pastor." Another regular feature, "Economy and Society" treated readers with expositions on the virtues of UNO's proposed "social-market economy" and long diatribes about the evil legacy of Sandinista economic policy.

For the most part, however, *La Prensa* weathered the transition well. Although the paper carried its share of pro-government stories and editorials, it largely avoided the excesses of "officialism" which had plagued the FSLN's *Barricada* during the 1980s. Like the other two dailies, *La Prensa* suffered a loss of readership due to the precipitous decline in purchasing power under UNO's economic-stabilization measures.

Under the Sandinistas, the state maintained a monopoly on television broadcasting through ownership of the country's two stations (Channels 2 and 6). The UNO-appointed director of the network, Carlos Briceño, instituted a thoroughgoing change in programming and initiated a process of substituting pro-Sandinista staff members with UNO activists and exiles brought back from Miami. Reports indicated that several groups – including the FSLN, COSEP, and U.S. televangelist Pat Robertson – had been authorized to open new channels, but by late 1990 the Chamorro government's monopoly remained intact.

While the Chamorro faction of UNO had a distinct advantage through its television monopoly and *La Prensa*, its weakest presence was to be found in the medium which is in many ways Nicaragua's most important: radio. With newspapers beyond the budget of the majority of Nicaraguans, and television largely limited to advantaged sectors of the urban population, radio is the key medium for reaching the broader population. There are approximately 40 radio stations currently operating in Nicaragua. The most influential are:

* Radio Nicaragua (formerly La Voz de Nicaragua) is the government's official station. Chamorro appointed Frank Arana, ex-director of the contras' Radio 15 de Septiembre, to head the

station. During the initial months of the Chamorro administration, Radio Nicaragua was largely outgunned by the older stations of the far right and the left which counted on established programming and loyal listener bases.

* Radio Corporación, part of the NED's "media project" during the elections campaign, has long been a stronghold of the far right. Since the arrival of the Chamorro government Corporación has provided militant support to the right wing of the UNO coalition, spearheaded by Vice President Virgilio Godoy.[47]

* Radio Católica belongs to the Catholic church hierarchy and is run under the direction of Cardinal Obando y Bravo's spokesman Bismarck Carballo. Although less virulent in tone than Corporación, the station also has staked out a position to the right of Chamorro. Católica has a large following among Nicaragua's devout Catholic majority.

* Radio Ya was founded by some 80 percent of the staff from the official Voz de Nicaragua under the Sandinistas who opted to set up a new station, complete with their own programming, rather than work at the old one under UNO direction. Even audience polls published in *La Prensa* confirmed that Radio Ya programming continued to be the most popular nationwide.[48]

* Radio Sandino was the FSLN's clandestine radio station during the guerrilla war against Somoza. It continues to be the official voice of the Sandinista Front.

* La Primerísima was the flagship station of the state-owned network of community stations, CORADEP, during the 1980s. After the Sandinista electoral defeat, it was turned over to the station's workers. CORADEP pioneered a series of projects in popular and participatory radio.

The three pro-revolutionary stations, in addition to the network of community stations set up in other parts of the country, are all expected to feel the pinch as advertising revenues dry up. During the 1980s a large part of their operating budgets came from selling advertising to state companies which are now either in the process of being privatized or have moved their ads over to the rightwing stations.

The drop in income from lost advertising also has hurt *Barricada* and *El Nuevo Diario*, the country's second and third-largest dailies, behind *La Prensa*. *Barricada*, official organ of the Sandinista Front and de facto mobilizer for government policy during the 1980s, has announced intentions to drop its status as the FSLN's paper. "We'll always have a revolution-

ary, progressive, and Sandinista editorial line," declared *Barricada* director Carlos Fernando Chamorro, President Chamorro's son, "but we'll
open ourselves to a greater plurality of opinions."[49]

*El Nuevo Diario* was formed as an independent, staff-owned daily in
1980 by some 80 percent of the staff and editors of *La Prensa* who had
resigned in protest over the rightward shift there. While the paper's
editorial stance is decidedly pro-revolutionary, much of its coverage tends
toward sensationalism. Since April 1990 *El Nuevo Diario* and La
Primerísima have become major forums for leftist critiques of the FSLN.

The plethora of new radio shows and publications include: *Análisis*, a
monthly magazine devoted to the economy; *Crítica*, also monthly, covering a wide range of social, political and economic themes; a weekly tabloid
*El Semanario*, directed by former Vice President Sergio Ramírez; and
*Novedades*, another weekly.

# The State of Health

Nicaraguans witnessed a dramatic increase in the provision of health
care during the early years of the Sandinista revolution.[50] But the contra
war and economic-austerity measures hit the health sector hard, and by
the end of the 1980s key indicators of the population's health had begun
to deteriorate. These trends are likely to continue under the UNO government as the demand for health services increases in proportion to the
declining public health conditions brought on by growing poverty and unemployment. Minister of Health Ernesto Salmerón—the Chamorros'
family physician—has established a positive working relationship with
health sector workers including those belonging to the pro-Sandinista
union FETSALUD.[51] He has, however, largely found his hands tied in
efforts to deal with the growing health crisis as a result of the drastic
budget restrictions prescribed by the economic-stabilization plan.

In Somoza's Nicaragua access to health care was essentially a luxury
for a privileged minority. A national social-security system provided for
the needs of only some 120,000 Nicaraguans while about 10 percent of the
rest could afford private treatment.[52] All others, the impoverished
majority, were left to fend for themselves. Nicaragua was one of the most
health-impoverished countries in Latin America.

The Sandinista government embarked upon a major program to
revamp the health system based on the conviction that access to decent
and affordable health services should be a basic human right guaranteed
to every citizen. The long-range goal was to create a national, socialized

health care system. Given the shortage of resources, it was agreed that in the short term, private health care would continue to exist alongside an expanded public system of hospitals, primary care clinics and mass-based health campaigns. To streamline the public sector, a National Unified Health System was created under the jurisdiction of the Ministry of Health.[53] In the initial years, health care and medicines in the public system were provided free of charge, but as austerity policies deepened during the latter part of the 1980s user fees were gradually introduced.

Substantial expansion was achieved in both curative and preventative medicine. More than 400 new health clinics and posts were opened and several major hospitals were built around the country. A new medical school was opened, expanding the capacity for doctor training from 50 to 500 per year. Where Somoza had allocated a scarce 3 percent of the national budget to health care, by 1986 the Sandinista government was budgeting 14 percent.[54]

But more than massive budget outlays, sophisticated physical installations, or expert medical personnel, Nicaragua's initiatives to improve the health of the nation were based on the direct participation of the population itself in health affairs. In 1981 and 1982 alone basic health training was given to some 80,000 *brigadistas*, volunteer paramedical health aides capable of carrying rudimentary services to even the most isolated corners of the nation.[55] In coordination with the popular organizations and local health officials, the *brigadistas* carried out annual nationwide health education campaigns, vaccination drives for the eradication of infectious diseases such as polio, and a malaria-control program.

Although serious problems and limitations remained, the revolution's achievements in the field of health care were formidable. In 1983, before the war began eroding the new health services, the World Health Organization declared Nicaragua a "Model Nation in Health Attention" in the underdeveloped world.[56] Nearly all major health and living standard indicators showed considerable improvements from 1979 to 1983, when the combination of war and economic crisis began to turn many of the trends around. Infant mortality, which stood at 121 deaths per 1000 live births before the triumph was cut almost in half by 1985, and both malaria and polio were completely eradicated.[57] Even life expectancy, where improvements usually are spread out over long time periods, had gone from 52 years before 1979 to 59 years by 1985.[58]

Even before the onset of serious difficulties in the late 1980s, problems and complaints were to be found. For one, the wealthy complained bitterly about having to wait in line for hospital services they considered inferior. They argued that those who could afford to pay should have the alternative of accessing higher quality care. A more widely felt problem came from the fact that the large initial expansions and free services stimulated an exaggerated demand, sending the public-health budget skyrocketing and overtaxing the weak infrastructure. Although several initiatives were undertaken to improve attention in the overcrowded hospitals, low salaries forced many doctors and technicians to dedicate the bulk of their efforts to private practice. During the 1980s more than one-fifth of all the country's doctors and medical technicians left the country altogether.

As in the education sector, the contras made the health workers and clinics explicit targets. In the northern war zones, at least 20 percent of all health clinics functioning in 1983 were either destroyed, attacked, or closed down due to threats by the contras. Some clinics were destroyed by contra attacks and rebuilt three times before being definitively abandoned. By 1987 more than a hundred health workers had been killed by the contras, including doctors and nurses from Germany, France, Spain, and Switzerland.[59] It is estimated that 15 percent of the population lost access to health care as a result. Similarly, vaccination campaigns had to be suspended in many rural areas due to contra activity. In others where they were not suspended, the campaigns were undermined by contra radio broadcasts "alerting" the population that the vaccines were actually "brainwashing serums from Russia and Cuba."[60] The military conflict itself placed an inordinate strain on the existing health care facilities. In 1987 an estimated 80 percent of patients in hospitals had war-related symptoms, and some 10 percent of the entire population was disabled, some from birth defects, but tens of thousands as a result of contra attacks.[61]

The growing economic crisis also has placed severe constraints on the country's general health situation, as dramatically exemplified in the case of diarrhea, the principal cause of death among children under five years of age. Most diarrhea in children is caused by low-quality drinking water or general unsanitary conditions in the home. In Managua, less than 50 percent of the population has access to safe water, in large measure due to the explosion of urban squatter settlements. In the rural areas, the figure is less than 10 percent. In all urban areas of the country, sewer systems reach less than 40 percent of the homes.[62]

Another worrisome trend tied to deteriorating economic conditions is the rise of malnutrition among children due to a decline in food consumption, particularly protein-rich staples such as beans, meat, and milk.

One source estimates that some 48 percent of all children are born into households with "inadequate living conditions."[63]

In the first half of 1990 more than 4,000 cases of measles were reported and some 200 children between the ages of two and four died in what constituted a serious setback to the progress which had been made in this field. By September, Minister of Health Salmerón reported that since the beginning of the year 1340 children had died of measles or diarrhea. Likewise as of July 1990 reports of malaria cases were up by 60 percent from the previous year.[64]

The control of epidemic diseases has been complicated by economic and political factors. Some health workers feel that the central government is holding back on budget outlays to the Ministry of Health in an effort to starve out the hospitals and clinics, thus paving the way for their privatization. The government contends that reduced funding is simply part of the general effort to cut spending. Meanwhile, problems have been encountered in the community-based vaccination campaigns, a project initiated under the Sandinistas. A shortage of volunteers to give the vaccinations has been aggravated by people who refuse to accept them. "People still believe that the vaccines we have are contaminated with the Sandinista virus," complained Salmerón. "Others say they won't cooperate with the UNO government because those vaccines aren't any good either."[65] The reduction and elimination of government subsidies for basic medicines has placed them far beyond the reach of large sectors of the population which could afford them before.

According to a report issued by Salmerón, 26 of the country's 30 hospitals have already reached the end of their useful life and eight should be rebuilt. Salmerón has declared publicly that he does not intend to privatize the hospitals, although he says he would welcome any investors interested in constructing new, private hospitals.[66] The minister of health also has announced plans to search abroad for funding for the crippled health sector, apparently convinced that adequate resources will not be forthcoming from the central government.

Some see a potential hidden bonus in the process of budget cutbacks at the Ministry of Health. Although in the short run they will lead to a reduction of services as personnel are laid off and primary care centers closed down, this same process will tend to stimulate a greater degree of community-level organizing around health needs. The reduction of dependence on the central government and increased reliance on people taking responsibility for their own solutions in the field of health could stimulate a broader dynamic of grassroots empowerment.

# Religion

"In this government," commented one observer of the Nicaraguan religious scene, "Obando plays the role of king while Violeta plays the prime minister."[67] Even *Newsweek* magazine described Cardinal Obando y Bravo as "the ideological power behind Chamorro's wobbly throne."[68] Indeed, it did not take long for the Catholic church hierarchy, under the firm leadership of Obando, to assume its new role as one of the key protagonists under the Chamorro administration. The strong bond between the president and the cardinal, a bond which had played an important role in catapulting UNO to its electoral victory in February 1990, was everywhere in evidence after Chamorro's inauguration.

Before setting foot in her new office, President Chamorro summoned Obando to bless the building with holy water. A few blocks down the street at the Ministry of Government (formerly Interior), Obando's mission of flushing out the diabolical spirits left behind by the Sandinistas and of blessing the premises for the new occupants – all under the watchful eyes of Nicaraguan television viewers – was saved for July 18, the day before the FSLN was to celebrate the 11th anniversary of the victory over Somoza. Just two weeks earlier Obando and Chamorro had participated in the groundbreaking ceremony which officially opened construction of Managua's new cathedral, a moment Obando had been waiting for since the 1972 earthquake left the old one in ruins. Beginning in May live television transmissions of Obando's Sunday mass, a practice which had also existed under Somoza, was reinitiated.[69]

If these signs pointed to the symbolic role the Catholic church would play during the 1990s, others made it clear that the changes would not be skin deep. "The fundamental task for the reconstruction of Nicaragua's social bases," wrote one of Chamorro's cabinet ministers, "is above all a spiritual task: the rechristianization of each and every Nicaraguan."[70] Progressive Catholics, the protestant churches, and ordinary Nicaraguans fearful of the conservative backlash and erosion of the separation of church and state, all braced for the onslaught.

## Religious Conflicts of the 1980s

Perhaps even more than the media or political parties, the religious terrain in Nicaragua was a battlefield for the playing out of ideological tensions after 1979.[71] Both the Catholic and evangelical churches were wracked by divisions between pro- and counter-revolutionary tendencies. In the end, the Catholic church's unrelenting opposition to revolutionary changes in Nicaragua succeeded in severely eroding the Sandinistas' legitimacy.

The Nicaraguan population traditionally is deeply religious. In 1979 an estimated 80 percent of all Nicaraguans belonged to the Catholic church, while there were several hundred thousand evangelicals. (In Nicaragua, the term *evangélico*, roughly synonymous with Protestant, describes all Christian churches that are not Roman Catholic.) The heavy influence of the Catholic church was due not only to its historical role as a pillar of Nicaraguan society, but also because it has remained ubiquitous: with 178 parishes in 143 municipalities, it is the only Nicaraguan organization with a presence throughout the entire country.

The dimensions of the conflict which would come to pervade the Catholic church and the tense relations between the Sandinista government and the hierarchy were largely unforeseen in 1979.[72] Notwithstanding Cardinal Obando's last-minute collaboration in Carter-sponsored efforts to avoid a Sandinista victory, after the triumph there was widespread optimism for a fruitful relationship on both sides. The church was assured a central role in national life as thousands of Christians took up the tasks of reconstruction, and several priests were appointed to high positions within the new government. In late 1980 the FSLN ratified its official position with the presentation of its "Document on Religion," guaranteeing total freedom of worship and respect for all religious beliefs. Earlier that year, the National Literacy Crusade was kicked off, under the leadership of Jesuit priest Father Fernando Cardenal, with the blessing of both the pope and Cardinal Obando.

But Nicaraguan conservatives' growing fear that the revolution was moving away from a reformist path, combined with intense pressures from the Vatican and Washington, changed all this. Nicaragua became the symbolic forefront of Vatican efforts under Pope John Paul II to roll back the progressive reforms begun by the Second Vatican Council in the 1960s and was an active site in the church's battle against the influence of liberation theology.

Washington's early moves to attract the hierarchy to its project of counterrevolution were based on three practical considerations: the considerable authority accrued to the church in a deeply religious and overwhelmingly Catholic country, the leadership qualities of Obando, and the belief that a religious persecution argument would help to isolate the Sandinista government internationally. Over the years, the hierarchy's anti-Sandinista activities would be bankrolled by a wide array of U.S. sources: AID; Catholic Relief Services (CRS); the neoconservative Institute on

Religion and Democracy (IRD); and important elements from the corporate right wing, such as WR Grace & Company.[73]

The pressures from Washington and the Vatican exacerbated existing divisions within the Nicaraguan Catholic church which centered around fundamentally opposed interpretations of politics and religion. Some in the church, particularly the bishops, expected the 1979 victory over Somoza to lead to a moderate, reformist government. Others — grouped around the movement within the Catholic church of progressive priests and lay persons known as the "popular church" — saw thoroughgoing structural change and revolutionary transformations as the only viable way to eliminate widespread poverty and injustice. Parallel to these divisions in the church structure, traditional sectors in Nicaraguan society stressed personal piety and the importance of authority and a hierarchical chain of command, emanating from the Vatican and passing through the Nicaraguan bishops. Others were strongly convinced that working within the revolution was the best way to fulfill their commitment to the poor — no matter what their superiors said.

The adversarial stance adopted by the Catholic church hierarchy was touched off by a series of clashes with the Sandinista government in mid-1982. The confrontational posture was reinforced and legitimized during Pope John Paul II's March 1983 visit to Nicaragua. Widespread expectations of an attempt to heal the emerging schisms between the popular church and the hierarchy were crushed during the pope's open-air mass, attended by some 700,000 people in Managua, in which he came down squarely on the side of the bishops. The stage was thus set for a crescendo of increasingly provocational moves by the hierarchy to delegitimize the government and do away with the popular church. Government leaders made it clear that although they were disposed to accept any amount of legitimate criticism and opposition from the hierarchy, open collusion with the counterrevolution would not be tolerated. The conflict reached its peak in mid-1986 with the expulsion of Bishop Pablo Antonio Vega for his lobbying efforts in Washington in support of then-President Reagan's $100 million contra-aid package.

Meanwhile, the pope's efforts to delegitimize the Nicaraguan "church of the poor" complicated an already difficult situation for progressive Nicaraguan Catholics. The popular church, which traces its roots back to the formation of the first Christian base communities in 1966, experienced great difficulty in adapting to post-triumph circumstances. Most of its activists became so involved in their work within the revolution that religious leadership dwindled. Consequently, the movement, which had enjoyed rapid growth during the war of liberation, largely stagnated. These limitations were aggravated by direct persecution at the hands of the conservative hierarchy, which consistently punished church members who failed to conform to its ideological convictions. A favorite tactic was transferring pro-revolutionary priests out of poor *barrios* and into middle-class neighborhoods, where their progressive message would fall on deaf ears. Priests in the government were forced either to resign or face expulsion from their religious orders.

But the spiral of conflicts gave way to a gradual easing of tensions and dialogue after 1986. As the prospects for a contra military victory began to unravel, the Vatican was the first to shift toward accommodation with the Sandinistas. Archbishop Paolo Giglio, an experienced troubleshooter and mediator, was appointed as the new papal nuncio and sent to Managua with orders to improve church-state relations. Shortly thereafter, President Ortega and Cardinal Obando y Bravo held talks for the first time in two years, agreeing to set up a government-episcopal commission charged with normalizing relations.

In 1987, with the momentum unleashed by the Esquipulas peace process, the government turned to Obando, naming him head of the National Reconciliation Commission and then mediator in cease-fire talks with the contras. The Sandinistas felt that Obando's strong influence among the contra leadership, and his broad legitimacy among the population, would help pave the way for an authentic process of peace and reconciliation in the context of the political opening and electoral reforms contemplated in the Esquipulas accords. Likewise, the FSLN government expected that the protagonist role given to Obando in the peace process would undermine anti-Sandinista sentiment among those sectors of the population who had followed the cardinal's lead in opposing the revolution. In the end, the FSLN's calculations proved erroneous. Obando capitalized on the opening for his own anti-Sandinista agenda and played an unabashedly pro-contra role as "mediator" in their negotiations with the government. Later, with the process of contra demobilization effectively stalled, Obando became a major supporter of Chamorro's bid for the presidency.

With the Chamorro government firmly installed, the Catholic church hierarchy wasted no time in moving forward with its ambitious agenda. "We have two themes," said Obando's spokesman Bismarck Carballo. "To promote the family in Nicaragua and unity within the church. The pope has asked that we promote a new evangelism, with new priests and new methods. We want to purify the church."[74] In essence, "promoting the family" means reimposing the traditional, conservative social order and moral values. In the short term, this translates into getting women back into the home and into the role of housewife and mother.

A glimpse into the new value system being promoted was provided by Minister of Education Sofonías Cisneros, a close associate of Obando. Speaking of the changes his ministry planned to institute in the sex education program, Cisneros commented: "[Family] planning is all right, but not on the basis of contraceptives and practices not approved by the church. Those types of gadgets won't be recommended any more....Sex is a gift from God [and] students are going to learn to use it in the way He expects them to, that is, for the purpose of procreation."[75]

Cisneros and his Vice Minister Humberto Belli are Obando's point men for revamping the nation's education system. Changes in the content of education have been given top priority by the church hierarchy for two reasons. First, during the 1980s education was under the direction of Father Fernando Cardenal, a Jesuit priest strongly committed to the revolutionary process. The current authorities say that education under the Sandinistas consisted of indoctrination and was a platform for the spreading of "dangerous doctrines" not sanctioned by the church. Second, although the Catholic church is ubiquitous, the school system is even more so, making it an ideal vehicle for Obando's mission of spreading conservative Catholic values. (See Education)

"Purifying the church" refers to a political house-sweeping performed within the church itself. According to Carballo, of 320 priests in Nicaragua, 20 are identified with the "popular church."[76] These progressive clergy will be weeded out and the presence of liberation theology and *sandinismo* in the church will be eliminated if the church hierarchy's purification agenda is successfully implemented.

Publicly, Obando's most controversial move since the UNO government's arrival has been the project to build a new cathedral in Managua. Obando named President Chamorro to head the committee charged with building the new structure. Also on the committee are Managua's reactionary Mayor Arnoldo Alemán, who donated 30 acres of city land for the project, and U.S. business tycoon Thomas Monaghan (Domino's Pizza), who promised to donate or raise at least half of the estimated $3 million in construction costs.[77] Monaghan's goal is to have the cathedral finished by 1992 in time for the pope's visit to Latin America commemorating the 500th anniversary of Columbus' landing in the Western hemisphere. Although many Catholics in Managua are clearly excited about the idea of having a new cathedral—particularly one built under the auspices of a Nicaraguan Cardinal and Violeta Chamorro—others see a contradiction in launching such an expensive project during times of harsh austerity and widespread poverty. The cathedral project also has been criticized by evangelicals as evidence that the government is playing favorites with the Catholic church.

Despite the generally cozy relationship between Obando and Chamorro, all has not been roses. On several occasions, Obando and the Catholic church hierarchy have criticized the government and tacitly given their approval and support to the Chamorro group's "tactical adversaries"—the rightwing extremists in UNO and the contras. In an effort to make sure the church does not come out on the short side of the stick in a potential confrontation, and to maximize positions in terms of isolating *sandinismo*, Obando has attempted to swim in both pools at the same time.

## City of God

Cardinal Obando's prominence in relation to the Chamorro government has overlapped with, and in some cases been overshadowed by, that of a little-known charismatic Catholic group, Ciudad de Dios (City of God). Prominent individuals from the group, estimated to have about 800 members, have taken influential cabinet and advisory posts in the Chamorro administration.

Founded in the mid-1970s as part of a conservative trend in the Catholic church which sought to counter the growing influence of the Latin American popular church movement, City of God was the Managua branch of Sword of the Spirit. In turn Sword of the Spirit was a subsidiary of the charismatic Word of God, to which Thomas Monaghan belongs, based in Ann Arbor, Michigan.

One observer, citing former members of City of God and Word of God, described the groups this way: "They practice 'shepherding discipleship,' which requires a member's total submission to a hierarchy of command. Authority, submission, and a belief that they are specially chosen by God are combined with layers of secrecy and ritual that keep members aloof from the rest of society."[78] For City of God members, life revolves around the search for direct, personal communication with God, a search which may lead to visions and mystical revelations.

City of God members opted to keep their distance from the anti-Somoza struggle, sticking to the belief that worldly injustice was divinely dictated. With the Sandinistas in power, however, many became active opponents, working in concert with Obando, COSEP, and *La Prensa* in a variety of initiatives which sought to topple the revolutionary government. One Nicaraguan analyst concluded that the City of God community believes that the Sandinistas and their actions are possessed by the devil, and that they have been chosen by God to eradicate that influence.[79]

The long-standing leader of the City of God community is Carlos Mántica, a close personal friend and adviser to President Chamorro. City of God members in the cabinet include Sofonías Cisneros and Humberto Belli; Petronio Delgado, Vice Minister of Health; and Ervin Krügger, Vice Minister of the Presidency. Many other high-ranking government officials are active with related groups in Nicaragua's charismatic movement, although they are not formally part of the City of God community.

Although it is unclear to what extent the spiritual beliefs of City of God members and other charismatics influence Chamorro's broader government program and policy initiatives, there is little doubt that those beliefs are at the forefront of UNO's plans to transform the ideological girders of Nicaraguan society. Through their posts in the leadership of the ministries of education and culture, as well as in *La Prensa* (the paper's Executive Vice President Jaime Chamorro is a member), City of God members are well positioned to propagate conservative beliefs and values which reinforce the government's broader agenda of social and economic counterrevolution. (See Education)

## Evangelicals on the Rise

Nicaragua's evangelical churches experienced rapid growth during the 1980s. By the end of the decade estimates of evangelical strength ran as high as one-fifth of the population.[80] This expansion was as much a product of the Sandinista government's policy of religious freedom as it was of the broader trend in Central America where the effects of war and economic crisis have provided fertile terrain for growth for dozens of evangelical denominations. With the arrival of the UNO government both conservative and progressive evangelicals openly expressed their fears that the cozy relations between Chamorro and Obando, as well as the sizable presence of charismatic Catholics in Chamorro's cabinet, threatened to elevate catholicism to the de facto position of official religion in Nicaragua. Progressive evangelicals felt doubly cornered with the initiation of a campaign by conservative denominations in Nicaragua and the United States to consolidate anti-Sandinista sentiment among all Nicaraguan Christians, regardless of their religious affiliation.

In general, the influence of the Catholic church is spread across all social sectors and classes in Nicaragua. In contrast, the evangelicals, particularly the pentecostal groups, tend to be concentrated more among the poor. And while catholicism is represented by a single church — albeit with internal divisions and a multiplicity of orders – evangelicals are spread across dozens of denominations.

The largest and oldest of the 118 non-Catholic denominations and groups are the Moravians (concentrated on the Atlantic coast), the Assemblies of God, and the Baptist Convention of Nicaragua.[81] The recent evangelical boom is largely attributable to the rapid growth of such pentecostal churches as Assemblies of God. Most of the country's pentecostal churches, which now account for some 85 percent of all Nicaraguan evangelicals, are recently arrived and are still relatively small. In part, this boom is explained by the fact that the evangelical religions offered a participatory, less hierarchical experience than the traditional Roman Catholic Church. In the war zones, Catholics were almost universally seen as being with the revolution – and thus a direct target of the contras – or openly against it. The evangelical option tended to offer more neutrality.

For the Sandinista revolution the growth of evangelicalism was a two-way street. Under the guidance and assistance of the IRD and the U.S. embassy in Managua, individual pastors linked to some of the evangelical groups became actively involved in counterrevolutionary activities.[82] More difficult to confront was the "numbing" effect of much of the pentecostals' other-worldly preaching, which consistently worked to undermine efforts by the Sandinistas to encourage the population to organize and mobilize in order to improve their daily lives.

On the other hand, with the exception of the Moravian church on the Atlantic coast, mainline protestant denominations like the Baptists were more supportive of the revolution. The bulk of progressive protestants are grouped together under the Evangelical Committee for Aid to Development (CEPAD), formed to assist relief efforts after the 1972 earthquake. CEPAD, which has grown to incorporate 49 member denominations, is an influential force at the national level and sponsors a wide array of social-development projects in the countryside. On the other end of the spectrum, a smaller split from CEPAD, the National Council of Evangelical Pastors of Nicaragua (CNPEN), is organized around several hundred conservative pastors. CNPEN enjoys close ties with the IRD and with numerous rightwing protestant groups in the United States.[83] While CNPEN members are not monolithically reactionary, the organizational leadership consistently adopted a counterrevolutionary posture during the 1980s.[84]

For most of the 1980s rightwing U.S. evangelical groups trumpeted the alleged lack of religious freedom under the Sandinistas. Their publications raised widespread alarm about religious persecution, with one organization, Christian Aid Mission, pointing to "a holocaust against evangelicals in Nicaragua." Some became actively involved in campaigns to send aid to the contra bases and refugee camps for their family members in Honduras. Beginning in 1988, however, these U.S. groups began focusing on the potential for evangelism within the country. As a result, dozens of U.S. evangelical pastors travelled to Nicaragua to mount countrywide evangelical crusades.

Jimmy Swaggart was the first of the major league televangelists to venture into enemy territory, preaching in Managua's Plaza of the Revolution in February 1988. Swaggart found the Sandinistas to be less than the devils he had characterized them to be for so many years. But ultimately his turnaround made little difference, as within days of his appearance, he fell from grace in the United States.

Evangelism in Depth (IINDEF), a Costa Rica-based organization associated with the Latin American Mission, spearheaded a nationwide evangelist crusade in 1989. Other U.S. groups that have recently established themselves in Nicaragua include the Christian Center for Renovation (associated with Trans World Missions), World Vision, and Caribbean Christian Ministries. Pat Robertson's Christian Broadcasting Network (CBN) set up a "Nicaragua Fund" in early 1989 to increase evangelical efforts in the country before the February 1990 elections; Robertson's *700 Club* appeared briefly in 1989 on Sandinista television, but technical and political problems eventually forced it off the air.[85] Along with the pentecostals, the Mormons and the Jehovah's Witnesses also have stepped up their campaigns of conversion in recent years.

Shortly after Chamorro's victory, CNPEN began working with Aid to Special Saints in Strategic Times (ASSIST), described by one researcher as "a California-based 'missionary' group specializing in covert activities against socialist states and progressive movements."[86] The goal of the CNPEN-ASSIST project was to establish "sister church" relationships between conservative churches in Nicaragua and the United States as a conduit for material and ideological support. In the wake of Chamorro's inauguration, CNPEN also launched an Alliance of Evangelical Churches to compete more directly with CEPAD. The flagship denomination of the new alliance was the Assemblies of God, which withdrew from CEPAD in August 1990.

The biggest campaign, however, Robertson's Project Light, burst onto the scene immediately after the February 1990 elections. The population was saturated – via television, radio, newspapers, and billboards – with the message "Now there will be more light, the light of Jesus." Many were shocked at the inappropriateness of some of the messages in the Nicaraguan context, a country wracked by war and poverty. One of the

Project Light newspaper ads, for example, featured a white man wearing a suit and tie (rarely seen in Nicaragua) sitting in a comfortable home complaining about his low salary and need for a raise. In a radio spot, Project Light presented a worker asking for a raise. Before his boss responds, the man "finds Jesus," allowing him thus to accept his employer's rejection with peaceful resignation.

The campaign and its organizers quickly became embroiled in public scandals. In the wake of an avalanche of negative reactions in the press the government canceled its commitment to air a series of CBN-produced television specials which had been designed to close the campaign in late March. In response, CBN opted to postpone the remainder of the project. But their hopes to revive the campaign under the Chamorro government were quickly dashed. Project Light's organizers complained that the new government's television officials had asked for excessively high rates for air time, and that they had insisted that materials would have to be presented for prior review by Cardinal Obando y Bravo. Obando's spokesman, Bismarck Carballo, had earlier referred to Project Light as an attempt to "buy followers using cheap proselytism."[87]

# Nongovernmental Organizations

After the electoral defeat of the Sandinistas, nongovernmental organizations (NGOs) began springing up throughout the country. There was the expected influx of NGOs associated with AID as well as those linked to the U.S. religious and political right wing. Post-election Nicaragua also experienced a blossoming of NGOs with ties to the FSLN. Suddenly cut off from the government infrastructure, Sandinista militants and former government officials hurriedly established NGOs to carry on their research work, popular organizing and education, and development programs. The new crop of NGOs joined an extensive network of local and foreign organizations that for the most part had worked closely with the Sandinista government.

During the 1960s and 1970s U.S. NGOs, most of which received AID funding, were well represented in Nicaragua. Among those with offices in the country were AIFLD, CARE, Catholic Relief Services, Foster Parents Plan, Partners of the Americas, Save the Children, and Technoserve. Several evangelical relief organizations such as World Vision and AMG International also managed programs in pre-Sandinista Nicaragua.

Besides these international NGOs, several local NGOs emerged during the Somoza years. Some of these groups, such as the Nicaraguan

Development Foundation (FUNDE), were business-oriented organizations that depended on AID and other foreign funding. Most other local NGOs were associated with the Catholic church, including CARITAS, Nicaraguan Radio Schools, and the John XXIII Institute for Social Action. CEPAD, formed to assist the 1972 earthquake victims, was the relief branch of the evangelical churches. Limited AID support, almost exclusively food aid and population planning assistance, was available to local NGOs. The some half-dozen NGOs that enjoyed institutional links with religious institutions were able to carry out important popular education work during the Somoza years in addition to their less political service programs.[88] But the overall repressive environment prevented a broader NGO community from emerging.

The revolutionary program of the Sandinista government attracted hundreds of progressive international NGOs, mostly European and Canadian, to Nicaragua. Some 75 foreign NGOs set up offices in the country while many more funded small service and development projects. Groups such as Tecnica and the Environmental Project on Central America (EPOCA) closely coordinated their projects with the government. In contrast to the often adversarial and distrustful relationship seen in other Central American countries, NGO representatives in Nicaragua largely reported excellent working relationships with the government. Not only did the local and international NGOs often coordinate their projects with the government but they also often teamed up with popular mass organizations such as UNAG and ATC. An estimated $30-50 million entered the country each year through NGOs, solidarity programs, and sister-city programs.[89]

During the Sandinista years most of the Nicaraguan NGOs were represented in an umbrella organization called the NGO Coordinator. In addition to the older NGOs, new organizations such as the parastatal Augusto C. Sandino Foundation (FACS), participated in this coalition.[90]

The termination of U.S. economic aid during the 1980s resulted in the departure of most U.S. NGOs.[91] During the 1989-1990 election campaign, as the U.S. destabilization effort switched from military to political tactics, the flow of U.S. political aid to the country gave rise to a network of NGOs linked to the UNO opposition, including Vía Cívica and the Youth Training Center (CEFOJ). (See U.S. Economic Aid) The resounding electoral defeat of the FSLN and the promise of U.S. economic aid opened the way for an influx of U.S. private organizations. Helping to resettle and establish development poles for the contras were among the early focuses of this rightwing humanitarian aid.

Among the first to show up were a few of the organizations that had supplied the contras, including AmeriCares, Cuban-American Medical Team, Friends of the Americas, Knights of Malta, and Civilian Material Assistance (CMA). AmeriCares—which has funded *La Prensa* and supported the contras—teamed up with the Knights of Malta, Central America Medical and Dental Foundation, and Cardinal Obando to send several shipments of humanitarian supplies into the country immediately after Chamorro's election victory. The shipment was received by a smiling Cardinal Obando, whose relief organization was working closely with repatriating contras. Marvin Bush, the president's son and nephew of AmeriCares president Prescott Bush, accompanied the second AmeriCares flight to Nicaragua, which arrived in Managua the day after Chamorro's inauguration.[92] The Knights of Malta had a small chapter in the country during the Somoza regime, but most members, including the organization's Cuban-born ambassador, left the country to live in the United States after July 1979.

Many of the U.S. NGOs that had programs during the Somoza era began to rush back into the country following Chamorro's victory. Project Hope, which brought its hospital ship to Nicaragua in 1967, returned to the country in 1990, with its medical supplies flown in by U.S. Air Force cargo planes. Food aid from the United States soon began flowing through the cardinal's social welfare organization COPROSA, as well as through CARE and the Adventist Development Relief Agency (ADRA).[93] The handout character of much of the early U.S. assistance programs was immediately apparent as Nicaraguans began lining up for discarded and often outdated supplies and medicines. Flying immense U.S. flags over its mobile clinics, Friends of the Americas handed out free drugs to poor people following the Chamorro inauguration.

It is likely that NGO operations in Nicaragua will follow the patterns seen in other Central American countries, where handout programs are combined with projects to promote exports and strengthen the private sector. NGO funding from the U.S. government also has an overtly political side seen in AID and National Endowment for Democracy support for such groups as the U.S.-based Center for Democracy and AIFLD. In coming years it is also likely that AID will attempt to establish an NGO coalition to combat the influence of those NGOs linked to the Sandinistas and popular organizations.

Remarkably, few of the international NGOs working in Nicaragua during the 1980s closed their operations following the inauguration of the Chamorro government. Some solidarity organizations like Tecnica experienced a sharp drop in volunteers but most NGOs vowed to continue and even increase their work. Rather than work directly through the government, many international NGOs are coordinating their programs with popular organizations and Sandinista-controlled municipal governments. Progressive Nicaraguan NGOs such as CEPAD reported discrimination during the first few months of the new government, having for the first time to pay taxes on imported humanitarian aid.

In its own version of privatization, the FSLN government during its lame-duck period promoted the formation of a multitude of new NGOs to avoid having its institutes and projects fall into the hands of the UNO government. The NGOs, run by Sandinista militants, also were established to build a new infrastructure to defend the revolution and to build a political base for its return to office in 1996. These NGOs form a social infrastructure of organizations that can provide technical services and information to the popular movement. NGOs are springing up not only on a national level but also locally and regionally to carry out programs formerly administered by government ministries, such as adult education and health services. The some two-dozen NGOs now dedicated to popular education projects are attempting to coordinate their work and even their fundraising.

Fernando Cardenal, former Education Minister, now runs the Nicaraguan Institute of Research and Popular Education; former Vice President Sergio Ramírez is president of the Institute of Nicaraguan Studies; Víctor Hugo Tinoco, formerly of the Foreign Ministry, directs the International Studies Center; Ernesto Cardenal, former Culture Minister, is vice president of the House of Three Worlds Foundation; and Miguel D'Escoto, former Foreign Minister, directs the El Madroño Foundation. Two Sandinista-linked community development organizations — the Popol Na Foundation, directed by former Vice Minister to the President Mónica Baltodano, and the Center for the Promotion of Community Development (CEPRODEC) — have been established. Dora María Téllez, a former Sandinista *comandante*, directs the Center for Health Studies (CEPS). There are also two new women's NGOs, the Nora Astorga Foundation and the Center of Research and Action for Women's Rights (CIAM).

# Women and Feminism

The most noticeable gains won by women in the context of the Sandinista revolution took place in two areas: changes in the legal superstructure and the incorporation of women into production and political life. The Nicaraguan Constitution, promulgated in January 1987, overturned the historic legal discrimination suffered by Nicaraguan women, establishing equality between the sexes as a fundamental right of all Nicaraguans. The constitution also obliges the state to remove, by all available means, obstacles hindering full equality. Modifications proposed by the women's movement, as well as input by women during open assemblies held to enrich the draft constitution, were instrumental in reformulating earlier draft versions of the document.

In addition to the constitutional clauses, a host of Nicaraguan laws addressing women's issues passed since 1979 are far more progressive than most in the Americas. They cover such areas as adoption, divorce, common-law marriage, and familial relations. These and other legal modifications empowered Nicaraguan women, backing their struggle to achieve greater equality with the force of law.

The participation of women in the work force and formal political life of the nation increased dramatically in the 1980s. By 1989 women represented 45 percent of the working population.[94] Nonetheless, for the most part the jobs open to women remained concentrated in the lower levels of the industrial pay scale, and women continued to predominate in commerce and the informal sector.

Some of the biggest advances were made in agriculture where women took over farming tasks long considered the exclusive domain of men.[95] The number of women directly involved in food production in the countryside soared, with women representing more than 35 percent of the year-round salaried agricultural work force, almost half of the seasonal workforce, and 44 percent of the cooperative movement.[96] Both the Rural Workers Association (ATC) and the Union of Farmers and Ranchers (UNAG) have women's secretariats which have been instrumental in improving the situation of women farmworkers and peasants.[97]

These inclusionary trends notwithstanding, women were conspicuously absent from the FSLN's top leadership body, the National Directorate. The directorate wielded immense powers in the party and government apparatus during the 1980s, and its nine-man composition was a gross misrepresentation of the gender proportions among the Sandinista membership and base. The presence and influence of women in the government and political life during the 1980s was thus largely limited to the intermediate leadership and grassroots levels.

As a result of the 1984 elections, 13 women were elected to the National Assembly, all representing the FSLN (none of the opposition party representatives were women). In the Sandinista government, women held about one-third of all leadership posts, including Minister of Health Dora

María Téllez and Police Chief Doris Tijerino (both elected in 1990 as FSLN representatives to the National Assembly).[98] Following the 1990 elections, nine of the FSLN's 39 representatives were women while six out of UNO's 51 representatives were women. Within the FSLN, women accounted for about 22 percent of the total party membership, and constituted 37 percent of the intermediate leadership.[99]

The FSLN-affiliated Nicaraguan Women's Association (AMNLAE) was one of the groups most negatively affected by the Sandinistas' ambivalent stance toward the popular organizations. (See Popular Organizing) In the early years of the revolution, AMNLAE rapidly expanded as women enthusiastically joined the tasks of reconstruction and took leading roles in the national literacy crusade and health campaigns. But later many in the women's movement, including sectors within AMNLAE, began insisting on the need to organize around more gender-specific issues. They called on the FSLN to confront more directly various ideological barriers, particularly the deeply ingrained, pervasive *machismo*. Proponents of this position were largely responsible for bringing thorny issues such as domestic violence, rape, sexual harassment, and abortion rights out into the open after years of conspicuous silence. Later, these same forces pushed for greater attention to the questions of AIDS victims in Nicaragua and the rights of a growing lesbian community.[100]

The predominant view among the Sandinista leadership, passed along to AMNLAE, was that the organization should focus its energies on the national priorities of defense and economic production and postpone the fight around gender-specific issues until after the war. As AMNLAE increasingly concentrated its organizing efforts around defense-related activities such as establishing support networks for the mothers and wives of draftees and of soldiers killed in combat, its membership dwindled.

Among the most visible successes of the women's movement has been the establishment of a network of women's legal support offices, the first of which was established in Managua in 1983 under the auspices of AMNLAE.[101] The original goal of providing free legal assistance to women was soon broadened to include a series of social-psychological, educational and paramedical services. By 1990 regional offices were operating in several cities around the country and there were 23 *casas de la mujer* or women's centers throughout the country. Although AMNLAE continues to play a role in the offices and centers, for the most part they are organizationally and financially independent.

The Center for Research and Action for Women's Rights (CIAM), formerly known as the Nicaraguan Women's Institute, was founded in 1987. The nongovernmental CIAM advocates political change in favor of women and its work revolves around research, sex education, and non-traditional vocational training for women. In 1989 a new private women's center called Ixchén (Indian goddess of the moon) opened in Managua. With a psychologist, social worker, gynecologist, and lawyer on its staff, Ixchén's three offices provide a variety of fee-based services, including pap smears and abortion referral. Most of the center's financing comes from feminist groups in Western Europe.

Despite the existence of a militant women's movement in Nicaragua, backed during the 1980s by a government which was at least in principle committed to the promotion of women's rights, several important factors constrained the pace of change. First, the Sandinistas' commitment to backing progressive change in favor of women was tempered by the hesitation to struggle against *machismo* within the party and government, and by the larger determination to prioritize the defense effort to the detriment of sector-specific demands. Many women became increasingly critical of the Sandinista leadership for failing to adopt a firmer stance in the face of conservative resistance to changes favoring women and for holding onto a conception of the organized women's movement as an auxiliary of the party apparatus.

Second, Nicaragua is a socially conservative country, particularly in the countryside. Despite many of the efforts sponsored by the Sandinistas and by the women's movement to promote an alternative vision of women's role in society, in the streets and in the homes attitudes often changed little. Third, the influential Catholic church hierarchy tenaciously resisted many of the government's policies regarding women. It opposed reforms in the areas of family life and education and the participation of women in the military, as well as rigidly insisting — even in the face of widespread opposition — on adherence to the papal encyclical making contraception a sin.[102]

## Women and the Chamorro Government

Women constituted one of the key constituencies targeted by the National Endowment for Democracy (NED) in its work around the 1989-1990 UNO electoral campaign. As part of the effort to persuade women to vote UNO, NED funds helped create the Nicaraguan Women's Movement (MMN) in early 1989. The MMN project never really got off the ground and its activities were largely confined to a tiny base around some of the rightwing politicians in UNO. One MMN leader confirmed that the group only has about 300 total members.[103]

Despite this pre-electoral outreach to women, during the first four months of the Chamorro administration it became painfully clear to

Nicaraguan women that the fact that their country now had the first woman president in Central American history could hardly be considered an advance for feminism. To the contrary, Violeta Chamorro in many ways epitomized the social conservatism of traditional Nicaragua and her close ties to the Catholic church hierarchy, together with the austerity policies of the UNO government, threatened to overturn many of the gains women had made during the 1980s.

Women soon were bearing a large part of the fallout from two broader trends initiated by the new government. First, as unemployment mushroomed, women became "last hired and first fired," reversing the trend of the 1980s toward greater incorporation of women into the formal sectors of the economy. The economic hardships faced by newly unemployed women — heads of households in the majority — were aggravated by cutbacks and cost increases in social services, particularly health and child care.

Second, the Catholic church's ideological crusade, strongly endorsed by President Chamorro, sought to reimpose traditional, conservative social values. (See Religion and Education) These changes were most graphically represented in the offensive in the field of reproductive rights. As part of the government's efforts to stamp out abortion — illegal but widely tolerated under the Sandinistas — Managua's women's hospital stopped the practice of performing therapeutic abortions, while pro-government media beamed powerful anti-abortion messages. Television viewers, for example, watched an "expert" from the International Organization for Human Life, invited from the United States to Managua by the Catholic church hierarchy, declare that abortion leads to "the abuse of sexual life, increased venereal disease, and increased fornication."[104] A television series on sex education, "Sex and Youth," was ordered taken off the air, and Ministry of Education officials engaged in a project to rewrite sex-education literature used in the nation's schools. According to numerous public declarations by church and education authorities, the use of all contraceptives other than the rhythm method will be proscribed.

In part as a response to the growing problem of unemployment among women, and to fill the void left by the government's cancellation of basic social services, a host of new nongovernmental organizations dedicated to womens issues have sprung up since April 1990. These groups are attempting to offer free or low-cost services to women, including legal assistance, sex education, family planning, and gynecologic attention.

Beginning in April 1990 AMNLAE expanded a debate over the nature and future of the organization which had been going on since long

before the Sandinista electoral defeat. As with the rest of the FSLN structures, the AMNLAE leadership will now be elected by its base instead of
appointed by the party. The organization also was moving toward a less
party-linked structure, opening the membership up to women of all political tendencies. Much of the internal debate focused on differences over
the most appropriate strategy for moving forward on gender-specific issues.

A prominent Nicaraguan feminist was asked recently if she felt
Nicaraguan women were in a better position when the country had a
*machista* revolutionary as president (Ortega), or with a socially conservative woman in that position (Chamorro). "Of course it was better
before. At least then we could negotiate, persuade, and politicize
him...there was a basis for dialogue."[105]

# Native Peoples

Nicaragua's ethnic communities — Creoles, Miskitos, Sumus, Ramas,
and Garífuna — share the vast expanses of the Atlantic coast with some
180,000 Spanish-speaking *mestizos*.[106] While the Atlantic coast region en-
compasses more than half of the nation's territory, its population of
roughly 300,000 is less than one-tenth of the national total. The Miskitos
are the largest of the three Indian peoples, numbering around 67,000 according to conservative estimates. They are followed by some 5,000 Sumus
and fewer than 600 Ramas. There are about 26,000 English-speaking
Afro-Americans, or Creoles, while the small Afro-Indian Garífuna group
numbers around 1,500.[107]

Although the influx of mestizos, who constitute the majority population in the region, has expanded the influence of Catholicism among
*costeños* (coastal population), the Moravian church continues to play a
dominant role on the coast. The Moravian church's general thrust that
"the kingdom of God is pure, and the kingdom of politics profane" contributed to the widespread apolitical orientation of the Atlantic coast
population before 1979. The conservative thrust of the Moravian church
on the coast historically was complemented by the influence of U.S. corporations — mainly timber, mining, and bananas — which operated there.
Despite its rich natural resource endowment, the Atlantic coast remains
the most economically underdeveloped region in the country, largely a
product of the enclave nature of foreign investments there which left a
legacy of paternalism and dependence.

The war against Somoza and the insurrection which toppled his dictatorship took place almost exclusively on the Pacific side of the country.

Nonetheless, the Sandinista victory in 1979 created, for the first time, the space and conditions in which Nicaragua's indigenous peoples could press for fulfillment of their historic demands. In the first year and a half of the revolution, the Sandinistas attempted to address the poverty and underdevelopment that characterized the area, investing heavily in social and productive infrastructure. They tried to respond to ethnically based demands as well, but in this unfamiliar terrain they quickly lost the ability to distinguish between legitimate demands of the people and confrontational ones voiced by Indian leaders with personal political aspirations. The FSLN's inexperience with ethnic politics and ignorance of the coast's complexities led to clashes with MISURASATA, an indigenous mass organization formed just after the Sandinista victory.

By early 1981 the rapid escalation of tensions led to a complete breakdown of relations between the government and MISURASATA. Within a year, two MISURASATA leaders — Steadman Fagoth and Brooklyn Rivera — led armed organizations and for the next three years the region was engulfed in war.

The migration of tens of thousands of Indian people to Costa Rica and Honduras and the internal displacement of entire communities contributed to a severe disruption in traditional lifestyles. Some 40,000 Miskitos and Sumus fled to Honduras and another 10,000 were displaced inside Nicaragua as a result of controversial government relocation programs.[108] The war threatened the very existence of the Sumus and the Ramas.

The English-speaking Creole population, concentrated along the southern part of the coast mainly in and around the city of Bluefields, also was affected by the war. Sporadic fighting took place on several points along the south coast and Bluefields itself was attacked by contras in 1985. In the face of economic decline and the tense military situation in the region, many Creoles — particularly draft-age males — opted to leave the country, headed for neighboring Costa Rica or for the United States.

## Peace and Autonomy

By 1985 relations between the indigenous population and the Sandinistas had begun to improve, largely as a result of reexamination by the government of its own views and policies.[109] The FSLN openly admitted many of its mistakes in its relations with the native population and rectified earlier policy shortcomings. The Miskito combatants, for their part, were tired of fighting and the Indian population had had enough of war.

A lengthy process of negotiations with both political leaders and field commanders of the Indian fighters led to a gradual lessening of hostilities.

But the factor which finally tipped the balance in favor of definitive peace on the Atlantic coast was the advance of the autonomy process. The first phase of that process drew to a close in September 1987 when, after two and a half years of grassroots consultations among the coastal communities, the National Assembly signed the Autonomy Statute into law. The statute, which incorporated a series of demands put forth by the indigenous groups and was backed by guarantees in the Nicaraguan constitution, symbolized the beginning of the end of war on the Atlantic coast.

The autonomy initiative, belittled by the Sandinistas' adversaries as a government ploy to temper indigenous nationalism, developed out of a broadly supported, grassroots movement among Nicaragua's ethnic population. In essence, autonomy aimed to guarantee self-rule and first-class citizenship for all ethnic groups on the Atlantic coast, while maintaining and developing their specific cultural identities as part of the Nicaraguan nation. Within this framework, the autonomy statute guaranteed the development and free use of native languages, recognized indigenous communal land ownership, and respected the rights of the different groups in regard to the development of natural resources.

The autonomy statute called for the installation of two 45-member coastal governments—one in the north, known as the North Atlantic Autonomous Region (RAAN), the other in the south or RAAS—comprised of directly elected representatives from each ethnic group. These councils are responsible for governing affairs such as regional trade with the Caribbean, distribution of basic goods, development of a plan for the rational use of the region's resources, and administration of health, education, and cultural services. The intent of the autonomy statute was for the regional governments to have control over finances as well. The central government would transfer all financing authority for the Atlantic coast to the autonomy councils and the councils were empowered to design a taxation plan. In addition, the councils were to administer a special development fund for the region, composed of contributions from bilateral and multilateral sources as well as the central government.

The autonomy statute is flexible by design, resembling a set of broad guidelines rather than a plan of action. While this flexibility was seen as necessary to guarantee respect for ethnic diversity and to leave room for the development of local initiative, it also has proved to be an obstacle in the implementation of autonomy. Conflicting concepts and interpretations of what autonomy really means in practice have emerged. While unity and cooperation are essential aspects for assuring the project's successful implementation, in reality the flexible nature of the statute often has tended to fuel existing inter-ethnic tensions and leadership rivalries within each group.

## UNO and the Coast: Wither Autonomy?

A new phase on the Atlantic coast — bringing both new promises and new threats — was opened up in 1990 by elections for the autonomous governments and the change in administrations in Managua from the FSLN to UNO.[110] Despite the tenacious continuity of old rivalries and the eruption of new ones, for the first time in a decade conflicts were now being played out on the political terrain, rather than the military one. By mid-1990 peace, at least peace defined as the absence of shooting, had become a reality on the coast.

On June 20, 1990 the last of some 2,000 Yatama contras handed in their weapons concluding the demobilization process on the coast. In negotiations with representatives from the UNO government in Managua, Yatama won a commitment for the establishment of three "development poles" for the former Miskito combatants and their families, with rights and responsibilities similar to those for the Nicaraguan Resistance (RN) in the Pacific. (See Guerrilla Opposition) The lack of a defined relationship between the new poles and the autonomous government, and the arms caches generally understood to be in the hands of rival Miskito factions, cast a shadow of doubt over how long the fragile peace might last.

On May 9, 1990 the new regional government authorities were formally sworn in. The RAAN — where the February 1990 elections had resulted in 22 seats for Yatama, 21 for the FSLN, and two for UNO — elected moderate Yatama activist Leonel Pantin as coordinator of its Autonomous Council, the highest representative of the autonomous government. In the RAAS — 23 seats for UNO, 18 for the FSLN and four for Yatama — the post went to Alvin Guthrie, who also was elected as an UNO deputy in the National Assembly and is head of the rightwing trade-union federation CUS.[111]

Although the government structures stipulated by the autonomy statute were thus successfully installed, a series of obstacles threatened to gut the autonomy process in practice. These included a revival of inter-ethnic tensions, as well as conflicts between the RAAS and the RAAN. Among the Miskitos, major differences over how autonomy should be applied existed, for example, between leaders like Brooklyn Rivera and Steadman Fagoth and between the different armed groups, Yatama and Kisan.

But perhaps the biggest threat to autonomy came from the central government in Managua. In April, Chamorro created the Institute for the Development of the Atlantic Coast (INDERA) and gave Brooklyn Rivera the ministerial post as its director. The creation of INDERA was not well received on the coast and many saw it as a direct attempt to undermine autonomy. The RAAS Autonomous Council sent a letter to Chamorro condemning INDERA as "antihistorical, illegal, and unconstitutional."[112] They were fearful both that Managua would attempt to use INDERA to usurp powers delegated to the regional governments, and that as head of the Institute Rivera would be well-placed to play favorites with his followers, for the most part Miskitos from the RAAN.

Many in the RAAN Autonomous Council also were critical of the move to establish INDERA. Yatama members and Sandinistas in the RAAN found themselves uniting to defend against any erosion in the authority of the autonomous governments. Fagoth and Rivera, bitter rivals for years until they reunited in 1989 in order to return to Nicaragua for the elections, once again found themselves at loggerheads, this time vying for control of the region's natural resources, a key aspect of the struggle for autonomy. INDERA is slated to control natural resource development on the coast, particularly those aspects relating to foreign investments and international marketing. Fagoth was appointed by the Autonomous Council as natural resources coordinator, and he maintains that control of fishing, timber, and mining is exclusively the responsibility of the autonomous governments.

# Refugees

Although to a lesser degree than in nearby El Salvador and Guatemala, the conflict in Nicaragua also produced a large-scale exodus from the country. Thousands of draft-age youths fled the country to avoid military service. Others sought to escape the desperate economic situation. Nearly all Nicaraguan refugees shared the conviction that as long as the Sandinistas remained in power, the country's two main ills – war and economic crisis – were not likely to go away. Conservative estimates say that between 1979 and 1987 more than 140,000 Nicaraguans, nearly 5 percent of the country's total population, left the country with the intent of taking up residence elsewhere.[113] Others insist that the figure is at least twice that high. Roberto Ferrey, a former member of the contra directorate and the director of Nicaragua's Repatriation Institute under Chamorro, estimated that if contras and their families were counted together with legal and illegal refugees, the total number of Nicaraguans who left the country over the last decade was half a million.[114]

With the exception of Miskito refugees from the Atlantic coast and contra family members, most of whom went to Costa Rica and Honduras, the majority of Nicaraguans who left since 1979 hoped to resettle in the United States. While some managed to fulfill their dreams, many others faced humiliating conditions among the unemployed, as undocumented workers, or in refugee camps and U.S. immigration detention centers. Although during some periods Washington granted Nicaraguans special treatment and allowed them to stay, the majority of asylum applications were turned down and some Nicaraguans were even deported.

## Refugees, Emigrants, and Displaced Persons

Several major waves of migration took place between 1979 and 1990. Even before the Sandinistas came to power, thousands of Nicaraguans had fled repression at the hands of Somoza's National Guard. The war of liberation alone generated an estimated 15,000 refugees. In the initial period after the 1979 Sandinista victory, nearly all of Somoza's associates and many upper-class families left, convinced that there was no place for them in a popular revolution. The bulk of this group either joined the contras or set up shop in Miami, home to the largest concentration of Nicaraguans outside the country.[115] The flight of the wealthy was complemented by a "brain drain." During the 1980s a third of the country's college-educated professionals left, including 22 percent of all doctors and medical technicians.[116]

In a concerted effort to lure back as many Nicaraguan entrepreneurs and professionals as possible, the Chamorro administration offered a series of generous incentives, including exemptions on import duties, special conditions for the return of confiscated properties, and investment privileges. For the most part, however, the self-exiled businessmen remained skeptical, adopting a "wait and see" attitude. In general, the exiles are "very closed-minded," commented Oscar Cerna, a Nicaraguan who owns a restaurant in Miami, during a visit to Managua. "They expect the new government to do everything for them and get rid of the Sandinistas completely. But once you come here, you see things are much more complex than that."[117]

It is expected that many in Miami's Nicaraguan community will eventually have no choice but to return as the Immigration and Naturalization Service (INS) policy of tolerance expires. In July 1990 the INS gave its certification that President Chamorro had asserted control over the country and had resisted "challenges" by the FSLN, thus ending a five-month suspension in the issuance of asylum denial letters. Some 12,000 rejected asylum seekers were expected to receive letters in the ensuing months, and 25,000 pending requests were not likely to be approved.[118] On the streets of Miami, many Nicaraguans declared that they would probably remain in the United States illegally before returning to their country against their will. According to Roberto Ferrey, former member of the contra directorate named by Chamorro to head the government's Repatriation Institute, since the Chamorro government cannot afford to pay transportation costs, those who do wish to return may have to wait until they are deported so that the U.S. government will pick up the tab.[119]

Following the flight of Nicaragua's elite sectors, the next major exodus took place on the Atlantic coast starting in 1982 with the eruption of military conflict there. Tens of thousands of *costeños*, mainly Miskitos, moved to United Nations High Commission for Refugees (UNHCR) or contra-sponsored refugee camps in Honduras and Costa Rica. As the peace process began to take hold on the Atlantic coast, many returned to Nicaragua and by the end of 1988 Miskitos in UNHCR camps in Honduras numbered fewer than 10,000.[120]

The largest single flow of Nicaraguans from the Pacific side of the country began following initiation of the draft in 1984. More than 30 percent of all Nicaraguans who left since 1979 were students, most of them draft-age youth unwilling to serve in the army. The contras, in conjunction with prominent Nicaraguan opposition figures and sectors of the Catholic church, set up an elaborate "underground railroad" network inside Nicaragua to shuttle draft resisters out of the country, and, often against their wishes, into contra camps in Honduras.[121]

Beginning in 1988, under the framework of the Esquipulas II Peace Accords, several repatriation projects for Nicaraguan refugees were initiated. With the war winding down, by mid-1989 more than 35,000 Nicaraguans had returned home, the highest repatriation rate in the region.[122] The repatriation process was accelerated after Chamorro assumed power. The UNHCR and the Honduran and Nicaraguan governments worked out an agreement to facilitate the return of refugees, contra family members, and the remaining Miskitos from Honduras.[123] A similar agreement with Costa Rica provided for the repatriation of more than 1,700 Nicaraguans there, mostly Creoles from the Atlantic coast port of Bluefields.[124] Between March and July of 1990 an estimated 10,000 refugees had repatriated.

According to Ferrey, Honduras was pushing for the return of all Nicaraguans, while the Costa Rican government had offered to provide legal status to those wishing to remain permanently in the country. Ferrey estimated that, with the exception of Nicaraguans in the United States, repatriation would be concluded by early 1991.[125] Once in Nicaragua, the refugees were to receive assistance from the U.S. Agency for International Development (AID), channeled through the OAS-sponsored International Commission for Support and Verification.

While the fate of Nicaraguan refugees outside the country received broad coverage in the media, less attention was given to the problem of those displaced from their homes inside Nicaragua. During the years of intense fighting in the Nicaraguan countryside, the military conflict resulted in the displacement of more than 354,800 Nicaraguans as well as the creation of 16,470 orphans.[126] Faced with the growing problem of internal refugees, in 1985 the government launched a resettlement program which relocated some 78,000 war-displaced *campesinos* into 202 new settlements.

The resettlement plan had a high initial cost, with expenses totaling more than $50 million, but the effort was deemed necessary in order to get the peasants out of resource-draining refugee camps and back into production. The contras' strategy of forcing the Sandinista government to relocate tens of thousands of *campesinos*, who were often reluctant to abandon their homes even in the face of the evident military threat, was largely successful in disrupting the rural economy — some 750,000 acres of farmland were abandoned — and in alienating an important part of the FSLN's base.[127]

# Environment

Beginning with President Violeta Chamorro's inauguration speech the UNO government has consistently professed a commitment to environmental protection. Chamorro appointed the country's best-known environmentalist, Jaime Incer, to head the Institute of Natural Resources and the Environment (IRENA, formerly DIRENA). Incer soon began speaking of ambitious plans to arrest environmental decay and to promote sustainable development practices. But many other Nicaraguan environmentalists remained skeptical. The deepest fears were that certain aspects of UNO's economic program — rejuvenation of agroexports like cotton, sugar, and beef; unregulated free-market policies; and the removal of restrictions on foreign investments — would rekindle the very factors which had led to devastation of the Nicaraguan environment in the first place. The Sandinistas had addressed and attempted to eliminate many of these factors.

By all accounts the legacy of the Somoza dictatorship in environmental terms was overwhelming. Deforestation was rampant on the vast lowlands of the Atlantic coast as a result of timber concessions granted to transnational lumber companies, and about one-third of the country's tropical rainforests had been leveled by agricultural colonization and cattle-ranching schemes which constantly pushed forward the agricultural frontier.[128] The two major lakes which cover a large portion of the south-central part of the country—Lake Nicaragua is the largest fresh water lake in the world—were contaminated by industrial pollution. Erosion resulting from the "cotton boom" of the 1950s in the arid western plains severely damaged topsoil conditions, bringing periodic dust storms, mud slides, and flash floods. More important, the dictatorship left in place a model of development and infrastructure which could serve only to perpetuate the cycle of environmental devastation.

The Sandinista government sponsored a variety of initiatives aimed at arresting environmental decay and at creating the social conditions necessary for long-term environmental protection and the sustainable use of natural resources.[129] An integral part of this strategy was the attempt to transform the prevailing agricultural model and land-tenure patterns.

As a result of the agricultural expansion underway since the 1950s large agroexport plantations and cattle ranches constantly ate away at Nicaragua's tropical rainforests. The Sandinista agrarian reform sought to break up many of the large plantations and to foster the creation of agricultural cooperatives and small family farms. It also sought to break the chronic dependence on a few export crops as well as to move toward national self-sufficiency in basic-grains production. This model, it was hoped, would help the country move away from the destructive and expensive "pesticide treadmill" bound up with export crop dependence.[130] In general, the new small landholders who benefited from the agrarian reform used fewer chemicals and grew a greater variety of food and export crops. Sustainable methods such as crop rotation and Integrated Pest Management (IPM) — a technique which attempts to reduce pesticide use by maximizing nonchemical pest controls — as well as terracing and reforestation practices to foster soil and watershed conservation, received official backing from the government.

The Sandinistas' concern for environmental protection, and its receptiveness to the concerns of national and foreign-based nongovernmental organizations working to promote ecologically sound policies, brought the following gains:

* Shortly after the 1979 victory the government nationalized Nicaragua's natural resources and forest lands and put an end to

the exploitation of forest, mineral, and aquatic resources by foreign companies. A ban on the export of endangered species also was implemented.

* The government imposed an official ban on the importation of ten hazardous pesticides – including DDT, aldrin, and dieldrin – and promoted a strategy to reduce dependence on imported agricultural chemicals through support for IPM programs and for pesticide use-reduction campaigns.

* A national parks system was created which was administered by DIRENA, the state environmental and natural resources ministry. Under the Sandinistas, DIRENA had targeted 18 percent of the country for eventual incorporation into protected national parklands.

* Both directly and through support to NGOs the government backed dozens of appropriate technology and alternative energy projects such as small-scale hydroelectric plants, solar ovens, fuel-efficient wood stoves, and windmill-powered generators and water pumps. Large-scale hydrothermal and geothermal electric plants were part of a strategy to reduce dependence on imported petroleum products.

* As part of the agrarian-reform process, up to two million trees per year were grown for use in reforestation projects and more than 700 miles of windbreaks were planted to arrest soil erosion.

* Nicaragua became a major participant in the international debate over environmental protection. Managua hosted the region's first conference on environmental problems in 1987, bringing together more than 150 environmentalists from the United States, Western Europe, and Latin America.[131] Two years later, more than one thousand delegates from some 60 countries around the world converged on the Nicaraguan capital for the "Fourth Biennial Congress on the Fate and Hope of the Earth."

* Environmental-protection clauses were incorporated into the constitution ratified in 1987.

* Two nongovernmental environmental groups were formed. The Nicaraguan Environmentalist Movement (MAN), launched in 1988 as the Nicaraguan equivalent of an environmental lobby, has some 20 national organizations affiliated. The group's main focus is to contribute to the recognition, recuperation, protection, and sustainable use of Nicaragua's natural resources.[132] MAN is an

outgrowth of the Nicaraguan Association of Biologists and Ecologists (ABEN) which also works on environmental issues.

Despite these advances the experience of the 1980s demonstrated that environmental protection takes more than good intentions. Particularly after 1985 the Sandinistas' objective of promoting environmentally sound practices was eroded and deprioritized by three factors: the war, economic-austerity policies, and differences within the government over the relationship between development policies and environmentalism.

Throughout Central America, war and militarization have had profound effects on the environment; Nicaragua was no exception. Contra activity in the countryside led to a direct curtailment of DIRENA's work, as more than 75 environmental-protection and natural-resource employees were kidnapped or killed by the contras during the 1980s. In 1983 Nicaragua's only tropical forest reserve, the Saslaya National Park, was closed after the contras kidnapped the park administrator and two rangers.[133] As part of their campaign to destroy infrastructure and development projects, the contras set fire to areas covered by reforestation projects and razed nurseries. It was in light of these activities that Nicaraguan environmentalists felt chills run down their spines when the Chamorro government announced that the main development pole for the resettlement of ex-contras would be located in the Río San Juan department, one of the country's most ecologically delicate zones.

When economic reforms were introduced to fuel the defense effort, sharp cutbacks were made in all but the most essential social and economic projects and environmental programs were among the first to face the budget ax. DIRENA, which had been set up in 1979 to coordinate all aspects of natural-resource management, saw its mandate and budget gradually whittled away after 1983. Many of DIRENA's ambitious plans, such as the creation of a large national parks system, remained on the drawing board. Nicaragua's IPM program, regarded by many as the most advanced in Latin America, was similarly reduced in the wake of austerity policies. "The pesticide crisis reflects the economic crisis," said environmental consultant Bill Hall. "The commitment is there, but it's on hold."[134]

Nicaragua's efforts to protect its forests, already curtailed by the effects of war and economic crisis, were dealt another heavy blow in October 1988 as Hurricane Joan destroyed some 10 percent of the country's tropical rainforests, advancing deforestation by 15 years in the space of four short hours. With large quantities of wood felled by the hurricane located in and around the contras' Río San Juan development pole, contra leaders were enthusiastic about a plan to generate jobs and income through extracting and processing the trees. Some environmentalists, however, have cautioned that the negative effects of such an operation could be devastating because the zone has few existing roads.

Despite these and other constraints, the poor state of environmental protection during the latter half of the 1980s is not wholly explained by political and economic factors. As Hall noted, "The ecological vision has respect, but it's not total—there is conflict and controversy over the role of ecological consciousness in development." This less-than-complete commitment to environmental protection became evident as the government began considering mega-scale development projects as a solution to economic underdevelopment. These included the possibility of building massive hydroelectric dams in the Miskito rainforest and consideration of linking the Atlantic and Pacific coasts with an extensive port and rail network or "dry canal"—both of which would result in the destruction of pristine environments.[135] Outright policy contradictions also played a role. For instance, Sandinista credit and subsidy policies, which aimed to stimulate agricultural production and to improve the situation of small holders and cooperatives, often ended up promoting the same practices which DIRENA was trying to eradicate, such as an unnecessary reliance on imported pesticides.[136]

Even without these shortcomings the dilemma faced by Sandinista policymakers was a difficult one. Many of the country's more serious environmental problems were intricately bound up with the model and structure of the economy inherited from Somoza. Many major reforms which could reduce poisoning of the environment would have inevitably triggered short-term economic losses, both in terms of local production and foreign-exchange earnings.[137]

During its first four months in office the Chamorro government demonstrated an approach to environmental issues rooted in pragmatism. In part, this meant taking a high-profile stance in favor of environmental protection and conservation and avoiding the adoption of specific initiatives which could generate significant levels of international criticism. For example, the Sí a Paz (Yes to Peace) international park in Río San Juan, included in the contras' initial proposal for the development poles, was placed off-limits and IRENA Minister Incer was included on the commission charged with delineating the exact location of the poles, ostensibly as part of an effort to minimize their environmental impact. Likewise, the government rejected an economically attractive proposal by a Miami-based businessman to use toxic waste as ballast in road-construction projects on the Atlantic coast. The lucrative deal apparently was rejected for fear of causing a backlash among environmentally conscious international donors and potential ecotourists.

Incer, who is reportedly an advocate of debt swaps and the promotion of ecotourism, expressed confidence that many governments and international organizations would be interested in funding environmental projects in Nicaragua. Incer also spoke of plans to set up a nationwide network of "ecology inspectors" who would be charged with controlling and regulating environmental conservation efforts and natural resource use. The project, to be coordinated with a national environmental education program, would be based on the division of the country into 35 "ecological districts."[138]

Although willing to give the benefit of the doubt to Chamorro regarding her proclaimed commitment to conservation, many Nicaraguan environmentalists questioned the extent to which ecologically sound policies would be compatible with the broader thrust of the government's economic and agrarian policies. Early policy decisions including austerity measures, privatization, and a renewed emphasis on agroexport crops produced by large private producers indicated that the economic model being pursued could lead only to the perpetuation of environmentally destructive practices.

## Chapter 5

# Foreign Influence

## U.S. Foreign Policy

Shortly after the 1990 election a group of Nicaraguan analysts observed: "The economy of this small country and the welfare of its people have never been a priority for the United States."[1] That essential truth is important to remember as Washington begins relations with a new government in Managua. From 1979 to 1990 Nicaragua was a foreign-policy priority for Washington — dominating presidential press conferences, State Department diplomatic maneuverings, and congressional debate. All Washington's preoccupation with and all the U.S. dollars spent on Nicaragua during the 1980s were directed toward destroying the Sandinistas' revolutionary project — not toward furthering democracy and development in Nicaragua.

The electoral defeat of Daniel Ortega must be counted as a victory for U.S. foreign policy. A combination of military, economic, and political tactics did remove the FSLN from power. The revolutionary party was replaced with a U.S.-backed political coalition shaped and financed by Washington. No longer was the U.S. embassy considered a hostile presence. Instead it was the new government's main financial supporter and economic consultant.

It was not the country's natural resources, its investment and trade potential, nor its geographical position that made Nicaragua a top foreign-policy concern for the United States. Rather it was the country's nationalism and its revolutionary spirit that drew U.S. attention. There is, of course, a long history to this conflictive relationship. In fact the entire history of Nicaragua since independence has largely been defined by the ongoing struggle against U.S. domination.

In the 1850s, for instance, U.S. mercenary William Walker declared himself president of Nicaragua but was soon chased out of the country. In the following years the U.S. government frequently intervened in local politics to support candidates that would do its bidding. In 1910 General José Santos Zelaya, a nationalist who made the mistake of negotiating new business deals with Great Britain and Japan, was ousted with the help of U.S. troops and Washington placed the country under a customs receivership. A few years later, in the mountains of Nueva Segovia, Washington fought its first counterinsurgency war in the southern hemisphere against Nicaraguan nationalist and Sandinista namesake Augusto César Sandino. Sandino represented no threat to U.S. economic interests, but he was challenging the U.S. right to preside over Central America as if it were its backyard. This nationalist sentiment needed to be crushed, and finally it was – not by U.S. Marines but by Washington's hand-picked allies in Nicaragua.

By the late 1970s the Somoza dictatorship was wearing out its usefulness to Washington. Instead of a faithful ally, Washington increasingly regarded Somoza as an embarrassment and an anachronism. More important, Somoza was no longer able to keep his country stable. As the Somoza regime tottered Washington desperately tried to construct a moderate alternative to the FSLN guerrillas. But faced with widespread popular support for the FSLN, Washington failed to stop the leftist advance of the Sandinistas. Once again *sandinismo* emerged as a challenge to U.S. control, and Washington decided it could not afford to have Nicaragua survive as an alternative model of political and economic development for the third world.

## Reagan's Crusade

President Ronald Reagan quickly grasped the ideological threat that Sandinista Nicaragua represented. During his eight years in the White House, the campaign against the FSLN took the form of a crusade and obsession. The counterrevolution became a passion that pushed aside legal restraints and more pragmatic solutions.

The extremes to which Washington was willing to go in pursuit of its objectives reflected the degree to which Nicaragua was a threat – not to its neighbors or to any real U.S. security interests, but to the way the U.S. government has traditionally viewed its interests in Latin America. Symbolically, revolutionary Nicaragua represented the antithesis of the U.S. vision of what reality should look like south of its borders. The small country held up an alternative model of socioeconomic change: one based on national sovereignty, political pluralism, a mixed economy, and improved living standards for the majority. The stakes of the conflict also rose to the extent that the White House, Pentagon, and CIA – spurred on by important forces from the New Right – conceived of the Nicaraguan counterrevolution as a litmus test for the Reagan doctrine and for the application of the precepts of low intensity conflict in a counterrevolutionary context.[2]

The original Reagan plan of counterrevolution sought to combine economic pressure, political manipulation, and support for the internal opposition. But the heart of the project consisted of military support for the armed contras. The goal was to throw the revolution into turmoil, provoking anti-Sandinista unrest and, eventually, an insurrection. The first CIA timetables had the contra leaders marching triumphantly into Managua by the end of 1983 to set up a new government.[3] Initial hopes were that the contras – with sufficient U.S. military backing – could do the job by themselves. If not, the Hondurans or a joint contingent of Central American troops could be brought in to help deal the final blow. In the worst of cases, the Pentagon could pull out its contingency plans for the direct deployment of U.S. troops.

The end of 1983 came and went, but the contras were no closer to Managua. The failure of the "rapid victory approach," combined with the ever-growing influence of low intensity conflict proponents among military and political strategists in Washington, brought about a gradual modification in the scope and nature of the anti-Sandinista campaign. The ultimate objective of getting rid of the Sandinistas would largely remain the same, but the methods and timetable were altered significantly.

The war increasingly acquired a new face. The contras began to wage a prolonged, grinding war of attrition against the government forces, while Washington increased pressures aimed at isolating the Sandinistas in the economic, diplomatic, and political terrains. The psychological and ideological dimension of the campaign became crucial, including the perpetual "threat" of an invasion. Under tremendous pressure from all sides, in the long run the Sandinista government would eventually either collapse, or give up – "say uncle" in Reagan's words. Some of the more farsighted strategists hoped that the campaign of destabilization would force the Sandinista leadership to make drastic compromises in its original political project and thereby lose the support of the Nicaraguan people.

While some in Washington had their doubts that such a strategy could actually succeed in destroying the revolution, they at least conceded that the war of attrition would send a powerful signal of U.S. resolve. "Washington believes," admitted Richard John Neuhaus, founding member of the neoconservative Institute on Religion and Democracy, "that Nicaragua must serve as a warning to the rest of Central America to never again challenge U.S. hegemony, because of the enormous economic and political costs. It's too bad that the [Nicaraguan] poor must suffer, but historically the poor have always suffered. Nicaragua must be a lesson to others."[4]

The attrition strategy—spearheaded by the massive destruction inflicted on the country by the contra army—was more successful in advancing the United States toward its goals than the earlier approach. For some Nicaraguans, economic hardships and war weariness began to make the revolution look like a "no win" alternative. But the fruits of the attrition strategy would not be fully harvested until long after Ronald Reagan had left the White House.

## A New Leaf under Bush

As Reagan's vice president, George Bush showed himself to be a strong supporter of the contras and the entire U.S. strategy of waging counterrevolutionary war against the Sandinista government. By the time Bush ascended to the presidency, however, the time had come to move away from the increasingly unproductive contra war and to focus on building a more effective internal opposition. President Bush put behind him the obsessive quality of Reagan's crusade against the Sandinistas but carried on his fundamental policy of seeking the final destruction of the Sandinistas. Although more careful to maintain his image as statesman, Bush continued the Reagan tradition of insulting the country's leaders, calling President Ortega an "unwanted animal at a garden party."[5]

Changing conditions in Central America had persuaded the Reagan State Department to reevaluate U.S. tactics, even to the extent of drawing up contra demobilization plans and a relocation strategy. Political rather than military options for ridding Nicaragua of the Sandinistas were increasingly being considered. Upon becoming president, Bush shifted away from the more aggressive policies of his predecessor and slowly began distancing himself from the contras.

Having referred to Reagan's Nicaragua policy as "the most divisive in recent history," Secretary of State James Baker stressed that Bush policy would seek to avoid the "excesses" which had characterized the previous eight years and would attempt to ground a new U.S. approach to Nicaragua in a broad, bipartisan consensus. Indeed, the bipartisan agreement reached in April 1989—which officially acknowledged U.S. support for the Central American peace process—pointed to a more pragmatic, multitrack approach that would keep several options open at the same time.

The key tactical dilemmas hinged upon what to do with the contras in light of Central America's resolve to disband them and how best to build up an internal anti-Sandinista coalition. The bipartisan accord placed the contras on the back burner. It tacitly accepted the inevitability of their eventual disbanding, while allowing the Bush administration to use "humanitarian aid" to keep the contra threat alive until after the 1990 election. This continued assistance to the contras, which violated the Esquipulas agreements, reminded Nicaraguan voters that six more years of Sandinista rule could mean six more years of war.

## Elections and their Aftermath

The disparate 14-party UNO coalition held together for the election and dealt the FSLN a shocking defeat. Some observers said that the UNO victory and the elections themselves were evidence of how wrongheaded the Reagan administration's militaristic approach had been, while contra supporters contended that it was the pressure of the counterrevolutionary resistance that forced the FSLN to sponsor the election. But there was hardly a dissenting voice in Washington that the Chamorro win constituted a victory for democracy, freedom, and economic progress. Since 1979 both sides of the aisle on Capitol Hill had been searching for a strategy to rid Central America of the Sandinista presence, and both Democrats and Republicans felt vindicated by the Chamorro landslide. Summing up this self-congratulatory atmosphere, a veteran *New York Times* reporter authored an opinion piece entitled, "Nicaragua, Victory for U.S. Fair Play."[6]

With Daniel Ortega a lame-duck president, Nicaragua suddenly lost its high place on Washington's priority list. Democrats asked why tiny Nicaragua should deserve special treatment in terms of economic aid while Eastern Europe was getting the short shrift. There were also new budget realities. The seemingly unlimited sums found by the Reagan administration to prop up Nicaragua's neighbors and tear down the Sandinista revolution were no longer available. There was also realpolitick to consider: Nicaragua could no longer be construed as a national-security threat which needed to be confronted with all of America's diplomatic, military, economic, and private resources.

Washington has by no means abandoned Nicaragua. But its commitment to support the new government and rebuild the country is not commensurate with its decade-long campaign to destabilize the Sandinista revolution. The National Endowment for Democracy (NED) is still funding programs in the country but no longer will millions of dollars be targeted for Nicaragua. The U.S. Agency for International Development (AID) has given Nicaragua special consideration the first year but the country cannot expect the kind of long-term commitment given the other Central American countries in the mid-1980s following the Kissinger

Commission recommendations. Rather than giving the new administration a grace period, Washington has indicated that it will be hard-nosed in insisting that a neoliberal restructuring program be implemented, no matter what its social and political consequences.

With the larger geopolitical preoccupations removed for the time being by the FSLN electoral defeat, the immediate focus of U.S. policy has been economic stabilization. Through its economic-aid program Washington is seeking to convert Nicaragua into a debtor in good standing with international financial institutions and a country that is once again fully integrated into the world capitalist market. Opening up the country to U.S. trade and investment is a priority of an array of U.S. government agencies. The United States also is interested in fortifying the local business elite, which functions not only as an economic partner but also as a trusted political ally. A chief focus of U.S. stabilization strategy is the privatization of state enterprises. The U.S. demand that state corporations and marketing boards be sold or dissolved closely relates to the broader political objective of rolling back the social gains of the revolution.

In its new foreign policy for Nicaragua, Washington is not just taking aim at the vestiges of the revolution—from agrarian reform to government control over international trade—but also looking to destroy *sandinismo* as a political and social force. This is a goal largely shared by the Chamorro administration and the UNO parties but there exist internal differences about how this might be best accomplished. The right mix of confrontation and cooptation, of neoliberal restructuring and gradual transformation, is being sought.

At least one part of the post-election strategy of counterrevolution is a carry-over from the earlier effort to build the internal opposition. Winning elections had been only one aspect of Washington's strategy of creating and supporting a wide range of civic, political, media, business, and labor organizations. Had the FSLN won the February 1990 election, these organizations would have formed the infrastructure of a broad opposition movement. As is, they will be used to build the the government's social base and to undermine the FSLN's own popular base of support.

Since the election this strategy of bolstering the anti-Sandinista infrastructure has been extended to the government itself—now open to massive U.S. penetration. On one level the U.S. embassy has demonstrated a clear interest in economically and politically stabilizing the Chamorro government, since the success of this government would be the best guarantee that the Sandinistas would not return to power in 1996. Washington is backing up the government with economic assistance, political aid and training (called "democracy-strengthening" assistance), support for new multilateral lending, and favored trade agreements.

Concerned that the pragmatists surrounding Chamorro have been too conciliatory toward the Sandinistas, however, the embassy has on another level supported UNO's rightwing factions. Like the embassy itself, groups such as the Superior Council of Private Enterprise (COSEP) business chamber, rightwing unions and political parties, and to some extent the Catholic hierarchy feel that there can be no progress in Nicaragua until *sandinismo* is eradicated. Rejecting the politics of negotiation and conciliation, the National Salvation Committees, UNO bands of workers and peasants, and various municipal governments have adopted a more confrontational approach. According to this scenario, *sandinismo* must be crushed not only for the good of Nicaragua but also for the future welfare of the entire region. Part of Washington's obsession with the FSLN stems from its fear that the Sandinista movement will continue to serve as a revolutionary model for popular movements elsewhere in the hemisphere.

Following UNO's election victory the U.S. embassy , which had long coordinated the internal opposition, started to bustle with new activity. Down to 15 staff before the election, the embassy began to swell immediately after Chamorro's inauguration and will soon equal in size the U.S. delegation in El Salvador – among the largest in the third world.[7] Some officials have moved over from Honduras where they were in charge of contra operations but dozens more are coming from Washington to set up the new AID mission and Department of Commerce office.

Veteran State Department troubleshooter Harry Shlaudeman was selected to direct the U.S. mission. Shlaudeman, a career diplomat, has a history of involvement in U.S.-guided political transitions in Latin America. He played a key role in the destruction of the Bosch government in the Dominican Republic in the mid-1960s, and he served as Deputy Chief of Mission in the early 1970s in Chile, where he facilitated collaboration between the CIA and internal forces working to destabilize the Allende government. More recently Shlaudeman served as an adviser to the Kissinger Commission on Central America and acted as the State Department's roving consultant in the region under President Reagan.[8]

Although Washington's immediate interest is in creating a stable government with a wide social base, its overriding goal is to crush the Sandinista alternative – even if this means the eventual destabilization of the current government. Both in seeking to rub out *sandinismo* and in demanding that an uncompromising program of privatization be implemented, Washington is blocking the development of a stable democratic society in Nicaragua—one that can only result from a policy of negotiation and conciliation. Once again, in the process of pursuing its narrowly conceived foreign-policy interests, the broad-based economic development and the welfare of the Nicaraguan people have again become the victims rather than the priorities of U.S. foreign policy.

# U.S. Trade and Investment

During the long years of Sandinista rule, the Nicaraguan-American Chamber of Commerce was all but moribund. Julio Virgil, a Nicaraguan businessman, kept the business chamber alive with an occasional mimeographed newsletter that circulated among some 60, mostly U.S., members. The Chamorro administration has promised to open the door wide for U.S. investment, but Virgil does not foresee a surge in U.S. business operations in the immediate future. Virgil, whose entire family left for the United States leaving him alone to run the family business, does not feel that the business climate has improved substantially even with the change in administration.[9] As in post-invasion Grenada, various U.S. government agencies have hosted trips to Nicaragua for prospective U.S. investors but few have put any money down yet.

## The Creeping Embargo

During the Somoza years the United States ranked as the country's most important trading partner—holding a 65 percent share of the Nicaraguan import market and purchasing nearly 60 percent of the country's exports in the 1970s.[10] As U.S.-Nicaragua tensions increased in the early 1980s, U.S. trade slipped and U.S. investors began to leave the country.

Although some U.S. traders and investors were scared off by the revolution, the most damaging moves against the U.S. economic position in Nicaragua came from Washington. In 1981 the Reagan administration cut off the trade and investment credits offered by the U.S. Export-Import Bank (Eximbank) and the Overseas Private Investment Corporation (OPIC). The next step in the escalating trade war came in 1983 when Washington slashed the country's sugar quota. That same year President Reagan ordered that all Nicaraguan consular and commercial offices in the United States be closed down—an action that further obstructed U.S. trade and investment in Nicaragua. The final blow was delivered in 1985 when the president announced a complete embargo against Nicaragua.

Under the provisions of the International Emergency Powers Act, the president could declare an embargo in a situation involving "any unusual and extraordinary threat to the national security, foreign policy, or economy of the United States."[11]

The embargo included a ban on all trade between the two countries. It also prohibited the national airline Aeronica from landing on U.S. soil and Nicaraguan ships from docking in U.S. ports. Exempted from the terms of the embargo were shipments to the U.S.-backed contras and their allies inside Nicaragua, as well as "donated items, such as food, clothing, and medicines intended to relieve human suffering."

The embargo declaration merely accelerated Nicaragua's efforts to diversify its trading partners. The diversification efforts, already well underway by 1985, were adopted as part of the government's nonalignment strategy and in expectation of an eventual U.S. embargo. When the embargo was announced, U.S. trade accounted for less than 15 percent of the country's commercial relations. Bananas were the leading Nicaraguan export to the United States, while imports from the United States included pesticides, fertilizers, irrigation equipment, industrial machinery, and spare parts.[12]

The main short- and medium-term effect of the embargo was a drop in production and in the provision of basic services, such as electricity, water, and transportation, due to the difficulty of acquiring spare parts for U.S.-manufactured equipment. But as time went on, Nicaragua was largely able to adapt to this situation by importing such parts and equipment through third countries. Despite repeated efforts by the White House, no other country formally joined the embargo. In fact, many U.S. allies in Western Europe acted to mitigate its effects.

Ironically, many assert that those Nicaraguans hardest hit by the suspension of commercial activity were the very sectors that Washington was attempting to bolster through other aspects of its policy. Leaders of COSEP repeatedly complained that the embargo was more damaging to the private sector than to the government. In early 1989 when rumor had it that the Bush transition team was toying with the idea of suspending the measure, opposition leader Carlos Huembes declared: "The embargo was a mistake from the beginning. The new administration in Washington should dump it."[13]

Despite a direct plea launched by several private business groups in Nicaragua and backed by Cardinal Obando y Bravo, the Bush administration decided to renew the embargo in May 1989, and again in November of that year. It was not until March 1990 that the embargo was finally lifted — an action that the U.S. Department of Commerce asserted would allow the United States to "resume its role as Nicaragua's most vital trading partner."[14]

## Beating the Drums for U.S. Business

After more than a decade of war and revolutionary government there was virtually no U.S. trade with Nicaragua and U.S. investment was confined to a few petroleum, chemical, food processing, and service industries. Soon after the Sandinista defeat Washington began the drive to renew its dominant trade position and to promote U.S. investment in Nicaragua.

On the trade front the U.S. Department of Commerce believes potential U.S. exports to Nicaragua could reach $1 billion annually for the next few years as the country reconstructs. Given that imports from all sources averaged only $800 million during the late 1980s, this will likely prove a wildly optimistic projection. Imports from Nicaragua will probably repeat the pattern of the 1970s, mostly traditional agroexports including beef and sugar. "Great potential" also exists for nontraditional exports such as winter vegetables and assembled manufactured goods.[15]

All of Washington's usual array of incentives and trade weapons are being quickly put into place. Most important is the economic-aid program whose dollars will be used, according to the agreements being signed with the Nicaraguan government, to buy mostly U.S. goods and services.[16] Eximbank took Nicaragua off its blacklist of Marxist-Leninist countries and approved short-term trade insurance. More important than the usual Eximbank trade insurance will be the Trade Credit Insurance Program (TCIP), a program that allows AID to use taxpayer funds to guarantee high-risk trade with Central America. Described by Eximbank as "kind of a loophole deal," TCIP is used by AID to increase U.S. exports to countries that have only minimal prospects of paying their bills.[17]

OPIC also has opened business again in Nicaragua and says it is "very bullish" about investment opportunities, particularly small business ventures in nontraditional agroexport production and seafood processing. Reminiscent of the post-invasion hype about U.S. investment rushing to Grenada, other government agencies such as the Caribbean Basin Information Center of the Commerce Department and the Private Sector Office of AID are searching for ways to promote U.S. investment in post-Sandinista Nicaragua. Besides having the embargo removed, Nicaragua has been welcomed into the backyard club of countries favored by the Caribbean Basin Initiative initiated in the early 1980s by President Reagan.

Part of the effort to increase U.S. investment and trade in the region is the campaign to have governments offer more generous tax breaks and investment incentives. Spearheading this campaign for the private sector is the Caribbean/Central America Action group (CCAA), part of David Rockefeller's Americas Society. Under the sponsorship of CCAA, such U.S. companies as Weil Brothers Cotton and Southern Shell are forming a Businessmen's Advisory Council on Nicaragua which will serve as a "pro bono sounding board to the Nicaraguan government as it moves to promote a free-market economy."[18]

Other U.S. agencies busy promoting U.S. investment include AID's Private Sector Office and the Caribbean Basin Information Center. Even FOMENTO, the Puerto Rican government's investment office, is promoting the establishment of twin-plant manufacturing enterprises in Nicaragua. The plants in Nicaragua would handle the most labor-intensive stages of manufacturing while the more capital-intensive operations would take place in Puerto Rico.[19]

At the end of the Ortega administration direct U.S. private investment did not go beyond the activities of some 36 transnational corporations and subsidiaries. These included such large companies as Exxon, United Brands, and Nabisco. (See Chart) Most enjoyed what they described as a cooperative working relationship with the government, their main complaint being the acute shortage of foreign exchange.[20]

A top priority for AID has been Nicaraguan government approval of new Foreign Investment and Export Promotion Laws because the existing laws "leave too much discretion to the government." As formulated in close consultation with U.S. government consultants, the new laws will give foreign investors all the "basic" guarantees and incentives, including duty-free imports for assembly manufacturing and the right to repatriate all profits.[21]

U.S. investment and trade are increasing, but there certainly has not been a flood of new business. The first major corporations to enter Nicaragua have been airline and shipping companies such as Continental and Sealand. Mining, lumber, and ranching companies—including Rosario Resources (AMAX), Robinson Lumber, and Peterson Ranching—that were notorious for their exploitative practices during the Somoza era have expressed interest in reinvesting. Standard Fruit, a Castle & Cooke subsidiary, has visited its old banana estates and is considering reinvesting in Nicaragua, as is United Brands. Standard Fruit left Nicaragua in 1982, after having broken a marketing contract with the new government.[22]

## U.S. Investment in Nicaragua
## 1987

| Nicaragua Firm | Business | U.S.Owner |
|---|---|---|
| Aceitera Corona SA | Mfg Cooking Oil | United Brands Co |
| Acumuladores Centroamericanos SA | Mfg Electric | Exide Corp |
| Ahlers SA* | Mfg Hygiene Prod | |
| Armando Mendoza Yescas & Asociados* | Consulting | |
| Bristol Myers de CA* | | Bristol Myers |
| Budget Rent-A-Car | Car Rental | Budget |
| Cia. Petrolera Chevron | Sale Petro Prod | Chevron Corp |
| Citizen Standard Life Ins. Co | Insurance | Citizen Standard Life Ins Co |
| Citibank NA | Banking | Citicorp |
| Electroquímica Pennwalt SA | Mfg Chemical Prod | Pennwalt Corp |
| Empaques Multiwall Ultrafort | Mfg Bags | St Regis Paper Co |
| Esso Standard Oil Ltd | Refining | Exxon Corp |
| Hercules de Centroamérica SA | Mfg Insecticides | Hercules Inc |
| Hotel Intercontinental | Hotel | Intercontinental Hotels Corp |
| Hotel Ticomo | Hotel | Huguette Fax de Thornton |
| IBM World Trade Corp | Sale Computer Equip | IBM World Trade Corp |
| Industria Cerámica CA, SA | Mfg Toilet Accessories | American Standard |
| Industrias Gemina SA | Mfg Flour Prod | General Mills Inc |
| Industrias Nabisco Cristal SA | Mfg Cookies, Crackers | Nabisco Brands Inc |
| Kativo de Nicaragua SA | Mfg Paints | HB Fuller |
| KEM Centroamericana | Sale Chemical Prod | KEM Mfg Corp |
| Mercadeo Industrial SA | | HB Fuller Co |
| Monsanto Agrícola de Nicaragua* | | Monsanto |
| Polymer SA | Mfg Plastic Prod | United Brands Co |
| Price Waterhouse | Consulting | Price Waterhouse |
| Sabores Cosco de CA | Mfg Food Flavourings | Cosco Intl Co |
| Targa Sasso Rent-A-Car | Car Rental | Avis |
| Texaco Caribbean Inc | Sale Gas | Transway Intl |
| United Marketing SA | Buy and Sell Food Prod | United Marketing |
| Xerox de Nicaragua SA | Sale Xerox Equipment | Xerox Corp |

Source: U.S. Embassy, "U.S. Investment in Nicaragua," March 1987.

* Indicates firm represents or has license contract with U.S. business.

The banana business illustrates many of the problems that may arise from U.S. reinvestment and renewed trade. After Standard Fruit withdrew from the country, the industry was nationalized and is now administered by the BANANIC state enterprise. Working with Pandel Brothers of California, the Sandinista government found a market for its bananas in the U.S. west coast market. But after the 1985 embargo, the country's banana exports were shipped to European markets. Rising prices and an expanding European market, as well as the increased efficiency of BANANIC, have increased the profitability of the banana business in Nicaragua. Privatization of the industry would deprive the government of an important source of income and endanger the bargaining position of the banana workers and the private banana growers. BANANIC officials feel that the entry of Nicaraguan bananas into the already saturated U.S. market would lower prices. In contrast, continued sales to European purchasers mean higher prices and offer the potential for a substantial expansion of the industry. As an added complication, the return of Standard Fruit or any other U.S. company would likely set off intense conflicts with the industry's 5,000 workers, ending years of calm labor-management relations.[23]

The U.S. Department of Commerce is advising potential U.S. investors that there are at least 160 state enterprises that will soon be privatized, "opening interesting opportunities for investors" in "publicly owned businesses ranging from a discotheque, hard-currency stores, and a luxury resort to sugar mills, beef slaughterhouses, a cement plant, textile factories, and beer and soft-drink processing plants."[24] AID has promised to provide the technical assistance necessary to facilitate this immense privatization process. While the investment opportunities may be attractive at first glance, the transfer of government properties to U.S. corporations will likely set off major labor conflicts and stir up the nationalist spirit of the Nicaraguan populace.

# U.S. Economic Aid

The main dispenser of U.S. economic aid, AID, is back in Managua after almost a decade's absence. Despite its official commitment to promote economic development for the poor, there was not much love lost between AID and the Nicaraguan people when the agency finally withdrew from the country.

During the 1960s and 1970s Nicaragua was a favored recipient of U.S. economic aid. AID's funds constituted as much as 15 percent of the government's budget. In the last half of the 1970s, the period when the

anti-Somoza struggle was most intense, the Somoza regime was the leading recipient in Central America of AID funds. Very little AID funding
trickled down to the poor, however. Most was explicitly designed either
to reward the government for remaining Washington's strongest ally in
Latin America or to support the business elite. In its 1978 congressional
budget presentation AID explained to Congress why the program was
needed in Nicaragua:

> There is a long-standing tradition of friendship and cooperation
> between the United States and Nicaragua. U.S. investment is wel-
> comed in Nicaragua's developing free-enterprise economy.
> Nicaragua's foreign policy stresses maintenance of the closest pos-
> sible ties with the United States.[25]

AID funding was instrumental in the creation of the Nicaraguan
Development Institute (INDE) and the Nicaraguan Development Foundation (FUNDE), which are associated with the Supreme Council of
Private Enterprise (COSEP). During the Somoza era AID hoped that
COSEP and affiliated groups would form a modernizing free-enterprise
alternative to the increasingly fragile dictatorship. In the first two years
of the Sandinista government, Washington attempted to funnel aid to
these groups for the purpose of supporting a business-oriented base of
opposition to the Sandinistas. In the 1970s AID funds also paid for the
training of National Guard officers and for a rural counterinsurgency
program.[26]

Unable to prevent the FSLN from assuming control of the new government, the Carter administration attempted to direct new economic aid to
the rightwing business sector and other private sector organizations
rather than channeling aid through the government itself. This aid was
regarded as a means to reduce the FSLN's influence and push the revolution toward a more moderate, reformist mold.

The Reagan team had a much more radical vision. The harsh anti-Sandinista positions outlined in the 1980 Republican platform were soon
translated into a twin track in the area of U.S. economic policy. The new
administration aimed to bring the revolution to its knees through a cutoff
in bilateral assistance and trade, combined with pressures on friendly
governments and multinational banks to do the same. It also channeled
covert and overt assistance for destabilization efforts to those forces inside Nicaragua most closely tied to U.S. interests and to the counterrevolution. These included COSEP, *La Prensa*, the Catholic church
hierarchy, and rightwing parties and unions.

Under Carter, the Congress approved — after lengthy and heated
debate and the inclusion of several unusual conditions — a $75 million aid

package for Nicaragua. The Sandinistas were put off by the fact that the bulk of the aid was destined explicitly for the private sector, and that the package as a whole contained politically motivated conditions. The government accepted the aid, however, largely under the belief that such a move would increase their chances of securing assistance from other donors.

Just two days after taking office, however, President Reagan suspended $15 million in undisbursed funds from the Carter package, all designated for government projects, pending a review of all assistance to Nicaragua. Secretary of State Alexander Haig called the action an attempt to "establish the substance and the atmosphere of the Reagan foreign policy."[27] In keeping with the new strategy, private-sector projects, including those covered by a $7.5 million appropriation for fiscal year 1981, would continue to receive funds. Managua later declared that it would refuse to allow the transfer of such funds, protesting that they were designated to help elements of the private sector that were actively aligning themselves with the counterrevolution.[28]

Although the cutoff in bilateral assistance from the United States was a serious blow, Nicaragua was eventually able to compensate by establishing aid programs with other countries, particularly in Western Europe and the Soviet Union. More painful were the U.S. pressures against assistance from the multinational banks, because many of these loans were destined for development projects that constituted an essential element of the Sandinistas long-term strategy for building an economy able to meet the basic needs of its population.

The Sandinista government got off to a good start with the multinational banks. This was largely based on its promises to live up to debt repayment commitments of the Somoza government and the presentation of attractive and viable development proposals. Before the advent of the Reagan administration, the World Bank and Inter-American Development Bank (IDB) had approved some $175 million in assistance to help in the reconstruction process, and another $150 million for several projects were widely believed to stand good chances of approval.

But in mid-1981 Washington began systematically to use its voting power as well as numerous delaying techniques to oppose all loans from the multinational banks for Nicaraguan development projects. World Bank and IDB lending to Nicaragua gradually slowed to a trickle. By 1984 Nicaragua had become the only Latin American member country which did not receive an IDB loan. On the heels of yet another IDB rejection of a Nicaraguan proposal, Central Bank President Joaquín Cuadra in April 1986 charged: "The bank has completely caved in to pressure from the

U.S. administration. It is ceasing to be an honest international lender and is becoming a political agency of the U.S. government."[29] All told, between 1981 and 1984 Nicaragua lost $400 million in loans and credits approved as bilateral and multilateral aid, subsequently blocked by the Reagan administration.[30]

Efforts to block loans from the multinational banks were paralleled by a U.S. campaign to shut off flows of economic aid from other countries. Although less successful, this economic sabotage campaign also produced some results. Mexico, for example, reversed its generous policy of aid and credit to Nicaragua in April 1985 as a direct result of U.S. pressure.[31]

## Support for Counterrevolution

The sources, recipients, and objectives behind U.S. funding for the internal opposition have closely followed the twists and turns of Washington's overall strategy against the Sandinistas, and the fate of the contras in particular. For the most part, this aid to the internal opposition was channeled through an international private network that was coordinated and largely funded by the U.S. government.

At first the contras were the focus of the assistance programs of the U.S. network. Working closely with the National Security Council and the CIA, private groups raised funds to support the counterrevolution. Groups like the U.S. Council for World Freedom and Civilian Material Assistance (CMA) provided the contras with military advisers, equipment, and mercenaries.[32] Most U.S. private groups, however, structured their fundraising efforts along humanitarian lines, providing food, medicine, and other nonlethal supplies to the contras and their families. The private "humanitarian-assistance" efforts of such rightwing organizations as Friends of the Americas were paralleled by similar campaigns by evangelical sects along the Nicaragua-Honduras border. Later, the U.S. Congress authorized a government humanitarian-assistance program, implemented by AID and the Pentagon, to complement and extend this private and very politicized humanitarianism.

Inside Nicaragua, direct and overt U.S. government aid to the Catholic church hierarchy and the private-sector elite had been suspended in 1981. But U.S. economic support for the internal opposition was never completely shut off. In the early 1980s the CIA became the main backer of internal opposition groups, including the newspaper *La Prensa*.[33] In addition to this clandestine funding, the internal opposition counted on other sources of U.S. government and private support. The American Institute for Free Labor Development (AIFLD), for instance, kept the rightwing CUS labor federation alive through training and travel programs for its leaders and social welfare services for its members.[34] AIFLD also coordinated various support networks for anti-Sandinista labor unions in Costa Rica, Venezuela, and in the United States.[35]

Anti-Sandinista religious bodies similarly benefited from U.S. assistance. The Catholic church's media and outreach programs relied on support from AID and such rightwing private organizations as the Heritage Foundation and the Institute for North-South Issues.[36] Rightwing evangelical groups received logistical and financial support from the U.S. embassies in Managua and San José. The embassy in Managua was perhaps the only one in the world to have a staffer assigned to religious affairs. According to an August 1986 report in the *Washington Post*, that person "cultivates and organizes protestant religious resistance to the Nicaraguan government and keeps track of the activity of church figures who favor the government." Through the U.S. embassy in San José, evangelical organizations working in Nicaragua received regular payments for their work.[37]

Beginning in 1984 the NED became a leading source of support for the internal opposition. NED, established in late 1983 and funded by Congress, functions as a quasi-private organization to channel U.S. Information Agency (USIA) and AID monies to foreign private organizations that support U.S. foreign-policy goals. NED has targeted Nicaragua for a large portion of its funds. In its early years, NED provided funds for several groups closely linked with Oliver North's contra support network, including the Friends of the Democratic Center in Central America (PRODEMCA), the Institute for North-South Issues, and the International Youth Commission.

Most NED support, however, flowed to the internal opposition through such U.S. organizations as Delphi International, AIFLD, Free Trade Union Institute (FTUI), Freedom House, and the Center for International Private Enterprise (CIPE). These funds were dispersed to the entire array of internal opposition groups, each of which were mobilized on UNO's behalf for the 1990 elections. They ranged from anti-Sandinista human rights organizations and civic-education groups like the Conservative Institute to political organizations like the Nicaraguan Democratic Coordinator (CDN).

As hopes to destabilize the revolution through military operations faded in the mid-1980s, increased attention was given to the internal opposition. But it was not until the late 1980s, with the prominence of the regional peace accords and the onset of the electoral campaign, that economic assistance to the internal opposition became the principal focus of U.S. counterrevolutionary operations. NED became the main instrument of this increased aid.[38]

## From Bullets to Ballots

NED's activities in Nicaragua have been a textbook example of the use of political aid to complement other instruments of U.S. interventionism: military aggression, economic destabilization, and anti-Sandinista propaganda. Unable to topple the Sandinistas through military pressure, the United States in late 1988 transferred the battle to the political arena. Using an array of individuals and groups it had supported for six years, NED constructed, organized, and guided its coalition of parties to success at the polls.

In the years preceding the elections, NED organized, sustained, and promoted the political forces which became UNO and its civic support network. Its Nicaraguan grantees were provided with material aid, as well as strategic and tactical guidance, from NED and the pass-through grantees which delivered NED assistance. NED supplied salaries, technical assistance, aid for infrastructure development, and training to help its Nicaraguan allies devise and implement anti-Sandinista strategies ranging from media campaigns to organizing efforts with targeted populations.

From 1984 to 1988 NED funneled more than $2 million to opposition groups ranging from human rights organizations to the media. The primary recipients were UNO candidate Chamorro's *La Prensa*, CUS and the CTN, the Nicaraguan Permanent Commission on Human Rights, and business associations and political parties associated with the CDN. NED's patronage allowed these groups, most of which operated with little popular support, to remain viable until the time of the elections when they were called upon to mobilize associated constituencies.

Between October 1988 and the elections in February 1990 NED supplied nearly $12 million for the electoral process in Nicaragua. Some of the money was used for election observer teams, the administrative costs of the pass-through grantees, and a required contribution to the Nicaraguan Supreme Electoral Council which oversaw the elections. The bulk, however, went to UNO and to its network of civic groups. Such groups included the Nicaraguan Women's Movement (MMN), Youth Training Center (CEFOJ), Vía Cívica, and the Institute for Electoral Promotion and Training.

In addition to those mentioned above, the increased NED funding flowed through the National Republican Institute for International Affairs, National Democratic Institute for International Affairs, International Foundation for Electoral Systems, the Center for Democracy, America's Development Foundation, and the Pro-Democracy Association (based in Costa Rica). Other U.S. private organizations not part of the NED network also joined the effort to support the internal opposition and defeat the Sandinistas in the 1990 election. These included the World Freedom Foundation and the Simón Bolívar Fund – each of which took care to demonstrate bipartisan consensus for their activities within Nicaragua.

Although the main thrust of the U.S. anti-Sandinista strategy was now overt, the CIA continued its clandestine operations in support of the internal opposition until the election. Between April and September 1989 the CIA funneled at least $5 million in covert funding to UNO for "housekeeping and political infrastructure."[39] After Congress insisted all aid to UNO be overt funding, the CIA allocated another $6 million for "regional programming" for covert operations outside Nicaragua designed to influence the elections.[40]

Capitalizing on the devastation wreaked by nearly a decade of U.S. military and economic aggression, NED's electoral campaign helped to defeat the Sandinistas and elect a new government headed by U.S. allies. NED was ultimately successful in ousting the FSLN, but both the process and the results of the UNO campaign raised serious questions about the "democracy-strengthening" character of NED. Its behavior seemed instead to be distinctly undemocratic.

Such massive external interference into the domestic political affairs of a sovereign country appears to violate in principle accepted democratic standards. The United States, reputedly the paragon of democratic practices, prohibits such foreign involvement in its own election campaigns. Along with being an external actor on the electoral scene, NED was also a highly partisan one. Rather than seeking impartially to build democratic institutions and develop political parties as democratic institutions, as it purportedly was doing, NED sought to topple the Sandinistas using the most expedient political tools.

NED funds glued together a fragmented opposition, torn by ideological and personal rivalries and dominated by reactionary elements. Those parties, including some of the country's most important, which chose not to participate in the UNO coalition were excluded from NED support. (See Politics) The FSLN, which also could have used some advice on building an effective party infrastructure, was of course excluded from this "democracy-strengthening" assistance.

Democracy did triumph in the February 1990 election, but the credit for the free vote and democratic transition goes largely to the FSLN, as most international observers noted. The expedient and fragile character of the UNO coalition became immediately evident after the election. The new government found itself without a strong political base, the constituent parties of UNO were as weak as ever, and the alliance had divided into "moderate" and "hardline" blocs.[41]

## Stabilization and Private-Sector Support

The 1979 victory of the FSLN altered the political landscape of Central America, causing Washington to let loose the floodgates of economic aid into the region. The United States surrounded Sandinista Nicaragua with an array of hostile governments fortified and stabilized with vast amounts of U.S. aid. Nearly $8 billion in U.S. economic aid from AID alone flowed into the region in the 1980s. With the UNO victory and the fading of the Sandinista "threat," Central America is no longer the top U.S. foreign-policy concern. As a result, aid for the entire region is likely to decrease dramatically in the early 1990s.

No longer the outcast in Washington's geopolitical lineup, Nicaragua has become just one more nation in the long line of underdeveloped nations seeking U.S. economic aid. The new Chamorro government expected and did receive special consideration from Congress and the White House in foreign-aid allocations for 1990 and 1991. But the aid package was neither as large nor did it arrive as fast as the Chamorro administration had expected. Washington spent billions of dollars in economic aid and billions more in military aid and maneuvers in its drive to isolate and destroy the Sandinistas. Yet its commitment to reconstruct and develop Nicaragua once the FSLN was gone from government proved less complete, and predictably so.

Washington seemed as surprised as most observers by the electoral triumph of UNO for it had no economic-aid package waiting for the new administration. The Chamorro transition team said that it needed at least $1.8 billion over three years to stabilize the country's finances and begin moving its economy forward. Although UNO's victory did not result in the downpour of dollars that many Nicaraguans had expected, Washington's support was nonetheless critical in bolstering the new government and setting its economic-policy direction.

Immediately following the election, the Bush administration authorized $30 million in emergency aid that did not require congressional approval. As part of its supplemental appropriations for 1990, Congress later approved $300 million and another $200 million for 1991. This direct economic aid will be complemented by the trade credits and investment insurance offered by OPIC and Eximbank. The White House also renewed the sugar import quota for Nicaragua — worth about $8 million annually in higher sugar prices.

## Where are the Dollars Going?

Administered largely by the Agency for International Development, the aid package reflects U.S. foreign-policy objectives in Nicaragua. Washington's foreign-aid policy in Nicaragua is multilayered and supports the various policy goals of destroying *sandinismo*, opening up the country to U.S. trade and investment, boosting the capitalist sector, stabilizing the economy, and shaping the new government. It is not necessarily an internally consistent program but overall does show Washington's determination to use increasingly scarce resources to debilitate the FSLN, impose a neoliberal economic program, and create an infrastructure of U.S.-sponsored programs and institutions.

With the balance-of-payments assistance and private-sector support projects dominating the package, the economic aid scheduled for Nicaragua resembles AID funding for other Central American countries. Actual development aid forms a minor part of the funding package. The small quantity of assistance that is directed toward the poor is more political than developmental in that it is designed to pacify the urban poor by partially easing the impact of AID-mandated structural-adjustment measures. As in the other Central American countries, AID also is sponsoring a "democracy-strengthening" program that provides funds and training to government institutions and private groups, most of which were part of the anti-Sandinista internal opposition.

The post-election aid package also includes more than $57 million for the repatriation and resettlement of the contras, their families, and other refugees.[42] A $1.4 million grant went to Cardinal Obando "for a monitoring network to assure the security of returning members of the resistance."[43] Of AID's 1990 grant of $300 million, $50 million is slated to pay part of Nicaragua's estimated $300 million in debt arrears. According to AID, a "considerable" portion of the 1991 aid package will go to covering debt arrears to the World Bank, IMF, and IDB.

The largest segment, $125 million, of the 1990 economic assistance is an Economic Support Fund (ESF) cash transfer for balance-of-payments support. This money goes directly to the country's Central Bank where it is used to purchase imports, including petroleum, agricultural inputs, and goods requested by the private sector to stimulate new productive enterprises. As stipulated in AID contracts, most of these imports, with the exception of petroleum, will be purchased from U.S. suppliers. AID says it will also use this balance-of-payments aid "to support the development of a policy-reform agenda and the initiation of reform actions."

Under the category of Development Assistance, a special focus will be projects that "permit the rehabilitation and modernization of private enterprise." This will include AID's support for the privatization of state enterprises. In much the same way that "shadow" or "parallel" administrative and policymaking institutions have been established by AID in other Central American countries, U.S. funds will provide "technical assistance and training in economic policymaking and public management."[44]

Education, health, agriculture, and employment-creation projects also will be funded by AID's Development Assistance budget. As expected, one of the first targets of the U.S.-sponsored overhaul of the country's social service structures was the educational system, where the U.S. embassy insisted on the immediate introduction of new school textbooks and the removal of the old ones tainted with *sandinismo*.[45] Additional U.S. funding will likely support the formulation of a new school curriculum and the privatization of higher education. AID also is planning an infrastructure repair and maintenance project that will provide temporary employment and give high visibility to the new government. These development-assistance projects will probably be characterized by political patronage, allowing the national and municipal governments to reward UNO supporters with jobs and benefits, while excluding and thereby weakening Sandinista unions and popular organizations.

Working together, AID and NED will be striving to strengthen the infrastructure of anti-Sandinista private institutions, including the media outlets, cooperatives, civic organizations, human rights groups, women's organizations, and think tanks. Political aid for what the U.S. government calls "democracy-strengthening" will come through a variety of channels, including direct NED funding, the international AID Democracy Initiatives program, and local AID funding. Approximately $650,000 to $700,000 remained from NED's election war chest, and this was divvied up among the U.S.-based Free Trade Union Institute (FTUI) for labor projects, *La Prensa*, three anti-Sandinista radio stations, the UNO transition team, a training program for UNO legislators, Via Cívica, Democracy Assistance Center (CAD), Youth Training Center (CEFOJ), and UNO's women's organization.[46]

In allocating the funds to FTUI, which is the AFL-CIO's umbrella organization for AIFLD and its two other international institutes, NED observed: "There is a danger that the democratic process will be undermined by post-election events....A successful organizing drive by independent trade unionists aimed at creating a viable democratic presence in communities and industries throughout Nicaragua is crucial to maintaining a stable transition period."[47] The U.S. embassy was counting on the U.S.-backed unions, grouped together in the Permanent Congress of Workers (CPT), to dominate the labor scene after the FSLN's defeat. But after the strikes of May and July 1990 the U.S. embassy found that the Sandinista unions were stronger than ever and that the U.S.-backed unions had little mobilizing power, despite all the funds that had been poured into them. Nevertheless, AID allocated $700,000 in 1990 for AIFLD, and NED funding to fortify the country's anti-Sandinista unions shows no sign of diminishing.

Under the FSLN government, *La Prensa* and three rightwing radio stations were the darlings of NED and AID "democracy-strengthening" programs. Spearheading the ideological and disinformation campaign against the Sandinistas, these media outlets received U.S. political aid on the grounds that they were victims of government censorship. Even though these media outlets have since become the voices of the government and the forces grouped together in the victorious UNO coalition, *La Prensa* and the radio stations have continued to receive U.S. funds. "It is imperative," states NED, "that the people of Nicaragua continue to have full access to information from the advocates of democracy concerning the future of their country and the case for a free society."[48]

Both the Nicaraguan Human Rights Association (ANPDH), the contra human rights organization formerly based in Tegucigalpa, and the Permanent Human Rights Commission (CPDH), the anti-Sandinista group closely associated with the Catholic church, will be receiving AID funds. AID's Office of Democracy Initiatives will be working closely with the National Assembly, municipal governments, and the Supreme Electoral Council. As part of the overall effort to fortify the anti-Sandinista political offensive, the U.S. Department of Justice also will sponsor programs with the new government and its judicial system.

With funds from AID's Washington office, the Washington-based Center for Democracy is setting up permanent offices in Managua. A center-right "democracy-building" institution headed by NED formulator, Allen Weinstein, the Center for Democracy will work in the legislative arena to undermine the strength of the FSLN and popular movement by advising and training UNO legislators and helping to formulate legislation.

It is still unclear to what extent NED will approve new funds to support anti-Sandinista organizations. Pulled by other target areas such as Eastern Europe and South Africa, NED will likely cut back on many of its former Nicaraguan programs and concentrate on new conservative institutes designed to shore up the counterrevolution's hold on government. Besides the projects described above, which used previously allocated funds, its only post-inauguration grant thus far has gone to the Nicaragua Municipal Leadership Training Institute.[49]

Food aid is also part of the expanding U.S. presence in Nicaragua. There are two components of this program that reflect the two different types of U.S. food aid. The larger program — called Food for Progress — involves the donation of wheat, corn, and other commodities to the government which then sells that food to private-sector millers and distributors who resell the commodities on the local market. Food for Progress does not pretend to be a development program but instead concentrates exclusively on inducing recipient governments to undertake free-market reforms. It serves as both balance-of-payments support (by obviating the need to use foreign exchange to purchase foodstuffs) and direct budgetary support by creating a new source of governmental revenue.[50]

In contrast to Food for Progress, the Title II program is a food-distribution program. The initial food-distribution program was administered by the Adventist Development Relief Agency (ADRA) and COPROSA, the social-service agency of the archbishop's office in Managua. CARE/USA is setting up another large Title II program in the *barrios* of Managua. This modified food-for-work program will function as a public-works and employment-generation project. To pay project costs, CARE and the city of Managua will sell the food commodities on the local market and then use this generated revenue to pay temporary workers. Similar urban-employment projects backed by U.S. food aid in other Central American countries have the stated political objective of reducing urban unrest resulting from U.S.-supported structural-adjustment programs.

Nicaraguans got their first taste of aid conditionality when they read the terms of the Food for Progress aid agreement signed one week after President Chamorro's inauguration. Like all U.S. assistance, the food aid came with strings attached. AID calls conditions attached to food aid agreements "self-help measures," but some Nicaraguans regarded the conditions as an insult and a challenge to national sovereignty. In return for its Food for Progress, the agreement obliged the Chamorro government to:

* Introduce into the National Assembly requests to annul or reform all decrees and orders that monopolize, control, and limit economic liberty.

* Seek to place in private hands all productive resources whose privatization would not contravene important public policies and which are presently property of the State.

* Covenant that all state enterprises...involved in the production of goods and services will be privatized within a framework of democratic productive property.[51]

For AID, its assistance package serves as a lever to force governments to institute policy reforms. Since the advent of the Reagan administration the policy reforms that AID pushes have had a distinctly neoliberal bent. It uses its economic assistance and food aid to ensure that recipient governments adhere to structural-adjustment programs that reduce the size of the public sector, promote private-sector investment, and liberalize trade. This pattern of conditionality is being repeated in Nicaragua with a special emphasis on the privatization of state enterprises. Among the conditions for its balance-of-payments support, AID has obligated the government to liberalize agricultural prices, abolish state marketing boards, and sell state-owned enterprises to private bidders.[52]

The AID Mission in Managua insists that it is not imposing an economic policy with its conditionality but only helping the new government fulfill its own plan. But, as AID officer Roger Noriega noted, "AID has experience around the world of what works, and we help people that help themselves. We aren't out to waste U.S. tax dollars on the wrong kind of policies."[53] Nicaragua having agreed to the right kind of policies, AID approved initial food shipments and cash transfers to the Chamorro government. And as Diane Ponasik, AID's Nicaragua Desk Officer in Washington, explained, "Before they get the next transfer, they have to prove that they are moving to meet the specified conditions."[54]

The withholding of promised aid because of a country's failure to implement agreed-upon policy reforms is not an idle threat, as government officials in Costa Rica and Honduras can testify. Only a few months after the $300 million aid package was authorized Nicaraguan officials were already expressing irritation at having the disbursement of those funds held up until new legislation regarding the private sector is pushed through the National Assembly.[55] As the source of the funds so critical to the government's economic stability, Washington can also impose new conditions at any time.

AID's hard-edged demands that the Chamorro government shrink the public sector and institute austerity measures regardless of their social costs contrasts with the U.S. government's own social-control programs in Nicaragua. While insisting that the government cut social services, AID is creating its own social service and food-aid programs. While obligating the government to chop the public-sector payroll, it is sponsoring its own employment-generation program. While forcing the government to pare down educational and health programs, AID is launching its own health and educational initiatives with private organizations.

Requirements that state enterprises be privatized, that a "framework of democratic private property" be installed, and that "economic liberty" prevail directly challenge the FSLN's professed commitment to defend certain advances of the revolution, like the agrarian reform and nationalization of international trade. If fully implemented these U.S. directives would violate the Chamorro administration's commitment to compromise and conciliation while contributing to further and possibly fatal social instability.

At the outset of the new Chamorro administration Foreign Minister Enrique Dreyfus asserted that "we will not sell our soul to the devil for any aid package."[56] But having relied on the United States to finance their way to power and having begged for U.S. dollars to stabilize the government, UNO administration officials may soon realize that their souls have already been mortgaged.

# U.S. Military Aid

Before July 1979 the Nicaraguan police and National Guard received extensive training and assistance from the U.S. government. No other country in the region had so many of its troops trained by U.S. counter-insurgency specialists.[57] A year before the Sandinista victory these aid programs were terminated, only to be replaced in the 1980s by funding for a counterrevolutionary war. But even with that war over and the Sandinistas out of power, U.S. police and military aid has not resumed. While bolstering the other armies in the region, despite their notorious human rights records, the U.S. government refuses to aid the Nicaraguan forces and insists that they be unilaterally cut back. Before renewing its military-aid program in Nicaragua, Washington has demanded the army be cleansed of its Sandinista officer corps.

Soon after Chamorro's inauguration U.S. military planes began arriving in Managua with shipments of surplus Department of Defense (DOD) medical supplies and other humanitarian supplies from U.S. private organizations such as Project Hope.[58] The DOD's Humanitarian Assistance Office, which has coordinated U.S. nonlethal aid to the contras and the Afghan *muhajedeen*, directed this effort to assist the repatriating contras and other returning Nicaraguans. Excess DOD property also was shipped to resupply the country's civilian hospitals.

Although there were no immediate plans to begin a military-aid program, the Drug Enforcement Administration (DEA) began working with the government and the police on drug interdiction soon after Chamorro took office. The DEA is also helping the country set up a more comprehensive anti-drug program that will work closely with DEA's regional office in Costa Rica.[59]

## Washington's War on Nicaragua

Immediately after their triumph in 1979 the Sandinistas petitioned Washington for military aid to shape the guerrilla force into a national army. Some in Washington supported the idea of providing such aid, in the hopes of assuring that Nicaragua would remain in the U.S. fold, but the hardline position won out and all requests for military aid were turned down.[60]

Instead Washington chose to mount a war against the Sandinista government just as it had chosen to wage a counterinsurgency war on Sandino's peasant army half a century before. The centerpiece of the destabilization campaign was the contra army, initially drawn from the remnants of the National Guard. During fiscal years 1982 through 1989 the contras received $343.89 million in direct U.S. government aid, $40.5 million in aid coordinated by the National Security Council (mainly through the Oliver North network), and $6.3 million in U.S. insurance and loans, for a total of $390.69 million.[61] (See Table) Hundreds of millions more were channeled to the contras through private organizations, foreign governments, and other indirect sources. In 1990 Washington allocated another $57 million for the repatriation of the contras and their families, including support for the new development poles.[62]

Regardless of the ebbs and flows in congressional support for the war, the Reagan administration was able to provide the contras with a steady stream of assistance. Funds were channeled covertly through the CIA, the Defense Department, and other governmental agencies. Covert funds also were directed through third countries, notably Israel, which sent arms captured from the Palestine Liberation Organization (PLO) in Lebanon and advisers to help train the contras at the behest of Washington. Finally, a host of private organizations, most of them linked to former U.S. military or intelligence personnel or the New Right, funneled cash, weapons, trainers, and even mercenaries to the contras, both before and after the fall of Lt. Col. Oliver North's operation.[63]

By 1986 this array of U.S.-backed funding sources had allowed the contras to become a powerful armed force, more numerous and with better weapons and training than the National Guard had enjoyed under Somoza. The contras' "army without a republic" even had its own incipient air force and navy. The United States provided several planes for use in resupply missions to forces inside Nicaragua, flown by contra pilots, and a fleet of artillery-equipped speedboats used in sabotage actions against Nicaraguan ports.

## U.S. Aid to the Contras
## 1982 - 1990

| Year | Source | Amount (millions of dollars) | Type |
|------|--------|--------|------|
| 1982 | CIA | $19.0* | Military |
| 1983 | CIA | 29.0* | Military |
| 1983-1985 | CIA | 3.0* | Political action |
| 1984 | CIA | 24.0** | Sabotage, infrastructure in Honduras |
| 1985-1986 | NSC | 40.5*** | Military |
| 1986 | State/CIA | 40.0* | Intelligence, training, other support |
| 1987 | DOD/CIA | 100.0** | Military, humanitarian, and to improve human rights record |
| 1988 | DOD/State/AID | 41.6** | Military, nonlethal aid, humanitarian, defense loans, AID expenses |
| 1989 | AID | 93.59** | Nonlethal aid, AID expenses, transportation, misc |
| 1990 | State | 10.0* | Emergency nonlethal aid |
| 1990 | AID | 47.0** | Repatriation aid |
| **Total** | | **$447.69** | |

Sources: "Previous U.S. and U.S.-Coordinated Aid to the Contras," Arms Control and Foreign Policy Caucus of the U.S. Congress, January 29, 1988, updated November 1989; "Report of the Congressional Committees Investigating the Iran-Contra Affair" (Washington: U.S. Government Printing Office, 1987); U.S. Embassy, "Nicaragua: A Commitment to Democracy, Reconciliation, and Reconstruction," no date.

    *According to press reports.

    **Congressionally appropriated funds.

    ***These funds were generated by arms sales to Iran ($3.8 million), donations from U.S. citizens ($2.7 million), and donations from Saudia Arabia and Taiwan ($34 million).

Starting in 1985 with the formation of the counterrevolutionary umbrella organization Nicaraguan Opposition Union (UNO), ever greater portions of aid to the contras were channeled toward political-propaganda activities. These included the maintenance of full-time staff at offices in Miami and Washington, human rights offices in Honduras and Europe, speaking tours for contra leaders, publications, and other forms of outreach to the public.

The contras also received direct benefits from the massive U.S. military presence in Honduras and the ongoing program of joint U.S.-Honduran military maneuvers. Two key aspects which allowed the contras to take the initiative in the early years of the war were the sophisticated resupply network – including land, air, and sea routes – and high-quality, timely intelligence on Sandinista troop movements, both provided to them thanks to the U.S. presence in Honduras. The maneuvers also served as an important, ongoing psychological stimulus for the often demoralized contra troops. Following many U.S.-Honduran exercises, arms and equipment were "left behind" for the contras.

U.S. forces also played a more direct role, particularly as military advisers to the contras, in key logistical and intelligence operations, and occasionally, in the execution of attacks. The mining of Nicaragua's harbors in 1984 was carried out by U.S. Navy SEAL special forces units.[64]

"Humanitarian aid" for the contras, introduced by the Reagan administration in 1985 as an elegant way to continue official bankrolling of the contra project while others put up the arms, had – with the April 1989 approval of a $50 million package – become a pragmatic maneuver aimed at gaining time. According to the Central American peace accords, U.S. aid to the contras during the late 1980s should have had but one purpose: to facilitate the disbanding, repatriation, and relocation of the contra army. (See Peace Process) Instead the 1989 aid permitted the contra army, with apparent U.S. approval, to continue its war of terror through February 1990. Following the Chamorro election victory, new commitments of U.S. aid at last supported the repatriation and resettlement process.

# Other Foreign Interests

After the Sandinista victory in July 1979 non-U.S. influence expanded in Nicaragua as the new government made a concerted effort to reduce its dependence on U.S. trade, aid, and investment. Economic relations with socialist nations, practically nonexistent before 1979, proved critically important during the 1980s. Although the influx of aid and advisers from socialist nations was the most dramatic change in the country's global economic relations, Nicaragua also experienced a sharp increase in Western European trade and assistance.

By mid-decade socialist countries were providing Nicaragua with nearly half its imports and purchasing one-fifth of its exports, while Western European and other industrial nations were supplying one-quarter of Nicaragua's imports and purchasing three-quarters of its exports.[65] Trade relations with the socialist countries and Western Europe had by the decade's end replaced the United States and other Central American countries as Nicaragua's principal trading partners.[66]

Major factors in Nicaragua's shifting trade and aid relations were the U.S. financial blockade and the trade embargo. After U.S. pressure resulted in the termination of multilateral aid, the country was forced to rely on a multitude of ever-changing bilateral aid agreements, usually for specific development projects, which made government planning difficult.

## Socialist Aid

Even before the Sandinistas overthrew the Somoza regime, Cuba was providing assistance to the FSLN. Although it provided training and arms, the Cuban aid was not decisive in the Sandinista victory. More arms came from Venezuela, Costa Rica, and Panama than from Cuba. Mexico and Colombia also provided political and material support to the FSLN guerrilla army.[67] In the first eight months of the revolutionary government, Cuba was the only socialist country to come forth with aid. In the early 1980s, however, assistance from the socialist bloc steadily increased as U.S. and Western aid declined.

The new Reagan White House canceled $9.6 million in wheat shipments to Nicaragua in February 1981. Within days the Soviet Union, Bulgaria, and East Germany announced they would ship 80,000 tons of grain to compensate for the U.S. program. Canada and several Western European countries also shipped wheat to Nicaragua. This response established a precedent which was repeated in years to come. Throughout the 1980s the socialist countries, in particular the Soviet Union and Cuba, responded to Nicaraguan calls for assistance, first after the U.S. cutoff of bilateral aid, then following the precipitous drop in multilateral aid, and also to compensate for the decreasing levels of aid from some U.S. allies. Trade agreements with the Council for Mutual Economic Assistance (COMECON) countries played a key role in providing Nicaragua with access to new markets as well as serving as a source of significant loans and credits.[68] Similarly the Soviet Union filled the gap in the military sphere when the contra war escalated and Managua found itself cut off from Western sources.

While also providing an important line of trade credits, most Soviet economic support to the Sandinista government — estimated at around $3 billion — was in the form of long-term assistance for medical, hydroelectric, and agricultural-development projects.[69] Trade relations with the Soviet bloc played a critical role in the survival of the FSLN government, particularly after the 1985 U.S. trade embargo. Annual exports to the Soviet Union hovered around $10 million throughout the 1980s, only a small percentage of total exports, but more than $50 million in annual imports from the Soviet Union made that country one of Nicaragua's chief sources of foreign supplies. After 1984, the year when Mexico ceded to U.S. pressure to halt oil deliveries to Nicaragua, the Soviet Union became the country's principal oil supplier. The changing focus of Soviet foreign policy in the late 1980s and the consolidation of the Central American peace process resulted in declining levels of economic aid. In 1989 the Soviet Union suspended arms shipments to Nicaragua, which according to an estimate by the U.S. Defense Intelligence Agency totaled $2.3 billion during the 1981-1988 period.[70]

Cuban support came mainly in the form of preferential trade agreements and the supply of skilled Cuban volunteers for economic-development projects and emergency relief operations. Nicaraguan exports to Cuba fell from a high of $11 million in 1981 to around $1.5 million by the end of the decade. Cuban imports rose sharply, however, topping $40 million in 1987 which made Cuba one of Nicaragua's main suppliers.

After U.S. pressure resulted in a drastic reduction in multilateral assistance, COMECON emerged as the main source of development aid. Between 1984 and 1986 the COMECON countries, together with Yugoslavia and China, supplied two-thirds of all grants, loans, and credits. COMECON assistance included support for irrigation projects, manufacturing plants, agricultural-development projects, hydroelectric plant construction, and the expansion of the country's gold mines.[71]

Trade relations with the COMECON countries had both advantages and disadvantages. COMECON products, particularly machinery and equipment, were less expensive than Western products. A Soviet tractor, for example, cost less than half as much as its U.S.-made equivalent. COMECON countries also offered preferential trade agreements that allowed Nicaragua to sell its exports at prices higher than world market averages. But the great distances involved, except for Cuba, meant higher transportation costs and longer waiting periods for spare parts. Trade agreements with an array of countries also created problems by bringing in many different makes and models of machinery and equipment, result-ing in compatibility problems.

The political upheaval in Eastern Europe and worsening economic problems in the Soviet Union and Cuba posed a threat to Nicaragua as it approached the 1990 elections. Cut off from all multilateral aid and most bilateral Western aid, the country had come to rely on the support of the socialist bloc nations. As this too began to dwindle the country's future economic prospects became more grim.

Following the Chamorro victory, the Soviet Union promised to honor its pre-election commitment of $288 million, most of which was in the form of petroleum. Ironically the Soviet aid was providing important sup-port for the Chamorro government while Washington's promised aid package was still lingering in Congress. It is unlikely, however, that Nicaragua can expect any more substantial Soviet aid in coming years.

The cutoff in Cuban aid after the election was more dramatic. When Cuban doctors and teachers began arriving in Nicaragua soon after the Sandinista victory, their presence stoked the anticommunist fervor of many Nicaraguans. Some communities demanded that the Cubans leave. But over the years the Cubans won the sympathy of the communities where they worked. Hardest hit will be the communities on the Atlantic coast that were beneficiaries of Cuban relief operations after Hurricane Joan struck in 1988. Immediately after the February 1990 election, the 350 Cuban construction workers who were building more than 1,000 homes in Puerto Cabezas stopped working and went home. Nicaraguans also benefited from Cuban scholarship programs which provided secondary and technical education to more than 3,000 students during the 1980s.[72] Minister of Education Sofonías Cisneros announced that Nicaragua would no longer allow teachers to be trained in Cuba "since the kind of teacher that Cuba can educate is not the kind we need."[73] Despite the Sandinista loss and hostility of many UNO militants, Cuba has demonstrated a continuing commitment to the Nicaraguan people, having returned its medical teams to the Atlantic coast at the request of the Ministry of Health and responding to the new government's call for international relief for victims of a flood disaster.

## Non-Socialist Aid

Although Western Europe's economic support for Nicaragua lagged behind the far-reaching sympathy the revolution enjoyed among the region's population, Western European economic assistance and trade was substantial in the 1980s. Close ties between Washington and some conservative governments, notably West Germany, the Netherlands, and

Great Britain, resulted in a restriction of bilateral aid to Nicaragua. Labor or socialist administrations in countries such as Italy, Spain, France, Austria, and Scandinavia contributed generously to Nicaragua. Sweden, which substantially increased its assistance after 1985, was an important supporter of the Sandinista government's development programs.[74]

By the end of the decade Nicaragua had also become the region's chief recipient of European Economic Community (EEC) development aid, receiving 40 percent of EEC aid to Central America since 1984 (at least half of this aid in the form of food donations). Most of the European aid, however, did not go directly to the Sandinista government but was channeled through nongovernmental organizations (NGOs).

European as well as Canadian NGOs concentrated their Central America aid in Nicaragua. They were attracted by the FSLN's encouragement of grassroots participation in development efforts and its commitment to improve the livelihood of the poor through redistributive reforms. Notable exceptions were two West German political foundations, the Konrad Adenauer and Naumann foundations, with programs that supported the contras and the internal opposition respectively.

Mexico and Venezuela were important sources of aid, mainly in the form of petroleum, during the first couple years of the FSLN government. As a result of pressure from Washington and the IMF, Venezuela ended its petroleum credits in 1982 and Mexico followed suit in 1984. Other significant non-socialist aid in the 1980s came from such United Nations' agencies as UNICEF, World Health Organization, World Food Program, and United Nations Development Program, which found the government's social program compatible with their own.[75]

Although Japan had no significant aid program in Nicaragua during the 1980s, it was an important trading partner, buying most of the country's cotton crop. Japan also signed an agreement with the FSLN government to study the feasibility of constructing an inter-oceanic canal through Nicaragua. Following the UNO victory, Japan promised to increase its development assistance to Nicaragua.

Aid and trade patterns are quickly changing as a result of the UNO victory. Most significant has been the increase in U.S. trade and assistance, although it is not expected that the United States will ever again so heavily dominate the country's foreign trade. The change in government opened up the country for new sources of aid from countries that had not supported the FSLN government as well as renewed aid from old trading partners. Venezuela and Mexico approved new petroleum credits, West Germany promised substantial economic assistance (the first time since

1982), and even Thatcher's Great Britain came through with a small amount of emergency aid for the new government.

Economic aid for the Chamorro administration did not, however, measure up to government expectations. Particularly disappointing was the failure of foreign donors, with the exception of the United States, to provide crucial balance-of-payments assistance. Reflecting the importance of such assistance, the FSLN joined in the search for foreign aid. FSLN representatives accompanied the government delegation to a June 1990 conference of nations and multilateral institutions interested in assisting Nicaragua. While noting their strong support for increased foreign assistance for the new government, the Sandinista representatives asserted that the FSLN would not allow the government to use the aid—much of which had been previously committed to the Ortega administration—to turn back the reforms of the revolution.

# Reference Notes

## Introduction

1. "El Drama de la Salud Infantil: Que No Se Apague Esta Sonrisa," *Pensamiento Propio*, October 1988, p.46.
2. Cited in Julia Preston, "The Defeat of the Sandinistas," *New York Review of Books*, April 12, 1990.
3. Known originally as the National Opposition Union, UNO changed its name to the National Organized Union following its election victory in February 1990.

## Chapter One

1. For an extensive review of politics during the Somoza period, see John A. Booth, *The End and the Beginning: The Nicaraguan Revolution* (Boulder: Westview Press, 1985); and Richard Millett, *Guardians of the Dynasty* (New York: Maryknoll, 1977).
2. For an excellent account of initial efforts at building a new state apparatus and popular democracy, see Thomas W. Walker, ed., *Nicaragua: The First Five Years* (New York: Praeger, 1985).
3. For detailed expositions on the question of popular hegemony in the Nicaraguan revolution, see Susanne Jonas and Nancy Stein, "The Construction of Democracy in Nicaragua," *Latin American Perspectives*, Summer 1990, pp.10-37; and Richard R. Fagen, Carmen Diana Deere, and José Luís Coraggio, eds., *Transition and Development: Problems of Third World Socialism* (New York: Monthly Review Press, 1986).
4. One good account of the construction of popular power is Gary Ruchwarger, *People in Power: Forging a Grassroots Democracy in Nicaragua* (South Hadley, MA: Bergin and Garvey, 1987).
5. Humberto Ortega, addressing the closing rally of the Literacy Crusade. Cited in George Black, *Triumph of the People* (London: Zed Books, 1981), pp.256-257.
6. For a detailed analysis of the constitution-drafting process and an analysis of the document itself, see Andrew Reding, "Nicaragua's New Constitution," *World Policy Journal*, Spring 1987.
7. For textual reproduction of the most important articles in the constitution, see *Barricada Internacional*, April 7, 1990, pp.6-7.
8. Much of this information is taken from "Setting the Rules of the Game: Nicaragua's Reformed Electoral Law," *Envío*, Instituto Histórico Centroamericano, June 1989, p.27. For more details on the division of state powers in Nicaragua and the democratic guarantees built into the model, see Alejandro Serrano Caldera, "Democracia y Estado de Derecho," *Pensamiento Propio*, July 1989, pp.23-25.
9. Losing presidential candidates are eligible to assume a seat in the legislature upon receiving more than one percent of the vote. As a result, from 1984-1990, the

National Assembly actually consisted of 96 representatives, and beginning in April 1990 it had 92 representatives.

10. For a book-length account of the history of elections and political parties in Nicaragua, see Oscar René Vargas, *Elecciones en Nicaragua* (Managua: Fundación Manolo Morales, 1989).

11. The most important of these was the Revolutionary Patriotic Front (FPR) which lasted from 1980 until 1984 when it was dissolved as the different forces jockeyed for position vis-a-vis national elections. The FPR included the FSLN, the Independent Liberal Party (PLI), the Popular Social Christian Party (PPSC), and the Nicaraguan Socialist Party (PSN).

12. Martin Edwin Andersen and Willard Dupree, "Nicaragua's Municipal Elections: The Report of an NDI Survey Mission," National Democratic Institute for International Affairs, October 31, 1988, p.3.

13. Cited in "Chamorro Takes a Chance," *Time*, May 7, 1990.

14. The Communists and Socialists, neither of which split, won three National Assembly seats each, also running on the UNO ticket.

15. Cited in "Nicaragua's 'Family' Style Bridges Political Chasms," *Los Angeles Times*, May 5, 1990, p.1.

16. Most of the UNO parties were splinters from the existing main party currents. With the exception of the Social Democrats and the leftwing parties, different factions of the tendencies represented in UNO also ran in the 1990 elections independent of UNO. The Independent Liberal Party, for example, won nearly 10 percent of the votes in the 1984 elections, but since then had divided into three factions, one of which remained outside UNO. One indication of the UNO parties' weak organizational base was the difficulty they had in finding pollwatchers to staff the 4,394 voting booths for election day. UNO leaders complained bitterly at the delays in arrival of U.S. funding, in part asserting that it constituted an obstacle in their efforts to mobilize pollwatchers. FSLN pollwatchers, as those in most countries, worked on a volunteer basis. Similarly, in four of the country's nine administrative regions, UNO was unable to fill candidate slates for municipal council posts.

17. Basic information on the parties is taken from "Political Parties in Nicaragua," *Envío*, July 1989, pp.23-24; "Political Parties and Alliances in Nicaragua," *Update*, Central American Historical Institute, Vol.6, No.34, October 28, 1987; and Elia María Kuant and Trish O'Kane, "Nicaragua: Political Parties and Elections 1990," *Working Paper*, CRIES, 1989.

18. These parties are: Social Conservatism Party (PSOC), Liberal Party of National Unity (PLIUN), Revolutionary Workers Party (PRT), Marxist-Leninist Party (MAP-ML), Social Christian Party (PSC), Central American Unification Party (PUCA), and the Democratic Conservative Party of Nicaragua (PCDN).

19. A nine-member National Directorate presided over the party from 1978 until April 1990, when General Humberto Ortega was relieved of his duties in the party in order to retain his position as chief of the army as stipulated in the March 27 Transition Protocol.

20. The best sources for writings on *sandinismo's* ideological roots are several books, published in Spanish, containing the works of FSLN founder Carlos Fonseca. Other useful sources are Donald C. Hodges, *Intellectual Foundations of the Nicaraguan Revolution* (Austin: University of Texas Press, 1986); Gabriele Invernizzi, et.al., eds., *Sandinistas: Entrevistas a Humberto Ortega, Jaime Wheelock y Bayardo Arce* (Managua: Editorial Vanguardia, 1986); and Dennis Gilbert, *Sandinistas: The Party and the Revolution* (Cambridge, MA: Basil Blackwell, 1988).

21. Cited in *New York Times*, October 21, 1984.

22. The official results were: FSLN, 67 percent; PCD, 13 percent; PLI, 9 percent; PPSC, 5 percent; and 2 percent each for the left parties PSN, PC de N, and MAP-ML.

23. Two reports from independent poll-watching delegations are: Latin American Studies Association, "Report of the LASA Delegation to Observe the Nicaraguan General Election of November 4, 1984," LASA Secretariat, University of Pittsburgh, 1984; and International Human Rights Law Group and Washington Office on Latin America, "A Political Opening in Nicaragua," December 1984. A comprehensive analysis of the 1984 elections and U.S. efforts to sabotage them is William I. Robinson and Kent Norsworthy, "Elections and U.S. Intervention in Nicaragua," *Latin American Perspectives*, Spring 1985, pp.83-110. The April 1985 edition of *Envío* contains an in-depth analysis of the electoral results.

24. See, for example, John Booth, "Election Amid War and Revolution: Toward Evaluating the 1984 Nicaraguan National Elections," in Paul Drake and Eduardo Silva, eds., *Elections and Democratization in Latin America, 1980-1985* (San Diego: University of California Press, 1986), p.58.

25. For more details on the forces behind the NED and its role in relation to U.S. foreign policy, see *National Endowment for Democracy: A Foreign Policy Branch Gone Awry* (Albuquerque: Council On Hemispheric Affairs and the Inter-Hemispheric Education Resource Center, March 1990).

26. For details on NED's Nicaragua project, see: ibid.; William I. Robinson, "Nicaragua: The Making of a 'Democratic' Opposition," *NACLA Report on the Americas*, February 1990, pp.7-11; William I. Robinson, "NED Overt Action: Intervention in the Nicaraguan Elections," *CovertAction Information Bulletin*, Winter 1990, pp.32-39 and Summer 1990, pp.31-34; Jacqueline Sharkey, "Nicaragua: Anatomy of an Election," *Common Cause Magazine*, May-June 1990, pp.20-29; and Holly Sklar, "Washington Wants to Buy Nicaragua's Elections Again," *Z Magazine*, December 1989.

27. The PPSC resigned from UNO, while the PSC and the PLIUN were expelled for having broken ranks and presented their own legislative candidates to the electoral registration authorities.

28. PSC leader Francisco Taboada, cited in Sharkey, op.cit., p.24.

29. Including the smaller municipal councils, UNO won a total of 100 municipalities and the FSLN, 31. National Assembly seats were divided as follows: the 14 parties belonging to UNO had a total of 51 seats; the FSLN, 39; one seat went to a Yatama (Miskito Indian organization) candidate who ran on the Social Christian Party ticket; and the Revolutionary Unity Movement (MUR) had one seat. For the specific breakdown by party and region, see Latin American Studies Association, *Electoral Democracy Under International Pressure* (Pittsburgh: University of Pittsburgh, March 1990).

30. For an observer delegation report, see ibid.

31. See Jack Spence, "Will Everything Be Better?," *Socialist Review*, March 1990, pp.115-132. This article sums up the main theories, and poses important questions regarding their general validity and implications. Also see Latin American Studies Association, *Electoral Democracy Under International Pressure*, op.cit.; James Petras, "Flawed Strategies Planted Seeds of Sandinista Defeat," *In These Times*, March 21, 1990; Carlos M. Vilas, "What Went Wrong" and George R. Vickers, "A Spider's Web," in *NACLA Report on the Americas*, June 1990; William M. LeoGrande, "Was the Left Wrong About Nicaragua?," and Paul Berman, "A Response to William M. LeoGrande," in *Tikkun*, May-June 1990; Julia Preston, "The Defeat of the Sandinistas," *New York Review of Books*, April 12, 1990; and Alma Guillermoprieto, "Letter from Managua," *The New Yorker*, March 26, 1990. A

lengthy account of the FSLN's own reflections on its electoral defeat was included in the resolutions from a party assembly held in June 1990. The resolutions are reproduced in full as a special supplement in *Barricada Internacional*, July 14, 1990.

32. Cited in Preston, op.cit. Appropriately, UNO's main campaign slogan was "UNO can change things."

33. This evidence is based on an analysis of poll data. See, for example, Spence, op.cit., pp.127-129.

34. Carlos M. Vilas, "What Went Wrong," *NACLA Report on the Americas*, June 1990, p.13.

35. The erroneous poll projections are analyzed in "After the Poll Wars: Explaining the Upset," *Envío*, March-April 1990, pp.30-35.

36. The historical tradition in Nicaragua, where elections had always been used to legitimize those in power and had never served to change from one government to another, also helps to explain the "protest vote" phenomenon. While some voters felt safe making a protest vote because they were convinced the FSLN would win by a large margin, others did so never actually conceiving that they could vote the government out. These interpretations are supported by observer accounts of the day after the elections. There were no UNO victory celebrations, and there was a widespread atmosphere of shock, remorse, and disbelief at what had occurred.

37. Cited in Latin American Studies Association, *Electoral Democracy Under International Pressure*, op.cit., p.40. For another account of the "protest vote," see Tim Coone, "The Sandinistas Lose Office But Not Power," *Financial Times*, reprinted in *World Press Review*, April 1990.

38. See *NACLA Report on the Americas*, June 1990, for more details on this.

39. The other members were Luís Sánchez and Carlos Hurtado for UNO, and Major General Joaquín Cuadra, the second-ranking military official behind Ortega, and Jaime Wheelock, Minister of Agrarian Reform, for the FSLN.

40. For a textual reproduction of the Transition Protocol, see *Barricada Internacional*, April 7, 1990, pp.12-13.

41. The remark was made during an April 5, 1990 press conference, cited in "Family Frictions," *Barricada Internacional*, April 12, 1990, p.3.

42. A lengthy exposition on this position can be found in Silvio De Franco, "Nicaragua en la Encrucijada: Reflexiones sobre las Tareas Críticas en su Nueva Etapa," *Pensamiento Centroamericano*, January-March 1990, pp.64-72. De Franco was later named by Chamorro to the post of Minister of Economy and Development.

43. Cited in *Barricada Internacional*, Special Supplement on Chamorro's Inauguration, May 5, 1990, p.3.

44. In fact, Chamorro had named two COSEP leaders to cabinet posts, but both refused the offer citing their opposition to her decision to allow General Humberto Ortega to remain in his post as head of the army. The political parties and COSEP had fully expected that the majority of ministerial posts would be assigned to them.

45. On many occasions throughout the campaign Chamorro referred to this "group of experts," insisting that she was little more than a symbol, "a bridge between the people and those experts." *La Prensa*, November 25, 1989, cited in "Los Reyes Magos de la Reina," *Pensamiento Propio*, May 1990, pp.24-25.

46. CORDENIC was formed under the auspices of the International Commission for Central American Recovery and Development, better known as the Sanford Commission, in which Chamorro appointees Enrique Dreyfus and Francisco Mayorga were representatives. See International Commission for Central American Recovery and Development, *Poverty and Hope: A Turning Point in Central America* (Durham, NC: Duke University Press, 1989).

47. "CORDENIC: Misión y Programa de Actividades, 1988," cited in *Envío*, July 1989, p.23. See also, "Los Reyes Magos de la Reina," op.cit.

48. Most CORDENIC members had either studied, taught, or occupied leadership positions at INCAE. Mayorga, as well as Chamorro's Minister of Economy and Development Silvio De Franco and Finance Minister Eduardo Pereira, had all been INCAE professors.

49. Together with AENIC--an association of some 70 directors of state, mixed and private enterprises led by Antonio Lacayo--CORDENIC was actively involved in pursuing dialogue with the Sandinista government over reshaping economic policy in 1988 and early 1989, at a time when COSEP boycotted all such initiatives.

50. The Chamorro government inherited a judiciary whose FSLN-appointed members' terms were set to expire in 1993. By late July 1990 Chamorro had dismissed the Court's president, Rodrigo Reyes, replacing him with Orlando Trejos, who had served as Labor Minister under Somoza. Reforms to the Organic Law of Tribunals also had been approved by the National Assembly expanding the high court from seven to nine members. See "Not Another One, Violeta," *Barricada Internacional*, August 11, 1990, p.19.

51. The first was during the July 1990 general strike, and the second in late September when President Chamorro was outside the country.

52. Cited in "UNO Politics," *Envío*, August-September 1990, p.27.

53. For a lengthy post-electoral examination of the situation in the municipal councils, see "Municipal Autonomy in Nicaragua," *Envío*, June 1990, pp.33-38.

54. The commission, which presented itself at a July 10, 1990 press conference, included National Assembly President Miriam Argüello, COSEP President Gilberto Cuadra, political leaders Agustín Jarquín and Elí Altamirano, and union leaders Carlos Huembes of the CTN and Roberto Moreno of the CAUS.

55. For more on the Commission, see "Thunder on the Right," *Envío*, August-September 1990, pp.26-28.

56. On June 16 and 17, 1990, some 300 FSLN leaders and grassroots representatives held an assembly outside of Managua to debate the party's past, present and future. The final resolutions from the assembly included a preliminary evaluation by the party of its errors, including mistakes in agrarian reform, relations with the Catholic church, the draft, and abuses committed by Sandinista militants. The complete text of the resolutions was reproduced as an eight-page special supplement in *Barricada Internacional*, July 14, 1990.

57. Cited in Preston, op.cit.

58. For a discussion of the FSLN's role as vanguard, see Bruce E. Wright, "Pluralism and Vanguardism in the Nicaraguan Revolution," *Latin American Perspectives*, Summer 1990, pp.38-54.

59. This estimate, which is close to the one used by Sandinista leaders, is cited in ibid.

60. See, for example, Aldo Díaz Lacayo, "The FSLN Congress and the National Directorate," and Carlos Tünnermann, "The Democratization of the FSLN," in *Barricada Internacional*, August 25, 1990, pp.16-17.

61. One who adopted this position publicly was General Humberto Ortega, who resigned his post in the National Directorate in April in order to remain at the head of the army. See interview with Ortega in *La Prensa*, September 12, 1990; and *El Nuevo Diario*, September 14, 1990.

62. Elections for the National Directorate were to be held during the February 1991 party congress.

63. Movement in this direction had already occurred by August 1990 as the pro-Sandinista farmers' union UNAG began operating in concert with demobilized

contras around land issues. For the opposing theoretical positions on this issue, see Orlando Núñez, "Pactos, Acuerdos y Alianzas," *Barricada*, June 14, 1990; and Alejandro Martínez Cuenca, "Alianzas y Convivencia Básica," *Barricada*, June 16, 1990.

64. An extensive account of Nicaragua's foreign policy under the Sandinistas is found in Mary Vanderlaan, *Revolution and Foreign Policy in Nicaragua* (Boulder: Westview Press, 1986).

65. This point became clear even before Chamorro's inauguration, when the president-elect successfully resisted pressure from Washington to reverse the decision to retain General Humberto Ortega in his post as army chief. It was reaffirmed during the July general strike when Chamorro reportedly turned down an offer of U.S. troops to restore order in the capital.

66. In terms of diplomatic relations, the only immediate change undertaken by the Chamorro team was in the Middle East. In 1982 the Sandinistas had broken relations with Israel, a staunch ally of Somoza which had kept military aid flowing to the National Guard after the United States cut off assistance. Instead the FSLN maintained close ties with the Palestine Liberation Organization (PLO). Chamorro quickly moved to reestablish ties with Israel and there was talk of bringing in the Israeli intelligence agency Mossad to reorganize the Nicaraguan intelligence apparatus. Although there was talk of a break in relations with Cuba, and hardline sectors of the government were actively sponsoring anti-Castro political activity by Cuban exiles in Managua, such a move seemed unlikely at the end of 1990.

67. For an in-depth analysis of foreign policy and the construction of a new national identity, see "Sandinista Foreign Policy: Strategies for Survival," *NACLA: Report on the Americas*, May-June 1985. Much of the material which follows is based on this excellent study. Also see "Nicaragua's Foreign Policy: Ten Years of Principles and Practice--An Interview with Alejandro Bendaña," *Envío*, August 1989, pp.25-38.

68. *Direction of Trade Statistics Yearbook* (Washington: International Monetary Fund, 1989), p.301.

69. For a comprehensive discussion of Nicaragua's efforts to diversify trading partners during the 1980s, see Michael E. Conroy, "Patterns of Changing External Trade in Revolutionary Nicaragua: Voluntary and Involuntary Trade Diversification," in Rose J. Spalding, ed., *The Political Economy of Revolutionary Nicaragua* (Boston: Allen and Unwin, 1987) pp.169-194; and Solon Barraclough, et.al., *Aid that Counts: The Western Contribution to Development and Survival in Nicaragua* (Managua: CRIES, 1988).

70. An extensive account of these efforts can be found in *NACLA: Report on the Americas*, May-June 1985.

71. Cited in *Barricada*, August 15, 1990.

72. For documentation of the bilateral attempts at resolving differences between Nicaragua and the United States, see "Nicaragua's Peace Initiatives with the United States," in Peter Rosset and John Vandermeer, eds., *Nicaragua: Unfinished Revolution* (New York: Grove Press, 1986), pp.57-61; and William M. LeoGrande, "Roll-back or Containment? The United States, Nicaragua, and the Search for Peace in Central America," in Bruce M. Bagley, ed., *Contadora and the Diplomacy of Peace in Central America*, Vol.1 (Boulder: Westview Press, 1987).

73. For more on the Sandinistas' stance regarding relations with the United States, see Víctor Hugo Tinoco, "After the Storm," *Barricada Internacional*, August 11, 1990, pp.8-11.

74. An extensive account of the peace process during the 1980s from the perspective of one of its chief protagonists is Víctor Hugo Tinoco, *Conflicto y Paz: El Proceso*

*Negociador Centroamericano* (Mexico: Editorial Mestiza, 1989). Tinoco was Vice Minister of Foreign Affairs during the Sandinista government.

75. Details on Nicaraguan amnesty programs, begun in 1983, can be found in "Waging Peace," *Envío*, January 1989, pp.12-15.

76. Some who accept that U.S. aggression placed the Sandinistas in a difficult position argue that making concessions in the framework of the peace process, and holding elections under the adverse conditions of war and economic crisis, was an unpardonable error on the part of the FSLN. While such arguments correctly identify some of the factors behind the Sandinistas' electoral defeat, they sidestep the more salient issue of the probable ramifications of alternative courses of action. Rejection of the Central American peace process, and cancellation of constitutionally mandated elections might have allowed the FSLN to hold onto its social base in the short run, but the ensuing economic and diplomatic isolation of the country, combined with a revival of the contra war, would have had devastating consequences. See, for example, James Petras, "Flawed Strategies Planted Seeds of Sandinista Defeat," *In These Times*, March 21, 1990.

77. It is important to note that this issue was not just limited to the question of U.S. pressures and the need to end the war in order to reduce defense spending. For example, in 1989 most Western European countries made continued economic assistance contingent upon the holding of internationally supervised elections.

78. For more on the contras' role vis-a-vis the elections, see David MacMichael, "The U.S. Plays the Contra Card," *The Nation*, February 5, 1990, pp.162-166.

79. The amnesty bill proposed by Chamorro was reformed by UNO representatives before being passed into law by the National Assembly. The FSLN voted unanimously for the original bill, but the reformed version overturned the amnesty passed by the FSLN during the transition period. The amended bill passed with 51 UNO votes plus one from Moisés Hassan against 37 FSLN votes.

80. For details, see *Barricada*, March 29, 1990. Additional information on the situation of the kidnap victims can be found in *Amnesty International Report 1989* (London: Amnesty International Publications, 1989), pp.140-141; "Where Is My Father?," *CEPAD Report*, May-June 1990; and in *Barricada Internacional*, August 11, 1990, pp.20-21.

81. A detailed explanation of why the ex-Guardsmen were given lenient treatment and of the deeper roots behind Nicaragua's human rights policy can be found in Tomás Borge, "On Human Rights in Nicaragua," in Tomás Borge, et.al., *Sandinistas Speak* (New York: Pathfinder Press, 1982), pp.85-104.

82. In 1988 alone, military prosecutors brought charges against 3,519 members of the armed forces, many of these for human rights abuses. More than 2,500 were found guilty and sentenced to jail terms. "Human Rights: Regional Commission Studies Nicaragua," *Envío*, July 1989, p.12. Amnesty International also discusses the FSLN's policy and practices regarding these matters in *Amnesty International Report 1990* (London: Amnesty International Publications, 1990), pp.175-178.

83. See *Envío*, December 1989, pp.15-16.

84. For an extensively documented account of contra atrocities against civilians, based on testimonies and first-hand field research, see Reed Brody, *Contra Terror in Nicaragua* (Boston: South End Press, 1985). Also see Americas Watch, "The Killings in Northern Nicaragua," October 1989.

85. *Amnesty International Report 1988* (London: Amnesty International Publications, 1988); *Human Rights in Nicaragua: August 1987-August 1988* (New York: Americas Watch, 1988).

86. Americas Watch, "The Killings in Northern Nicaragua," cited in *Envío*, December 1989, p.13.

87. For a detailed account of the history of the CPDH and its activities, see "Opposition Rights Group Continues Attack," *Envío*, March 1989, pp.19-25.
88. Paul Laverty, "Human Rights Report--The CPDH: Can it be Trusted?," Scottish Medical Aid to Nicaragua, cited in *Envío*, March 1989. The CPDH receives no monies directly from the NED, but NED funds have been used to translate, publish, and distribute the group's bulletins.
89. See U.S. Department of State, "Country Reports on Human Rights Practices for 1988," (Washington, February 1989), p.645; and Americas Watch, "Human Rights in Nicaragua August 1987-August 1988," cited in *Envío*, January 1989.

## Chapter Two

1. The Chamorro government, the FSLN, and General Ortega all agreed on the need to change the name of the EPS. Soon after Chamorro's inauguration, Ortega proposed adopting "Army for the Defense of National Sovereignty" (EDSN), the name which Sandino had given to his guerrilla forces in the 1920s and 1930s. At the time of this writing, no agreement had been reached and the army, now formally cut off from the Sandinista party, continued to be known as the EPS.
2. For more on the National Guard, see Richard Millett, *Guardians of the Dynasty* (New York: Maryknoll, 1977).
3. An explanation of the defensive character of Nicaragua's armed forces can be found in Lt. Col. Edward King, ret., "Analysis of the Military Situation in Nicaragua," April 1985. King gathered the material for his report on several visits to the region, where he went as part of U.S. congressional fact-finding missions.
4. For a detailed account of Sandinista military doctrine and the evolution of the EPS, see William I. Robinson and Kent Norsworthy, *David and Goliath: The U.S. War Against Nicaragua* (New York: Monthly Review Press, 1987), pp.251-260.
5. "Patriotic Military Service: The Front Line in the Defense of the Revolution," *Barricada Internacional*, December 8, 1988, p.11.
6. "The War: A Long and Inconclusive Story," *Barricada Internacional*, May 5, 1990.
7. These figures are from the International Institute of Strategic Studies, cited in *Barricada Internacional*, June 30, 1990, p.12.
8. For an analysis of how the EPS views its role under the new circumstances, see Rodolfo Castro, "El General en su Laberinto," *Pensamiento Propio*, September 1990, pp.25-27.
9. See Oswaldo Lacayo, second in command of the EPS Chiefs of Staff, cited in *La Crónica*, September 1-7, 1989; and an interview with EPS Chiefs of Staff head Joaquín Cuadra, "El Mayor Acierto: Un Ejército Popular," *Pensamiento Propio*, July 1989, pp.6-9.
10. *Barricada Internacional*, June 30, 1990, p.13.
11. The first phase also included the disarming of civilians. See Gabriela Selser, "Nicaraguan Army is Reduced," *Barricada Internacional*, June 30, 1990, pp.12-13; and Mary Speck, "Nicaraguan Army to be Cut in Half," *Washington Post*, June 16, 1990, p.A16.
12. *Washington Report on the Hemisphere*, July 11, 1990, p.6.
13. Cited in Richard Bourdeaux, "Nicaragua's Army will be Cut in Half, Sandinista Military Chief Asserts," *Los Angeles Times*, April 27, 1990, p.A16. Although the EPS is clearly a powerful actor in the national balance between pro- and counter-revolutionary tendencies, it is in a qualitatively different position than the powerful armies of northern Central America in terms of issues such as impunity and autonomy vis-a-vis the civilian governments. Furthermore, the EPS' institutional

mandate precludes any possibility of its use as an instrument of repression against the population. For more information on the army as a power bloc in Guatemala, El Salvador, and Honduras, see Richard Bourdeaux, "Reining in the Latin Tiger," *Los Angeles Times*, September 2, 1990, p.A1.

14. See Bourdeaux, "Reining in the Latin Tiger," ibid., and *New York Times*, September 18, 1990.

15. *La Prensa*, July 21, 1990.

16. In April, U.S. press reports indicated that the Mossad had accepted a petition by Chamorro to have Mossad agents reorganize the Sandinista foreign intelligence apparatus, a report which was denied by Hurtado. See Bill Gertz, "Nicaragua Asks Israeli Spies for Help," *Washington Times*, April 25, 1990.

17. Throughout the 1980s as alliances in the anti-Sandinista camp were formed, broken and reformed in accordance with the political exigencies of the moment, dozens of contra groups and front organizations came and went. From the beginning the contra landscape was dominated by the Nicaraguan Democratic Force (FDN), operating out of Honduras. In 1982, the Democratic Revolutionary Alliance (ARDE) was formed in Costa Rica. Armed groups on the Atlantic Coast included Misura, Misurasata, Kisan and Yatama. The last of several contra umbrella organizations, the Nicaraguan Resistance (RN) oversaw demobilization of most contra forces in mid-1990. A detailed account of the multitude of contra groupings can be found in Robinson and Norsworthy, *David and Goliath*, op.cit.

18. In April 1984, the CIA informed Congress that the contra army totaled 15,000 men. The contras themselves frequently claimed 20,000, while the Nicaraguan government estimated between 12,000 and 16,000. See Peter Kornbluh, *Nicaragua: The Price of Intervention* (Washington: Institute for Policy Studies, 1987), p.55.

19. Interview by *Barricada* special correspondent Guillermo Cortés with Edgar Chamorro in Miami, published in *Barricada*, December 9, 1985.

20. In mid-1985 one study concluded that 46 of 48 command positions in the contra movement were held by former National Guard members. See "Who Are the Contras?," a report by the Arms Control and Foreign Policy Caucus of the U.S. Congress, April 18, 1985.

21. See Instituto Nacional de Estadísticas y Census, *Diez Años en Cifras*, July 1989.

22. For more information on low intensity warfare and its application in Nicaragua, see Robinson and Norsworthy, *David and Goliath*, op.cit.; Peter Kornbluh, *Nicaragua: The Price of Intervention* (Washington: Institute for Policy Studies, 1987); Holly Sklar, *Washington's War on Nicaragua* (Boston: South End Press, 1988); Deborah Barry and Rodolfo Castro, *Centroamérica: La Guerra de Baja Intensidad* (San José, Costa Rica: DEI, 1987); and Sara Miles, "The Real War: Low Intensity Conflict in Central America," *NACLA Report on the Americas*, April-May 1986.

23. For an account of the transformation of the contra army and the rise of the new leadership, see Raúl Marín, "Los Ultimos 'Paladines'," *Pensamiento Propio*, May 1990, pp.26-28.

24. See David MacMichael, "The U.S. Plays the Contra Card," *The Nation*, February 5, 1990, pp.162-166.

25. This figure comes from United Nations Security Council, "ONUCA: Report of the Secretary General," June 29, 1990. On July 5, ONUCA brought the total up to 19,613. Of those, 16,408 had turned in arms, while the rest were listed as "unarmed couriers." The bulk of demobilized contras belonged to the Nicaraguan Democratic Force (FDN). Under separate negotiations with the government, the Miskito organization Yatama demobilized 1,612 troops and a separate group, the Southern Front, another 1,630. Most observers agreed that several thousand Nicaraguans who "demobilized" were actually contra family members or civilian supporters who

were given arms so as to enter the process and thus become eligible for the special privileges--three months' worth of food and medical attention and participation in the development poles--which accompanied it.

26. For more details on the development poles, see Richard Bourdeaux, "Contras to Get Own Colony in Deal to Disarm," *Los Angeles Times*, May 6, 1990; and "Serán una Realidad los Polos de Desarrollo?," *Pensamiento Propio*, August 1990, pp.30-32.

27. See *Pensamiento Propio*, ibid.

28. Lee Hockstader, "Former Contras Scatter from Special Enclaves," *Washington Post*, July 15, 1990, p.A23.

29. The new party was under the leadership of Oscar Sobalvarro. Former contra chief Israel Galeano complained at having been displaced, insisting that the full Nicaraguan Resistance command had not been present at the meeting in which Sobalvarro was "elected."

30. *Barricada*, August 16, 1990.

## Chapter Three

1. By 1983, when most of the major changes in ownership had already taken place, the structure of the mixed economy measured in terms of percent contribution to GDP was as follows: state, 40 percent; capitalist, 29 percent; and small producers, 31 percent. In the economy's two major productive areas, agroexports and industry, the capitalist sector was responsible for 42 and 49 percent of production, respectively. Cited in Eduardo Baumeister and Oscar Neira Cuadra, "The Making of a Mixed Economy: Class Struggle and State Policy in the Nicaraguan Transition," in Richard R. Fagen, Carmen Diana Deere, and José Luís Coraggio, eds., *Transition and Development: Problems of Third World Socialism* (New York: Monthly Review Press, 1986), p.188.

2. See, for example, ibid.; Carlos M. Vilas, "Socialismo en Nicaragua," *Nueva Sociedad*, No.91, September-October 1987, pp.159-75; Orlando Nuñez Soto, *Transición y Lucha de Clases en Nicaragua, 1979-1986* (Mexico: Siglo XXI, 1987); and Jaime Wheelock Román, *Entre la Crisis y la Agresión: La Reforma Agraria Sandinista* (Managua: Editorial Nueva Nicaragua, 1985).

3. Stahler-Sholk, citing figures used by Richard Harris and Carlos Vilas, reports the following estimates. Urban class structure: 25 percent artisans or self-employed; 24 percent property owners; 21 percent informal services or unemployed; 20 percent proletariat; and 10 percent salaried petty bourgeoisie. Rural class structure: 38 percent poor peasants; 29 percent proletariat; 22 percent medium peasants; 8 percent wealthy peasants; and 2 percent bourgeoisie. See Richard Stahler-Sholk, "Stabilization, Destabilization, and the Popular Classes in Nicaragua, 1979-1988," *Latin American Research Review*, Fall 1990, p.83.

4. In 1979 Nicaragua's GNP dropped by 26 percent as production ground to a near-standstill. Direct infrastructure damage alone was close to $500 million. Tom Barry and Debra Preusch, *The Soft War: The Uses and Abuses of U.S. Economic Aid in Central America* (New York: Grove Press, 1988), p.219. Only $3.5 million in reserves, not enough to pay for two days of imports, was left behind after Somoza's looting. George Black, *Triumph of the People* (London: Zed Books, 1981), p.201. The Sandinistas assumed responsibility for repaying the foreign debt accumulated by the dictatorship in the 1970s, calculated at roughly $1.6 billion.

5. World Bank, *Nicaragua: The Challenge of Reconstruction*, Report No. 3524-NI (Washington: World Bank, 1981)

6. "Country Profile: Nicaragua, Costa Rica, Panama, 1989-1990," *The Economist Intelligence Unit* (London), 1989, p.15.

7. For a comprehensive discussion of the Sandinistas' efforts to achieve food self-sufficiency, see Joseph Collins, et.al., *What Difference Could a Revolution Make? Food and Farming in the New Nicaragua* (New York: Grove Press, 1986).

8. U.S. pressure resulted in a precipitous drop in financing to Nicaragua from multilateral development banks. In 1979, these sources provided 78 percent of all Nicaragua's contracted borrowing; by 1984 the figure was down to zero. See Stahler-Sholk, "Stabilization, Destabilization, and the Popular Classes in Nicaragua," op.cit., p.56.

9. It is important to note that planning for a major economic-adjustment package and monetary reform had begun as early as 1982 and recognition of the need for such measures was made publicly the following year. In 1984 the package was tabled in part out of fear of provoking a recession in an electoral year. Subsequently, questions related to the contra military threat and the need to sustain defense spending played a major role in delaying the measures, which were finally implemented in 1988. See "Operación 'Berta'," *Barricada*, March 1-3, 1988.

10. The Economic Commission for Latin America (CEPAL) calculated damages from the hurricane at $848 million, more than 3 times Nicaragua's average annual exports during this period. Despite the magnitude of the disaster, Nicaragua received almost no international relief assistance.

11. All data in this section is extracted from "The UNO Agenda for Economic Recovery," *Regionews from Managua*, April 1, 1990.

12. For one retrospective analysis of the 100-day plan, see Semia Guermas and Oscar Neira Cuadra, "Aterrizaje Forzoso: Demagogia y Realidad," *Pensamiento Propio*, September 1990, pp.28-31. *La Prensa* also ran a lengthy, somewhat critical balance of this period on its editorial page. See Javier Morales, "El Plan Económico de Nicaragua," *La Prensa*, August 26 and 27, 1990.

13. These figures are cited in Morales, ibid., August 27, 1990, p.4.

14. See an April 2, 1990 *Barricada* interview with COSEP president Gilberto Cuadra, "Privatize it All," reproduced in *Regionews from Managua*, CRIES, April 20, 1990. COSEP's views on privatization can also be found in "Dos Empresarios Exponen Problemas de Privatización," *La Prensa*, August 27, 1990, p.3.

15. See U.S. Agency for International Development, "Food for Progress Agreement Between AID and Government of the Republic of Nicaragua: Economic Stabilization and Recovery Program," May 3, 1990.

16. Excerpts from a *Barricada* interview with Krügger reproduced in "The Keyword is Privatization," *Barricada Internacional*, June 30, 1990, pp.10-11.

17. *The Economist Intelligence Unit*, op.cit., p.18.

18. In 1978, 47.8 percent of the arable land was owned by just 0.7 percent of the population while more than half the rural population was crammed onto 2.1 percent of the land. A full 20 percent of all farmland was owned by Somoza and his closest associates. Cited in "Who Owns the Land?," *CEPAD Report*, May-June 1990.

19. A comprehensive discussion of Nicaragua's agrarian-reform program can be found in Collins, et.al., op.cit.

20. Statistically, this meant that more than 6.7 million acres of farmland were turned over to 120,000 rural families. Vice Minister of Agriculture and Agrarian Reform Alonso Porras, cited in *Envío*, August 1989, p.17; and "Who Owns the Land?," op.cit.

21. For lengthy expositions on Sandinista agrarian policies and land reform, see Wheelock, op.cit.; Laura J. Enriquez, "The Dilemmas of Agro-Export Planning in Revolutionary Nicaragua," in Thomas W. Walker, ed., *Nicaragua: The First Five Years* (New York: Praeger, 1985); and Carmen Diana Deere, Peter Marchetti, and Nola Reinhardt, "The Peasantry and the Development of Sandinista Agrarian Policy: 1979-1984," *Latin American Research Review*, Fall 1985, pp.75-109.

22. Paul Rice, "Growing with Experience: Eight Years of Agrarian Reform," *Nicaraguan Perspectives*, Fall 1987, p.20. Much of the analysis presented here is based on Rice's excellent study.

23. For a discussion of the different views among the Sandinistas regarding alliances in the countryside, see David Kaimowitz, "Nicaraguan Debates on Agrarian Structure and their Implications for Agricultural Policy and the Rural Poor," *Journal of Peasant Studies*, October 1986, pp.100-117.

24. Between 1983 and 1988, 31,000 families benefited from this program. "Who Owns the Land?," op.cit.

25. As a result, by mid-1989 the state accounted for only 38 percent of the land area which had been affected by the agrarian reform (and less than 15 percent of the country's total farmland), with the remaining 62 percent divided between production cooperatives, credit and service cooperatives, and small and medium individual producers. Eduardo Baumeister, "Y las Tierras Cambiaron de Dueños," *Pensamiento Propio*, July 1989, p.34.

26. All figures in this paragraph are taken from ibid., p.34.

27. Before 1979 only about 6,000 farmers, the country's big agroexport growers, had access to credit. Under the Sandinistas, more than 75 percent of all farmers took advantage of the easy credit terms offered by the nationalized banking system. Although the 1988 economic reforms introduced tight restrictions on credit and more realistic interest rates, in practice these policies were applied flexibly. Under the UNO government, in addition to the high interest rates, many farmers have been reluctant to seek credits from the banks as they would be required to put their property titles up as collateral.

28. See, for example, Tablada's declarations on the occasion of INRA's eleventh anniversary, in "INRA Profundizará la Reforma Agraria Dice su Director," *La Prensa*, July 17, 1990.

29. FNT communique, August 31, 1990, cited in *Regionews from Managua*, September 21, 1990.

30. "Godoy Backers Seize Cooperatives," *Envío*, August-September 1990, pp.28-30.

31. "Tensions Feared in the Countryside," *Barricada Internacional*, May 5, 1990, p.6.

32. For a report on land takeovers on the cooperatives, see "Godoy Backers Seize Cooperatives," op.cit.

33. Many cooperatives were incorporated into the Territorial Militias or other defense structures. During the course of the war, contra attacks against the cooperatives resulted in the killing of 5,400 cooperative members, the kidnapping of 3,100, and the destruction of 1,350 homes.

34. Unless otherwise noted, figures used here regarding cooperatives and the information on FENICOOP are taken from "Tensions Feared in the Countryside," op.cit., pp.6-7. For a more lengthy account on the role and formation of cooperatives during the 1980s, see "Cooperativas: Un Nuevo Giro," *Envío*, June 1987, pp.13-38.

35. Cited in "Banano, Dulce Banano...," *Pensamiento Propio*, August 1990, p.9.

36. See ibid.

37. See *La Prensa*, May 22, 1990.

38. A profile of the Nicaraguan industrial sector can be found in Richard L. Harris, "The Economic Transformation and Industrial Development of Nicaragua," in Richard L. Harris and Carlos M. Vilas, eds., *Nicaragua: a Revolution Under Siege* (London: Zed Books, 1985). Another excellent overview is provided in Claes Brundenius, "Industrial Development Strategies in Revolutionary Nicaragua," in Rose J. Spalding, ed., *The Political Economy of Revolutionary Nicaragua* (Boston: Allen and Unwin, Inc., 1987), pp.85-104.

39. *Envío*, June 1989, p.13.

40. Roser Solá Monserrat, *Geografía y Estructura Económicas de Nicaragua* (Managua: Universidad Centroamericana, 1989), p.183.

41. For a detailed account of the banking system and credit policy under the Sandinista government, see Laura J. Enriquez and Rose J. Spalding, "Banking Systems and Revolutionary Change: The Politics of Agricultural Credit in Nicaragua," in Spalding, op.cit., pp.105-125.

42. See *This Week in Central America*, July 30, 1990, p.180.

43. The statistics cited here on the foreign debt are the official ones used by Nicaragua's Central Bank. See "The Foreign Debt: Things Could be Worse," *Barricada Internacional*, June 16, 1990, p.9.

44. See *Envío*, July 1990, p.16.

## Chapter Four

1. Philip Wheaton and Yvonne Dilling, *Nicaragua: A People's Revolution* (Washington: EPICA Task Force, 1980), p.84, citing *Barricada*, July 26, 1979.

2. Richard Stahler-Sholk, "Nicaragua," in Gerald Michael Greenfield and Sheldon L. Maram, eds., *Latin America Labor Organizations* (New York: Greenwood Press, 1987), p.555.

3. Luís Serra,"Entre Las Bases y El Poder," *Pensamiento Propio*, December 1988. For a broader discussion of class alliances in terms of the government's stabilization policies see Richard Stahler-Sholk, "Stabilization, Destabilization, and the Popular Classes in Nicaragua, 1979-1988," *Latin American Research Review*, Fall 1990.

4. E.V.K. Fitzgerald, "Stabilization and Economic Justice: The Case of Nicaragua," in Kwan S. Kim and David F. Ruccio, eds., *Debt and Development in Latin America* (Notre Dame, IN: University of Notre Dame Press, 1985).

5. Stahler-Sholk, "Stabilization, Destabilization, and the Popular Classes in Nicaragua," op.cit., pp.67-68.

6. Serra, op.cit.

7. Ibid.

8. Gary Ruchwarger, *People in Power: Forging a Grassroots Democracy in Nicaragua* (Massachusetts: Bergin and Garvey Publishers, 1987), p.242.

9. UNAG producers accounted for most of the country's production of corn and beans, while state and capitalist producers accounted for significant shares of rice, sorghum, and beef production as well as sugar and cottonseed oil production.

10. Serra, op.cit.

11. "Nicaragua: Low Intensity War and Revolutionary Maneuvering," *Envío*, May 1990, p.28.

12. From excerpts from a speech by Tomás Borge on the revolution and democracy in *Envío*, June 1990, p.44.

13. "From Military to Social Confrontation," *Envío*, July 1990, p.11.

14. This history of Nicaraguan unions is drawn largely from Stahler-Sholk, "Nicaragua," op.cit.
15. "Creating a New Power," *Barricada Internacional*, Special Supplement, May 1989. For information on the labor movement during the 1980s also see: Harris and Vilas, "The Workers' Movement in the Sandinista Revolution," op.cit., pp.120-150; Stahler-Sholk, "Nicaragua," ibid.; and Stahler-Sholk, "Stabilization, Destabilization, and the Popular Classes in Nicaragua," op.cit.
16. *Barricada Internacional*, May 1989, p.2.
17. Stahler-Sholk, "Nicaragua," op.cit., p.557.
18. For an excellent discussion of economic stabilization and its effect on the popular sectors see: Stahler-Sholk, "Stabilization, Destabilization, and the Popular Classes in Nicaragua," op.cit.
19. These members of the FNT were formerly grouped together in the Nicaraguan Labor Coordinating Group (CSN), established in November 1981 to unite the country's labor confederations. The anti-Sandinista socialist unions, CGT-I, CAUS, and FO, were early members of the CSN but soon disaffiliated. CTN declined to participate, and CUS initially joined but immediately quit.
20. Trish O'Kane, "El Nuevo Panorama Sindical," *Pensamiento Propio*, September 1990.
21. Deena Abu-Lughod, "Trade Unions Fight It Out," *Barricada International*, May 19, 1990, p.7.
22. Newly organized unions registered between January and August 1990 include: FNT, 247 unions, 23,000 workers; CTN, 21 unions, 1,865 workers; Independent, 16 unions, 1,404 workers; CAUS, 8 unions, 787 workers; CUS, 15 unions, 603 workers; CTN-A, 11 unions, 583 workers; and CGT-I, 9 unions, 575 workers. Ministry of Labor, cited in O'Kane, op.cit.
23. Abu-Lughod, op.cit.
24. For an overview of Sandinista changes in the education system during the 1980s, see Desiree Pallais, "Renovación en los Textos," *Pensamiento Propio*, August 1989, pp.33-35.
25. Cited in "Rewriting History," *Barricada Internacional*, June 2, 1990, p.17.
26. Belli was instrumental in the propaganda war against the Sandinista government. He received financial and logistical support from the CIA for his anti-Sandinista volume, *Nicaragua: Christians Under Fire*. During the 1980s, Belli, a former *La Prensa* editor, was active with the Puebla Institute, an anti-Sandinista human rights organization. See, for example, Edgar Chamorro, *Packaging the Contras: A Case of CIA Disinformation* (New York: Institute for Media Analysis, Inc., 1987).
27. "Rewriting History," op.cit., p.17.
28. Cited in "The Pope's Man Always Rings Twice," *Newsweek*, August 6, 1990.
29. The textbook change was opposed both for ideological reasons--many Sandinista educators asserted that the content of the AID-funded readers was inappropriate to Nicaraguan reality--as well as for pedagogical ones--education professionals pointed out that, irrespective of the content, the two readers were based on fundamentally different teaching methodologies.
30. This figure was cited in an FNT communique released on August 30, 1990.
31. See reports on ANDEN congress in *Barricada*, August 19 and 20, 1990.
32. "The Placement of Students from Central America," a PIER Workshop Report, 1987, p.181.
33. Robert Arnove and Tony Dewees, "Education and Revolutionary Transformation," *Nicaraguan Perspectives*, Fall 1987, p.30. This article provides an excellent overview and evaluation of the changes in education introduced since the triumph.

34. Ibid., p.31.

35. *Nicaragua Through Our Eyes*, Committee of U.S. Citizens Living in Nicaragua (CUSCLIN), July 1989, p.9.

36. These statistics were included in a September 1987 letter sent by Fernando Cardenal, Nicaraguan Minister of Education, to the U.S. Secretary of Education, cited in *Update*, October 26, 1987, p.2.

37. For one good overview of developments in the Nicaraguan media during the early 1980s, see the chapter by John Spicer Nichols in Thomas W. Walker, ed., *Nicaragua: The First Five Years* (New York: Praeger, 1985).

38. In turn, NED's electoral "media project" provided continuity under the Chamorro government to a series of destabilization initiatives which had been waged through the media during the 1980s. The media component of Washington's campaign to oust the Sandinistas was multifaceted. It's two most high-profile aspects were covert and overt support to *La Prensa* (See "CIA Psychological Warfare Operations: Case Studies in Chile, Jamaica, and Nicaragua," *Science for the People*, January-February 1982; and John Spicer Nichols, "La Prensa: The CIA Connection," *Columbia Journalism Review*, July-August 1988) and the attempt to assure that anti-Sandinista content would dominate Nicaragua's radio waves. See Howard Frederick "Electronic Penetration in Low Intensity Warfare: The Case of Nicaragua," in Thomas W. Walker, ed., *Reagan versus the Sandinistas: The Undeclared War on Nicaragua* (Boulder: Westview Press, 1987) and Edgar Chamorro, op.cit., pp.24-30 and 37-45.

39. The FSLN was formally committed to freedom of the press, and the 1987 constitution forbids prior censorship. In exercising censorship against *La Prensa* during the mid 1980s, the Sandinistas argued that under wartime conditions, opposition forces aligned with the foreign power sponsoring the aggression--the United States government--could not be allowed to play the role of open accomplice to destabilization.

40. Michael Massing, "Nicaragua's Free-fire Journalism," *Columbia Journalism Review*, July-August 1988, p.1.

41. For more information on these themes, see "Nicaragua's New Media Law: Freedom and Social Responsibility," in *Envío*, July 1989, pp.25-32; Armand Mattelart, ed., *Communicating in Popular Nicaragua* (New York: International General, 1986); and Carlos Fernando Chamorro, "Frontpage Battlefront," *Barricada Internacional*, July 8, 1989, p.36.

42. Cited in "The Battle for Public Opinion," *Barricada Internacional*, June 2, 1990.

43. For details on the suspension of *Extravisión*, and on other limits to press freedoms, see "Nicaragua: Los Problemas de la Libertad de Expresión," *Inforpress Centroamericana*, August 16, 1990, pp.9-10.

44. According to one report, the bill was written by Reynerio Montiel, a former adviser to Somoza Colonel Alberto Luna who wrote and enforced the "Black Code." See articles on the bill in *La Prensa* and *Barricada*, August 28 and 29, 1990.

45. One relative exception to this was the weekly newspaper *La Crónica*. The paper had a pluralist editorial staff and its content, although sharply anti-Sandinista, offered a broad range of opinions on current affairs. In mid-1990, *La Crónica* closed down operations amidst a scandal over misappropriated finances.

46. Violeta Chamorro is *La Prensa's* publisher, while her daughter Cristiana--who is the wife of top Chamorro aide and Minister of the Presidency Antonio Lacayo--is co-director.

47. During the July 1990 general strike, the station's Managua offices became the operational base for a group of some 300 armed rightwing vigilantes, while its broadcasts served as a platform for Godoy's political destabilization activities.

Before the strike concluded, the station's transmitter was destroyed in a bomb attack. It was back on the air within weeks.

48. Cited in "The Battle for Public Opinion," op.cit., p.12.

49. Ibid., p.13.

50. An extensive account of changes in health care in Nicaragua under the Sandinistas can be found in Richard Garfield, *Health and Revolution: The Nicaraguan Experience* (London: Oxfam, 1989).

51. FETSALUD represents 17,000 of the health care system's 23,000 workers. "A Poor State of Health," *Barricada Internacional*, July 28, 1990, p.23.

52. Dr. Antonio Jarquín, "Socialist Rationale for Private Medicine," *Links*, NCAHRN, Winter 1989-1990, p.16.

53. For a discussion of the national health system set up by the Ministry of Health, see Patricia Obregón, "Expectativas y Realidades," *Pensamiento Propio*, July 1989, pp.36-38.

54. Cited in David Henson, "Ten Years of Revolutionary Accomplishments," *EPOCA Update*, Spring 1990, p.8.

55. Ibid., p.16.

56. *CEPAD Report*, January-February 1989.

57. "El Drama de la Salud Infantil: Que no se Apague Esta Sonrisa," *Pensamiento Propio*, October 1988, p.45.

58. Richard M. Garfield and Eugenio Taboada, "Health Services Reforms in Revolutionary Nicaragua," in Peter Rosset and John Vandermeer, eds., *Nicaragua: Unfinished Revolution* (New York: Grove Press, 1986), p.430.

59. Stephen Kinzer, *New York Times*, March 23, 1987, cited in ibid.

60. Unitarian Universalist Service Committee, "Health as a Human Right in "Nicaragua: The Impact of Low Intensity Conflict," September 1987.

61. Henson, op.cit., p.9.

62. "El Drama de la Salud Infantil," op.cit., p.46.

63. *Envío*, January 1989.

64. "A Poor State of Health," op.cit., p.22.

65. Ibid., p.23.

66. Salmerón's declarations were reproduced in a lengthy article in *Barricada*, August 12, 1990.

67. Father Xabier Gorrostiaga, Director of CRIES, cited in "New Cathedral Provokes Criticism," *CEPAD Report*, May-June 1990.

68. "The Pope's Man Always Rings Twice," op.cit.

69. Television in Nicaragua is state-owned. Both the Sandinista opposition and some evangelical groups have complained bitterly that they are charged exorbitant rates for air time, while Obando's mass is aired free of charge.

70. Silvio De Franco, "Nicaragua en la Encrucijada: Reflexiones sobre las Tareas Críticas en su Nueva Etapa," *Pensamiento Centroamericano*, January-March 1990, p.70. De Franco serves as Minister of Economy and Development in the Chamorro government.

71. One major account of struggle in the Nicaraguan church during the 1980s is Michael Dodson and Laura Nuzzi O'Shaughnessy, *Nicaragua's Other Revolution: Religious Faith and Political Struggle* (Chapel Hill, NC: University of North Carolina Press, 1989).

72. Informative accounts of the history of this conflict can be found in Alfonso Dubois, "La Iglesia en Nicaragua: El Proyecto Tras el Cardenal," *Pensamiento Propio*, March 1986, pp.22-27; "Church-State Relations: A Chronology," *Envío*, November

and December 1987; Penny Lernoux, "The Struggle for Nicaragua's Soul: The Church in Revolution and War," *Sojourners*, May 1989; and an interview with Monseñor Bosco Vivas, "Los Vericuetos de una Relación," *Pensamiento Propio*, July 1989, pp.51-53.

73. The link with CRS is documented in Ana María Escurra, *El Vaticano y la Administración Reagan* (Mexico: Ediciones Nuevomar, 1984), p.51.

74. "The Pope's Man Always Rings Twice," op.cit.

75. "For the Purpose of Procreation," *Barricada Internacional*, June 16, 1990, p.15.

76. Interview by Debra Preusch with Bismarck Carballo, Managua, July 20, 1990.

77. For more information on the cathedral project and on Monaghan, see Russ Bellant, "Nicaraguan Government Appointments Linked with U.S. Charismatic Group," *National Catholic Reporter*, July 27, 1990, p.6; "Managua Cathedral Drive Faces Opposition," *National Catholic Reporter*, July 13, 1990, p.3; and "New Cathedral Provokes Criticism: Church-State Relations Come under Fire," *CEPAD Report*, May-June 1990.

78. Cited in Bellant, op.cit., p.6.

79. See Noel Irías, "Ciudad de Dios," *Crítica*, June 1990, p.7.

80. For lengthy accounts on evangelicals in Nicaragua during the 1980s, see Abelino Martínez, *Las Sectas en Nicaragua: Oferta y Demanda de Salvación* (San José, Costa Rica: DEI, 1989); and David Stoll, *Is Latin America Turning Protestant?* (Berkeley: University of California Press, 1990). Paul Jeffrey, "Church Fray Spurs Liberation Theology," *The Guardian* (New York), July 1989. Two brief accounts of the impact of evangelism in Nicaragua during the 1980s are "Pentecostals in Nicaragua," *Update*, Central American Historical Institute, March 10, 1987, p.2; and Edwin Saballos, "Los Conservadores Tienen el Protagonismo," *Pensamiento Propio*, July 1989, pp.54-56.

81. James and Margaret Goff, "The Church Confronting Change: Organized Religion and Liberation Theology in Revolutionary Society," *Nicaraguan Perspectives*, Summer-Fall 1989, p.7.

82. It should be noted that in some cases the government moved against what it perceived as subversive acts without reasonable cause or based on mythical charges. For a detailed account of some of the more prominent counterrevolutionary activities of evangelical leaders and their connections to the U.S. embassy, see Paul Jeffrey, "Evangelicals: Facts and Fictions," *Christianity and Crisis*, October 20, 1986, pp.366-68; "U.S. Aiding Nicaragua's Church Opposition," *Sojourners*, November 1986; and "The Other Invasion," *CEPAD Report*, July-August 1989.

83. Many of these sects form part of the "Shepherding" movement and include Chapel Hill Harvester Church in Atlanta, Georgia; the Crossroads Community Church in Vancouver, Washington; and congregations associated with Shepherding guru Dennis Peacocke.

84. *CEPAD Report*, July-August 1989.

85. Ibid.

86. Sara Diamond, "Christian Right Sows Division in Ranks of Nicaraguan Faithful," *Guardian*, August 1, 1990.

87. Cited in "U.S. Evangelist's Expensive Nicaraguan Campaign Encounters Rocky Ground," *CEPAD Report*, March-April 1990. Most of the material presented here on Project Light is taken from this article and from "Briefly: More Problems for Robertson," *CEPAD Report*, May-June 1990.

88. For an overview of pre-1990 NGOs see: *Documento Base Presentado por la Coordinadora Nacional de ONG*, c.1988.

89. Solon Barraclough, et.al., *Aid that Counts: The Western Contribution to Development and Survival in Nicaragua* (Managua: CRIES, 1988), p.10.

90. At the start of the Chamorro government the members of the NGO Coordinator were the following: Asociación para el Desarrollo de los Pueblos (ADP), Centro de Educación Promocional Agraria (CEPA), CEPAD, Centro Ecuménico Antonio Valdivieso (CAV), Eje Ecuménico de Nicaragua, Escuelas Radiofónicas de Nicaragua (ERN), FACS, Instituto de Acción Social Juan XXIII, Instituto de Investigaciones Económicas y Sociales (INIES), and Instituto de Promoción Humana (INPRHU).

91. One of the few NGOs to stay was the Wisconsin Partners, which is respected for its rural development work in Nicaragua.

92. *CEPAD Report*, January-February 1990 and March-April 1990.

93. Other U.S. NGOs that have signed grant agreements with AID include National Association for the Partners of the Americas, Pan American Development Foundation, and World Rehabilitation Fund. Others that have expressed interest in working with U.S. government funds in Nicaragua include Catholic Relief Services, International Rescue Committee, Mercy Corps, and Save the Children. Interviews by Debra Preusch with Roger Noriega, AID Nicaragua, July 16, 1990; and with Roberto Ferrey, Repatriation Institute, July 18, 1990.

94. Mónica Baltodano, "Women: Ten Years of Achievement and Hope," *Barricada Internacional*, July 8, 1989, p.24.

95. For a lengthy discussion of the role of women in the agricultural sector during the Sandinista government, see Gary Ruchwarger, *Struggling for Survival: Workers, Women, and Class on a Nicaraguan State Farm* (Boulder: Westview Press, 1989).

96. *Envío*, December 1987, p.20, and ibid.

97. For details on the issue of women's integration into the rural economy, see Carmen Herrera, "El Dilema de las Campesinas," *Pensamiento Propio*, May 1989, pp.38-40.

98. *Envío*, December 1987, p.19.

99. Maxine Molyneux, "La Mujer: Activismo sin Emancipación," *Pensamiento Propio*, June-July 1985.

100. One of the leading spokespersons for the feminist movement in Nicaragua is Sofía Montenegro, an editor of the FSLN daily *Barricada*. See "Futuro, en Femenino," *Pensamiento Propio*, August 1990, pp.38-40.

101. For more details on the legal offices, see "New Legal Protection for Women in Nicaragua," *Update*, March 25, 1987.

102. Molyneux, op.cit.

103. Interview by Debra Preusch with Francis Blandon, Managua, July 21, 1990.

104. Cited in "All God's Children...," *Barricada Internacional*, July 28, 1990, p.19.

105. "Futuro, en Femenino," op.cit., p.40.

106. For a lengthy account of the situation of Nicaragua's ethnic communities during the 1980s, see Carlos M. Villas, *State, Class, and Ethnicity in Nicaragua: Capitalist Modernization and Revolutionary Change on the Atlantic Coast* (Boulder: Lynne Reinner, 1989).

107. Due to the extreme isolation of the Atlantic coast, no real census has been conducted. The estimates used here are cited in Philippe Bourgois, "Nicaragua's Ethnic Minorities in the Revolution," in Rosset and Vandermeer, eds., op.cit., p.459.

108. Jonas Bernstein, "Uneasy Truce for Coastal Indians," *Insight*, May 23 1988.

109. For detailed accounts of the peace and autonomy processes, see "The Atlantic Coast: Peace Has Taken Hold," *Envío*, June 1988; and "From Separatism to Autonomy: Ten Years on the Atlantic Coast," *Envío*, April 1989.

110. For an early analysis of the elections' impact on the autonomy process, see "Será Ahora una Realidad la Autonomía?," *Pensamiento Propio*, June 1990, pp.27-29.

111. For more details and analysis on the election results, see "Atlantic Coast: What Fate Autonomy?," *Envío*, March-April 1990, pp.17-20.

112. Cited in "At Last, the War Ends," *CEPAD Report*, May-June 1990.

113. Nicaraguan Director of Immigration, cited in *Los Angeles Times*, November 20, 1988.

114. Roberto Ferrey, cited in "Contras: A Government Priority," *Barricada Internacional*, June 2, 1990, p.8.

115. One source cites the INS as claiming that more than 100,000 Nicaraguans have entered the Miami area in the last ten years. See "El Búmeran de la Migración," *Pensamiento Propio*, January-February 1989.

116. Brook Larmer, "Nicaraguans Grapple with Economic Despair," *Christian Science Monitor*, January 23, 1989; *Envío*, January 1989.

117. Cited in "A Nicaraguan Capitalist Returns," *Boston Globe*, April 30, 1990, p.2.

118. Associated Press cable, July 20, 1990, cited in Latin America Data Base, *Central America Update*, July 25, 1990. The same source says that in FY1989, the INS granted just under 6,000 requests for asylum from Nicaraguans, denying more than 10,000.

119. *Barricada Internacional*, June 2, 1990, p.8.

120. U.S. Committee for Refugees, *World Refugee Survey: 1988 in Review* (New York, 1989).

121. See, for example, William I. Robinson and Kent Norsworthy, *David and Goliath: The U.S. War Against Nicaragua* (New York: Monthly Review Press, 1987), p.135.

122. Gabriela Selser, "Home is Where the Heart Is," *Barricada Internacional*, October 28, 1989, p.5.

123. The Mexican news agency NOTIMEX reported that as of mid-July 1990, there were an estimated 20,000 Nicaraguan refugees in the UNHCR camps in Honduras, plus another 30,000 contra family members holding special Honduran immigration permits. See Latin America Data Base, *Central America Update*, July 22, 1990.

124. See Latin America Data Base, *Central America Update*, July 20, 1990.

125. Interview by Debra Preusch with Roberto Ferrey, July 18, 1990.

126. Both figures are from "Nicaragua in Numbers: Ten Years of Aggression," *Nicaragua Through Our Eyes*, July 1989, p.9.

127. Information on internal refugees and resettlement camps taken from Robinson and Norsworthy, *David and Goliath*, op.cit., pp 136, 267-268; and from "Contras: A Government Priority," op.cit.

128. *Sierra Club Yodeler*, May 1988.

129. Much of the information in this section is taken from: David Henson, "Elections in Nicaragua: The Environmental Impact," *EPOCA Update*, Spring 1990, pp.1-10.

130. For an excellent account of the "pesticide treadmill" and Nicaragua's experiments with IPM, see Sean L. Swezey, Douglas L. Murray, and Rainer G. Daxl, "Nicaragua's Revolution in Pesticide Policy," *Environment*, January-February 1986. Also see Sally Gladstone, "Alternative Pest Control in Nicaragua," *Global Pesticide Monitor*, May 1990.

131. Bill Hall and Joshua Karliner, *Greenpeace*, Vol.12, No.4.

132. An exposition of MAN's viewpoints can be found in an interview with María Luisa Robleto, "Hay que Integrar la Ecología al Desarrollo," *Pensamiento Propio*, September 1988.

133. *Cultural Survival Quarterly*, Vol.11, No.3, pp.38-45.

134. Bill Weinberg, *War on the Land: The Politics of Ecology and the Ecology of Politics in Central America* (forthcoming).

135. Ibid.

136. One good critique of the effect of credit and subsidy policies on pesticide use can be found in Allan J. Hruska, "Government Pesticide Policy in Nicaragua, 1985-1989," *Global Pesticide Monitor*, May 1990, pp.3-5.

137. For a detailed description of this dilemma, including case studies, see Nick Young, "El Culto de los Químicos: Una Herencia Mortal," *Pensamiento Propio*, April 1989, pp 41-43.

130. See "Sandinismo Atentó contra Ecología Nacional," *La Prensa*, July 14, 1990.

## Chapter Five

1. *Envío*, June 1990, p.5.

2. Detailed examinations of the Reagan doctrine and low intensity warfare can be found in William I. Robinson and Kent Norsworthy, *David and Goliath: The U.S. War Against Nicaragua* (New York: Monthly Review Press, 1987); Sara Miles, "The Real War: Low Intensity Conflict in Central America," *NACLA Report on the Americas*, April-May 1986; Deborah Barry, Jose R. Castro, and Raúl Vergara, "Nicaragua: País Sitiado," *Cuadernos de Pensamiento Propio*, CRIES, 1986; and Michael T. Klare and Peter Kornbluh, eds., *Low Intensity Warfare* (New York: Pantheon Books, 1988).

3. *Miami Herald*, February 24, 1985, cited in Robinson and Norsworthy, *David and Goliath*, ibid., p.47.

4. Cited in Penny Lernoux, "The Struggle for Nicaragua's Soul, a Church in Revolution and War," *Sojourners*, May 14, 1989, p.23.

5. *Chicago Tribune*, October 29, 1989.

6. *New York Times*, March 1, 1990.

7. Interview by Debra Preusch with Douglas Gray, State Department Nicaragua Desk Officer, September 6, 1990.

8. Grant Fisher, "U.S. Ambassador Shlaudeman: Front Man for Counterrevolution," *NICCA Bulletin*, Nicaragua Center for Community Action, July-August 1990; and *Washington Post*, May 10, 1990.

9. Interview by Tom Barry with Julio Virgil, July 23, 1990.

10. U.S. Department of Commerce, "Business Opportunities in Nicaragua," May 1990.

11. For a complete summary of Washington's trade war see: Tom Barry, *The Destabilization of Nicaragua* (Albuquerque: Resource Center, 1986).

12. "Country Profile: Nicaragua, Costa Rica, and Panama, 1989-1990," *The Economist Intelligence Unit*, 1989, p.25.

13. "Anti-Sandinistas Urge End to U.S. Embargo," *New York Times,* January 12, 1989.

14. U.S. Department of Commerce, op.cit.

15. Ibid.

16. Interview by Debra Preusch with Diane Ponasik, AID's Nicaragua Desk Officer, September 4, 1990.

17. Interview by Debra Preusch with Bob Chadwick, Eximbank, June 19, 1990.

18. CCAA Press Release, May 22, 1990.

19. These twin plant operations would benefit from the provisions of Section 936 of the U.S. Tax Code which permits tax-free investments in Puerto Rico. To be eligible for this program, the Nicaraguan government will be expected to sign an extensive

Tax Information Exchange Agreement with the United States. Only Jamaica, Barbados, the Dominican Republic, Trinidad and Tobago, Grenada, and Dominica have signed this agreement which gives the IRS free access to government financial records. Interview by Debra Preusch with Luisa Cerar, FOMENTO, September 6, 1990.

20. The authors of one survey of the managers of transnationals with operations in Nicaragua concluded that these companies have "survived, grown, and generated profits" in Nicaragua since 1979. See James E. Austin and John C. Ickis, "Managing After the Revolutionaries Have Won," *Harvard Business Review*, May-June 1986, pp.103-109.

21. Interview by Debra Preusch with Julie Rauner, U.S. Department of Commerce Nicaragua Desk Officer, September 6, 1990.

22. Standard Fruit is one of several companies that have outstanding OPIC claims against Nicaragua, and the Nicaraguan government also has a suit pending against Standard Fruit. These will have to be resolved before Standard Fruit and other companies receive OPIC insurance to reinvest in the country.

23. Roberto Torres, "Banano, Dulce Banano," *Pensamiento Propio*, August 1990.

24. U.S. Department of Commerce, op.cit.

25. U.S. Agency for International Development, *Congressional Presentation FY1978, Annex III* (Washington: AID, 1977).

26. For more on AID programs in 1960s and 1970s see: *Human Rights in Nicaragua, Guatemala, and El Salvador: Implications for U.S. Policy*, Hearings Before the Subcommittee on International Relations, House of Representatives, July 8 and 9 1976; *Testimony of Penny Lernoux in Foreign Assistance and Related Agencies Appropriations for 1978*, Hearings before a Subcommittee of the Committee on Appropriations, Part III, 1977, p.551; Tom Barry, op.cit., pp.3-6.

27. Peter Kornbluh, *Nicaragua: The Price of Intervention* (Washington: Institute for Policy Studies, 1987), p.98.

28. For these statistics, and a more detailed description of this period, see Tom Barry and Debra Preusch, *The Soft War: The Use and Abuses of U.S. Economic Aid to Central America* (New York: Grove Press, 1988), pp.200-205, and ibid., pp.97-98.

29. *Envío*, April 1989, p.16.

30. E.V.K. Fitzgerald, "Stabilization and Economic Justice: The Case of Nicaragua," in Kwan S. Kim and David F. Ruccio, eds., *Debt and Development in Latin America* (Notre Dame, IN: University of Notre Dame Press, 1985), pp.195-213.

31. Peter Kornbluh, "Uncle Sam's Money War Against the Sandinistas," *Washington Post*, August 27, 1989.

32. Formerly known as Civilian Military Assistance, CMA is a paramilitary group of retired U.S. soldiers and officers led by Tom Posey which now calls itself Civilian Material (sometimes Materiel) Assistance.

33. See, for example, Bob Woodward, *Veil: The Secret Wars of the CIA* (New York: Simon and Schuster, 1987), p.113; and John Spicer Nichols, "La Prensa: The CIA Connection," *Columbia Journalism Review*, July-August, 1988.

34. See, for example, "Nicaragua: Special Campesino Program" and "Exchange Trip to Central America, June 12-18, 1988," in Quarterly Report to the National Endowment for Democracy from the Free Trade Union Institute, Second Quarter 1988. Also see Quarterly Reports for the Third Quarter 1988 and July 1, 1989 - September 30, 1989.

35. Certain aspects of this AIFLD-backed international network on behalf of the CUS and CPT can be found in the Grant Agreement between the NED and FTUI, No.89-34.2, signed in November 1989; and "FY1989 Proposal: Nicaragua Election

Supplemental," Proposal to the National Endowment for Democracy from the Free Trade Union Institute, August 22, 1989.

36. Ana María Excurra, *Agresión Ideológica Contra la Revolución Sandinista* (Mexico: Ediciones Nuevomar, 1983), pp.50-51; *Report of the Congressional Committees Investigating the Iran-Contra Affair*, Appendix B (Washington: U.S. Government Printing Office, 1987), Vol.12, pp.53-70, Vol.19, pp.276-281, and Vol.26, pp.20-36, 56-57; and "Nicaraguan Internal Opposition Receives U.S. Funds," *Washington Report on the Hemisphere*, March 16, 1988.

37. *CEPAD Report*, July-August 1989.

38. Detailed accounts of NED's extensive activities around the Nicaraguan electoral process can be found in Holly Sklar, "Washington Wants to Buy Nicaragua's Election Again," *Z Magazine*, December 1989; and William I. Robinson, "Intervention in Nicaraguan Elections," *CovertAction Information Bulletin*, Winter 1990.

39. *Newsweek*, September 25, 1989 and October 9, 1989. Also see: William I. Robinson, "Nicaraguan 'Electoral Coup'," *CovertAction Information Bulletin*, Summer 1990, p.32.

40. *Newsweek*, March 12, 1990; and Robinson, ibid.

41. For a thorough description and analysis of NED's Nicaragua and global operations see *National Endowment for Democracy: A Foreign Policy Branch Gone Awry* (Albuquerque: Council On Hemispheric Affairs and the Inter-Hemispheric Education Resource Center, March 1990).

42. This $57 million-plus estimate comes from an information sheet distributed by AID. It includes $5.7 million from the Survival Assistance for Civilian Victims of Civil Strife program, $1.405 million earmarked for repatriation efforts by Cardinal Obando's office, $250,000 for a "Basic Support for the Resistance" program, $330,000 for rehabilitation programs for the resistance, and $3 million for the assistance provided to the contras by the Organization of American States and the United Nations High Commission of Refugees (UNHCR) through the International Commission for Assistance and Verification. Of AID's FY1990 supplemental grant, $47 million is scheduled for the repatriation of the resistance and refugees, of which $30 million is directly targeted for contra resettlement programs, including the new development poles.

43. U.S. Embassy, "Status of AID Programs in Nicaragua," no date.

44. "Shadow governments" refer to AID-funded agencies and private institutes that formulate government policy and oversee government programs. See: Barry and Preusch, op.cit., pp.3-70.

45. Mary Jo McConahay, "Battle for Minds of Nicaraguan Youth," Pacific News Service, July 16, 1990.

46. A preliminary breakdown of the balance left from NED's election support grants is as follows: $107,000 for pro-U.S. labor unions through FTUI; $75,000 to civic, women's, and youth groups through the Costa Rica-based Democracy Assistance Center (CAD); $40,000 for Center for Youth Development; $250,000 to $300,000 for the Chamorro transition team, $125,000 to *La Prensa*; and $50,000 to three rightwing radio stations. Information from NED document obtained by William Robinson of Agencia Nueva Nicaragua and cited in Jack Colhoun, "With Aid to Chamorro, the U.S. Seeks to Neutralize the Sandinistas," *Alert!*, CISPES, May 1990.

47. Ibid.

48. Internal NED memo cited in Jack Colhoun, "U.S. Aids Sandinista Rivals to Bolster UNO," *The Guardian*, June 6, 1990.

49. Interview by Beth Sims with Peter Kosciewicz, NED Public Information Officer, September 19, 1990.

50. The high level of executive discretion in the allocation of Food for Progress makes this a highly politicized program. As described in National Security Council Memorandum No.156 (January 1985), "This judicious use of aid...will reduce the political risks to leaders of the third world countries committed to undertaking agricultural reform during a transition period of economic hardship." NSDD Memorandum No.167 (April 1985) stresses that before all other criteria, "U.S. strategic and foreign-policy interests must be served by the Food for Progress program."

51. U.S. Agency for International Development, "Food for Progress Agreement Between AID and Government of the Republic of Nicaragua: Economic Stabilization and Recovery Program," May 3, 1990.

52. Interview by Debra Preusch with Diane Ponasik, AID Washington, September 4, 1990.

53. Interview by Debra Preusch with Roger Noriega, AID Managua, July 16, 1990.

54. Debra Preusch, Diane Ponasik.

55. *La Prensa Latina*, September 7, 1990.

56. *Barricada*, June 19, 1990.

57. Tom Barry, Debra Preusch, and Beth Wood, *Dollars and Dictators* (New York: Grove Press, 1983), pp.66-73. The U.S. Public Safety Program (1961-1973) trained 81 Nicaraguan police, and the International Military Education Program (IMET) trained 5,740 between 1950 and 1978. Between 1950 and 1980 Nicaragua received $13 million in military aid for the National Guard.

58. Interview by Debra Preusch with Thomas Von Hare, Department of Defense Humanitarian Assistance Office, September 6, 1990.

59. Interview by Debra Preusch with Bill Ruzzamenti, Drug Enforcement Administration, September 21, 1990.

60. For a colorful and detailed account of Nicaragua's attempts to secure military aid from the United States, see "Sandinista Foreign Policy: Strategies for Survival," *NACLA Report on the Americas*, May-June 1985, pp.23-27.

61. "Previous U.S. and U.S.-Coordinated Aid to the Contras," Arms Control and Foreign Policy Caucus of the U.S. Congress, January 29, 1988, updated November 1989.

62. This $57 million includes more than $10 million in emergency aid which did not require congressional approval and $47 million approved by Congress as part of the $300 million supplemental authorization for 1990. U.S. Embassy, "Nicaragua: A Commitment to Democracy, Reconciliation, and Reconstruction," no date.

63. One extensive account of the channels used for assistance to the contras is Peter Dale Scott and Jane Hunter, *The Iran-Contra Connection: Secret Teams and Covert Operations in the Reagan Era* (Boston: South End Press, 1987).

64. For further documentation of the direct role played by U.S. forces, see Robinson and Norsworthy, *David and Goliath*, op.cit., pp.100-102 and 161-163.

65. Solon Barraclough, et.al., *Aid That Counts: The Western Contribution to Development and Survival in Nicaragua* (Managua, CRIES, 1988), p.19.

66. Ibid.

67. John Lamperti, *What Are We Afraid Of? An Assessment of the 'Communist Threat' in Central America* (Boston: South End Press, 1988), p.26. Also see: Robert Armstrong, Marc Edelman, and Robert Matthews, "Sandinista Foreign Policy: Strategies for Survival," *NACLA Report on the Americas*, May-June 1985.

68. During the 1980s the COMECON included the Soviet Union, East Germany, Bulgaria, Czechoslovakia, Hungary, Poland, Romania, Mongolia, Cuba, and Vietnam.

69. "USSR and Nicaragua: Closer Relations," *Barricada Internacional*, October 14, 1989.

70. Robert E. Sanchez, "Soviet Approach to Central America," *Congressional Research Review*, February 1989.

71. Barraclough, et.al., op.cit., p.17-18.

72. Scarlet Cuadra, "Cuba: Unconditional Aid," *Barricada Internacional*, May 5, 1990.

73. "Foreign Cooperation Notes," *Regionews from Managua*, July 4, 1990.

74. Barraclough, et.al., op.cit., p.25.

75. Ibid., p.17.

# Statistics

## Population

| | |
|---|---|
| Population: | 3,500,000 (1989)[1] |
|   Urban Population: | 59.4% (1988)[2] |
|   Population Density: | 75.8 per sq. mi. (1989)[1] |
|   Annual Growth Rate: | 3.4% (1980-1988)[2] |
| Literacy: | 88% (1981)[1] |
| Ethnic Composition (1981): | |
|   Miskito: | 3% |
|   Creole: | 1% |
|   Sumu: | 0.3% |
|   Garífuna: | 0.06% |
|   Rama: | 0.03% |
| Religion: | |
|   Catholic: | 85% |
|   Protestant: | 15% (1988)[3] |

## Health

| | |
|---|---|
| Life Expectancy at Birth (1989):[1] | |
|   Male: | 61 years |
|   Female: | 63 years |
| Infant Mortality per 1,000 Live Births: | 65 (1989)[1] |

## Economy

| | |
|---|---|
| GDP (1987, in 1986 dollars):[4] | $3,079 million |
| Per Capita GDP: | $819 (1988)[2] |
| Income Distribution (1980):[5] | |
|   Poorest 20% of Population: | 3% |
|   30% Below the Mean: | 13% |
|   30% Above the Mean: | 26% |
|   Richest 20%: | 58% |
| Rural Population in Absolute Poverty: | 57%[6] |
|   (Absolute poverty is the inability to afford food providing minimum nutritional requirements.) | |
| Land Distribution:[7] | |
|   Small and Medium Farmers: | 77.8% |
|   Large Farmers: | 7.5% |

| | |
|---|---|
| State-owned: | 11.7% |
| War Zones: | 3% |
| External Public Debt: | |
| 1970: | $147 million[8] |
| 1989: | $9,200 million[9] |
| Trade Balance: | -$410.8 million (1989)[9] |
| External Debt as % of GNP: | 207.8% (1987)[10] |
| Property & Income Taxes as % of Current Revenues: | 18.2% (1988)[2] |
| Labor Force by Sector (1986):[1] | |
| Agriculture: | 44% |
| Service: | 43% |
| Industry: | 13% |
| Unemployment and Underemployment: | 38.3% (1989)[9] |
| Top Agricultural Products: | Coffee, Cotton, Beef, Sugar[4] |

## U.S. Economic Aid[11]
### (millions of dollars)

| | 1946-1979 | 1980-1988 | 1989 | 1990 | 1991* |
|---|---|---|---|---|---|
| Development Assistance | 226.9 | 0 | 0 | 132.0** | 100.0 |
| ESF | 8.0 | 54.7 | 2.0[#] | 187.0[##] | 100.0 |
| PL480 Food Aid | 25.5 | 19.4 | 0 | 22.6 | 0 |
| Peace Corps | 7.5 | 0 | 0 | 0 | 0 |
| Total | 267.9 | 74.1 | 2.0 | 341.6 | 200.0 |

## U.S. Military Aid[11]
### (millions of dollars)

| | 1946-1979 | 1980-1988 | 1989 | 1990 | 1991* |
|---|---|---|---|---|---|
| MAP | 7.8 | 0 | 0 | 0 | 0 |
| FMS | 8.0 | 0 | 0 | 0 | 0 |
| IMET | 11.6 | 0 | 0 | 0 | 0 |
| Total | 27.4 | 0 | 0 | 0 | 0 |

*Requested

**Includes $57 million in aid for repatriation and resettlement

[#]Funding through the National Endowment for Democracy

[##]Includes $9 million in pre-election political aid

Sources: 1) CIA, World Factbook 1989; 2) Inter-American Development Bank, Economic and Social Progress in Latin America: 1989 Report; 3) "USIS Brief on Nicaragua," January 1, 1989; 4) Inter-American Development Bank, Economic and Social Progress in Latin America: 1988 Report; 5) CEPAL Review, April 1984; 6) Tom Barry, Roots of Rebellion: Land and Hunger in Central America (Boston: South End Press, 1987); 7) CIERA, cited in Barricada International, April 8, 1989; 8) World Bank, World Development Report 1988; 9) Fundación Internacional para el Desafío

Económico Global, Nicaragua, September 1990; 10) "Nicaragua, Costa Rica, Panama: Country Profile, 1989-1990," Economist Intelligence Unit, 1989; 11) U.S. Agency for International Development, Office of Planning and Budgeting, U.S. Overseas Loans and Grants: Obligations and Loan Authorizations July 1, 1945-September 30, 1983; U.S. Agency for International Development, Office of Planning and Budgeting, U.S. Overseas Loans and Grants: Obligations and Loan Authorizations July 1, 1945-September 30, 1988; U.S. Agency for International Development, Fiscal Year 1990 Summary Tables; U.S. Embassy Fact Sheet, May 1990.

# Chronology

1821    Central America declares its independence from Spain.

1833    U.S. troops intervene briefly in Nicaragua.

1852    Liberals and Conservatives finally agree to name Managua as the capital.

1854    In the first major U.S. intervention, the U.S. Navy burns down a Nicaraguan town following an insult to millionaire Cornelius Vanderbilt.

1855    In order to secure the rights to a canal for the United States, mercenary William Walker hires an army, invades Nicaragua, and declares himself president. Walker reestablishes slavery in the country and is subsequently recognized by Washington.

1857    Walker is overthrown and constitutional rule reestablished.

1860    Under the Treaty of Managua, part of the Atlantic coast is declared a reserve under British protection, although Nicaraguan sovereignty over the region is recognized.

1893    Nationalist José Santos Zelaya comes to power.

1894    U.S. troops intervene four times in the next five years.

        The Atlantic coast is "reincorporated" and the British pull out.

1905    The British relinquish all claims to the Mosquito coast in the Harrison-Altamirano Treaty, granting certain protections to Miskito and Creole populations.

1910    U.S. troops intervene.

1911    United States places Nicaragua under customs receivership, controlling the country's revenues for the next 38 years.

1912    U.S. Marines begin 20 years of repeated occupation of Nicaragua.

1916    Bryan-Chamorro Treaty confirms status as U.S. protectorate.

        Conservative Emiliano Chamorro elected president.

1926    U.S. Marines land and occupy the country almost continuously until 1933, mounting what would become Central America's first counterinsurgency war against a peasant army, led by Augusto C. Sandino, the "General of Free Men."

1927    On June 16, U.S. planes launched the first aerial bombardment of a civilian population in history as part of effort to defeat Sandino and his supporters. More than 300 residents of Ocotal lose their lives.

1932    Liberal Juan Bautista Sacasa elected president.

1933    After failing to defeat Sandino's guerrilla army, the Marines withdraw, having established the Nicaraguan National Guard with Anastasio Somoza García as commander-in-chief.

| 1934 | Sandino is murdered. |
|------|----------------------|
| 1936 | Sacasa removed by Somoza's forces; presidential election won by Somoza. |
| 1950 | Somoza reelected; new constitution promulgated. |
| 1956 | Somoza assassinated; National Assembly selects his son Luís to complete the term in office. |
| 1957 | Luís Somoza elected president. |
| 1961 | Carlos Fonseca, Tomás Borge, and Silvio Mayorga form the FSLN. |
| 1963 | Somoza associate René Schick elected president. |
| 1964 | With the National Guard as the centerpiece, the United States sponsors the formation of CONDECA to coordinate Central American military action against "internal subversion." |
| 1967 | Luís Somoza dies; his brother Anastasio Somoza Debayle elected president. |
| 1971 | Congress dissolves itself, abrogates the constitution, and transfers executive power to President Somoza pending new constitution. |
| 1972 | Earthquake devastates Managua; Somoza named chairman of National Emergency Committee and declares martial law. |
| 1974 | Somoza reelected. |
|      | FSLN raid in Managua. |
| 1977 | Martial law lifted. |
|      | Formation of Group of 12 (Los Doce), prominent Nicaraguan political figures and intellectuals opposed to the regime. |
|      | Major FSLN offensive. |
| 1978 | Pedro Joaquín Chamorro, editor of La Prensa and leading opposition figure, is assassinated. |
|      | National Guard sent in to break national strike. |
|      | Formation of the Nicaraguan Democratic Movement (MDN). |
|      | Formation of the Broad Opposition Front (FAO). |
|      | FSLN commandos seize National Palace. |
|      | FSLN-led insurrection takes Masaya, León, Chinandega, and Estelí for several days. |
| **1979** | |
| Jan. | Formation of the National Patriotic Front (FPN). |
| June | FSLN units take León and Matagalpa, and begin march on Managua. |
| July | The FSLN triumphantly enters Managua and installs a revolutionary government. |
| **1980** | |
| Mar. | Revolutionary government launches massive National Literacy Crusade which reduces illiteracy from more than 50 percent to 13 percent in five months. |
| May | Inauguration of the Council of State. |
|      | U.S. Congress approves $75 million economic-aid package for Nicaragua. |
| 1981 | Health care campaigns reduce infant mortality rate 40 percent in relation to pre-revolutionary figures. |
|      | Promulgation of the Agrarian Reform Law. |
| Mar. | United States cuts off $9.8 million in food aid to Nicaragua. |
| Apr. | Washington suspends all bilateral aid to Nicaragua, but continues support to private sector and Catholic church. |

Nov.  Reagan administration authorizes $19 million to destabilize Nicaraguan government, giving the CIA a green light to organize ex-National Guardsmen into a counterrevolutionary army based in Honduras.

1982

Jan.  In the wake of increasing contra activity on the Atlantic coast, the government decides to relocate Miskito communities from the Río Coco further inland at the Tasba Pri resettlement. Some 10,000 Miskitos flee to Honduras.

Mar.  Following contra destruction of two bridges in the north, the government declares a state of emergency.

June  U.S. Congress approves $5.1 million in economic assistance for the Nicaraguan private sector.

Oct.  Standard Fruit violates its agreement to administer banana industry until 1985 when it announces its immediate withdrawal from Nicaragua, leaving 3500 unemployed.

Nov.  U.S. Congress approves $24 million in covert aid to the contras.

1983

Jan.  The Contadora Group, formed by Mexico, Venezuela, Colombia, and Panama, declares an avoidance of the outbreak of war between Nicaragua and Honduras to be the initial focus of its negotiating mission.

Feb.  More than 5,000 U.S. and Honduran troops take part in the Big Pine military maneuvers near the Nicaraguan border.

Mar.  First large-scale invasion of contras from Honduran territory. In the United Nations Nicaragua denounces U.S. support for the contras; only El Salvador, Honduras, and the United States vote against the Nicaraguan motion.

Pope John Paul II visits Nicaragua.

May  Washington reduces Nicaragua's sugar import quota by 90 percent.

June  U.S. Treasury Department announces official policy of opposing all multilateral loans to Nicaragua.

Patriotic Military Service (draft) instituted.

Sep.  The contras launch their "Black September" offensive, including sea- and air-based attacks against petroleum installations and key economic infrastructure, and ground attacks against the principal entry points on the country's northern and southern borders.

Oct.  CONDECA is reestablished with the explicit goal of pressuring Nicaragua, and the FDN immediately solicits CONDECA's support in its contra war.

Contra offensive deepens with heavy fighting in the north and south, eight aerial attacks, and sabotage actions against the ports of Corinto and Sandino.

Dec.  Government implements an amnesty program for contras who lay down their arms.

1984

Mar.  CIA and Navy units assist the contras in the mining of Nicaraguan harbors in gross violation of international law. Seven ships are damaged by the mines.

Apr.  Diverse sectors of the international community condemn the U.S. mining of Nicaraguan ports.

More than 35,000 U.S. troops surround Nicaragua as the Pentagon simultaneously stages maneuvers off the Atlantic and Pacific coasts and in Honduras.

| | |
|---|---|
| May | The International Court of Justice orders the United States to suspend support for the contras and the mining of Nicaraguan ports. |
| Sep. | Two members of Civilian Military Assistance, a rightwing U.S. group aiding the contras, are shot down in a helicopter flying over Nicaragua. |
| | Nicaragua agrees to proposed Contadora Peace Plan; Reagan administration asks Honduras, El Salvador, and Costa Rica to demand changes in the plan. |
| Nov. | Nicaragua holds first free elections in history. The FSLN's candidate Daniel Ortega is elected to a six-year presidential term with 67 percent of the vote against six opposition parties. Reagan denounces the elections as a sham. |

**1985**

| | |
|---|---|
| Feb. | Economic stabilization package implemented. |
| May | White House declares trade embargo against Nicaragua. |
| June | U.S. Congress approves $27 million in "humanitarian" aid to the contras. |

**1986**

| | |
|---|---|
| June | $100 million contra aid package approved by U.S. Congress. |
| Oct. | U.S. mercenary Eugene Hasenfus shot down and captured during a contra resupply mission. |
| Nov. | Iran-Contra scandal breaks in Washington. |

**1987**

| | |
|---|---|
| Jan. | New constitution signed. |
| Aug. | Presidents of Costa Rica, El Salvador, Guatemala, Honduras, and Nicaragua sign the Esquipulas II Peace Accords. |
| | Nicaragua becomes the first signatory to the Esquipulas accords to form a National Reconciliation Commission. |
| Sep. | National Assembly approves the Autonomy Statute for the Atlantic region. |
| | La Prensa is allowed to resume publication after a one-year suspension; the church hierarchy's Radio Católica is permitted to resume broadcasting. The government announces an end to all prior censorship of the media. |
| | President Ortega announces a unilateral suspension of offensive military operations for the month of October to cover three zones totaling 1,450 square kilometers. |
| Nov. | Following several meetings with House Speaker Jim Wright, President Ortega announces a new 11-point proposal for achieving a cease-fire, disarmament, amnesty, and the integration of the contras into civilian life. Nicaragua also agrees to name Cardinal Obando y Bravo as mediator between the government and the contras. |
| | Nicaragua releases 985 political prisoners, 200 of whom are ex-National Guardsmen. |
| Dec. | The first in a series of indirect meetings is held between the contras and the Nicaraguan government in Santo Domingo under the mediation of Obando. Among other things, the contras demand a general amnesty, an end to the military draft, the creation of new police and military forces, and the dismantling of "military" cooperatives. |

**1988**

| | |
|---|---|
| Jan. | Nicaragua announces its willingness to enter into direct talks with the contras and lifts the five-year state of emergency. |

| | |
|---|---|
| Feb. | Economic reform measures decreed, spearheaded by a currency change. |
| Mar. | Provisional government-contra cease-fire signed in Sapoá. |
| June | After another round of dialogue with the government, the contras break off peace talks. |
| Oct. | Hurricane Joan passes through Nicaragua, leaving an estimated $800 million in damages. |

**1989**

| | |
|---|---|
| Feb. | The Costa del Sol summit of Central American presidents calls for the elaboration of a plan to disband the contra army. |
| Mar. | Following a pardon granted by the National Assembly, 1,894 ex-National Guardsmen are freed from prison. |
| Apr. | U.S. Congressional Bipartisan Accord results in the approval of $49.75 million in non-lethal aid to keep the contras intact. |
| June | In compliance with the Costa del Sol accords, Nicaragua's media and electoral laws are modified. |
| Aug. | President Ortega and representatives from 20 opposition parties sign an accord further modifying the electoral law and procedures, suspending the draft during the campaign period, and calling on the Central American presidents to approve a contra demobilization plan. |
| | The Central American presidents approve a plan to have a United Nations force oversee contra demobilization, to be completed by December 5th. |
| Sep. | National Opposition Union (UNO) selects La Prensa's Violeta Chamorro and the Independent Liberal Party's (PLI) Virgilio Godoy to lead the opposition ticket in the 1990 presidential elections. |
| | U.S. Congress approves overt aid to support the "election process." In reality the aid is used to back the UNO campaign. |
| Nov. | Following a sharp escalation in contra attacks against civilians, the government suspends its unilateral cease fire and launches an offensive. |
| | Representatives from the government and contras meet face to face for the first time in over a year to work out a plan for contra demobilization. After 12 days of meetings, the talks are suspended. |
| Dec. | UNO campaign rally in Masatepe degenerates into riot. An FSLN activist is killed. |

**1990**

| | |
|---|---|
| Jan. | U.S.-based polling firm announces that its latest surveys have increased the FSLN's probable margin of victory for February's elections. The latest poll shows Daniel Ortega with 51 percent of respondents' preference and Violeta Chamorro with 24 percent. |
| Feb. | UNO's closing campaign rally draws an estimated 60,000 people, by far the largest opposition rally since 1979. Three days later an estimated 400,000 attend the FSLN's closing rally. |
| | UNO's electoral upset gives Violeta Chamorro 54.7 percent of the vote to Daniel Ortega's 40.8 percent, margins which were closely maintained in races for legislative seats. |
| Mar. | Contra forces transfer en masse from their base camps in Honduras into the Nicaraguan countryside to avoid demobilization. |
| | Washington formally lifts the five-year trade embargo against Nicaragua. |

FSLN and UNO negotiators sign a Transition Protocol stipulating the basic conditions for the transfer of power on April 25. The document calls for strict adherence to the existing legal order and constitution, including respect for the "structural integrity" of the security forces.

Apr.  Violeta Chamorro assumes the presidency and names her cabinet. General Humberto Ortega remains as head of the Armed Forces.

May   After several days of talks, contra leader Israel Galeano signs an agreement promising to begin disarming his troops on May 8 in order to conclude by the previously agreed upon date of June 10. The accord promises a series of incentives for the contras, including the establishment of semi-autonomous "development poles."

A nationwide public-sector strike drags on for five days before ending with a negotiated accord.

President Chamorro sends reform proposals to the legislature on the University Autonomy Law, the Civil Service Law, and the Labor Code, and issues two decrees calling for the rollback of Sandinista agrarian reform.

Congress approves an aid package for Nicaragua totaling more than over $300 million.

June  Contra demobilization officially ends. 19,613 armed and unarmed contras were demobilized and became eligible for international and Nicaraguan government assistance programs.

The army initiates a plan to cut its ranks in half, to 41,000 troops, by the end of the year.

July  A nationwide general strike, called by the pro-Sandinista National Workers Federation (FNT) paralyzes the country. The compromise accord signed by union representatives and the government is systematically violated by the latter in the following days and weeks.

---

Sources: Gerald Greenfield and Sheldon Maran, eds., Labor Organizations in Latin America (New York: Greenwood Press, 1987); "Chronology of Key Events in the Atlantic Coast, 1979-89," Envío, April 1989, p. 30; "For the Record: Chronology of Nicaragua's Compliance," Central America Bulletin, June 1988, pp. 8-9; Conflict in Central America (London: Longman Group UK Limited, 1987), pp.68-70; Tom Barry and Debra Preusch, The Central America Fact Book (New York: Grove Press, 1986), pp.312-318.

# Abbreviations

| | |
|---|---|
| ABEN | Nicaraguan Association of Biologists and Ecologists |
| ADRA | Adventist Development Relief Agency |
| AID | U.S. Agency for International Development |
| AIFLD | American Institute for Free Labor Development |
| AMNLAE | Nicaraguan Women's Association |
| ANC | Conservative National Action |
| ANDEN | National Educators Association |
| ANPDH | Nicaraguan Human Rights Association |
| APP | Area of Peoples Property |
| ARDE | Democratic Revolutionary Alliance |
| ATC | Rural Workers Association |
| CAUS | Trade Union Action and Unity Confederation |
| CAV | Antonio Valdivieso Ecumenical Center |
| CDC | Civilian Defense Committee |
| CDN | Nicaraguan Democratic Coordinator |
| CDS | Sandinista Defense Committee |
| CEFOJ | Youth Training Center |
| CENIDH | Nicaraguan Human Rights Center |
| CEPAD | Evangelical Committee for Aid to Development |
| CEPRODEC | Center for the Promotion of Community Development |
| CEPS | Center for Health Studies |
| CGT | General Confederation of Workers |
| CGT-I | Independent General Confederation of Workers |
| CIAM | Center for Research and Action for Women's Rights |
| CIAV | Commission for Support and Verification |
| CIDCA | Center for Research and Documentation on the Atlantic Coast |
| CLT | Workers Struggle Committee |
| CMA | Civilian Material Assistance |
| CNES | National Council for Higher Education |
| CNPEN | National Council of Evangelical Pastors of Nicaragua |
| CNPPDH | National Commission for the Promotion and Protection of Human Rights |
| CONAPRO | National Confederation of Professionals |
| CORDENIC | Commission for the Reconstruction and Development of Nicaragua |

| CORNAP | National Corporation of the Public Sector |
| COSEP | Superior Council of Private Enterprise |
| CPDH | Permanent Human Rights Commission |
| CPT | Permanent Workers Congress |
| CRIES | Regional Coordinator for Social and Economic Research |
| CRN | National Reconciliation Commission |
| CRS | Catholic Relief Services |
| CSE | Supreme Electoral Council |
| CST | Sandinista Workers Central |
| CTC | Committee of Agricultural Workers |
| CTN | Nicaraguan Workers Confederation |
| CTN-A | Autonomous Nicaraguan Workers Central |
| CUS | Confederation of Trade Union Unity |
| CUSCLIN | Committee of U.S. Citizens Living in Nicaragua |
| EPS | Sandinista People's Army |
| FACS | Augusto C. Sandino Foundation |
| FDN | Nicaraguan Democratic Force |
| FES | Federation of Secondary School Students |
| FETSALUD | Federation of Health Workers |
| FNT | National Workers Federation |
| FO | Workers Front |
| FSLN | Sandinista National Liberation Front |
| FUNDE | Nicaraguan Development Foundation |
| INCAE | Central American Institute of Business Administration |
| INDE | Nicaraguan Development Institute |
| INDERA | Institute for the Development of the Atlantic Coast |
| INIES | Nicaraguan Institute for Economic and Social Research |
| INRA | Agrarian Reform Institute |
| IRENA | Institute of Natural Resources and the Environment |
| JS | Sandinista Youth |
| MAN | Nicaraguan Environmentalist Movement |
| MAP-ML | Marxist-Leninist Popular Action Movement |
| MDN | Nicaraguan Democratic Movement |
| MISURASATA | Miskitos, Sumus, Ramas, Sandinistas Working Together |
| MMN | Nicaraguan Women's Movement |
| MPS | Sandinista People's Militia |
| MPU | United People's Movement |
| MUR | Revolutionary Unity Movement |
| NED | National Endowment for Democracy |
| NGO | Nongovernmental Organization |
| ONUCA | United Nations Observer Group in Central America |
| PALI | Neo-Liberal Party |
| PAN | National Action Party |
| PAPC | Popular Conservative Alliance Party |
| PC de N | Communist Party of Nicaragua |

| | |
|---|---|
| PCD | Democratic Conservative Party |
| PCN | Nicaraguan Communist Party |
| PCS | Social Conservative Party |
| PDCN | National Democratic Confidence Party |
| PIAC | Central American Integrationist Party |
| PLC | Constitutionalist Liberal Party |
| PLI | Independent Liberal Party |
| PLIUN | Independent Liberal Party for National Unity |
| PNC | National Conservative Party |
| POI-RN | Internal Order Police-Nicaraguan Resistance |
| PPSC | Popular Social Christian Party |
| PRT | Revolutionary Workers Party |
| PSC | Social Christian Party |
| PSD | Social Democratic Party |
| PSN | Nicaraguan Socialist Party |
| PUCA | Central American Unity Party |
| RAAN | North Atlantic Autonomous Region |
| RAAS | South Atlantic Autonomous Region |
| RN | Nicaraguan Resistance |
| SMP | Patriotic Military Service |
| UNAG | National Union of Farmers and Ranchers |
| UNE | National Employees Union |
| UNEN | National Nicaraguan Student Union |
| UNO | National Organized Union (National Opposition Union) |
| UPN | Nicaraguan Journalists Union |

# Bibliography

The following periodicals are useful sources of information and analysis on Nicaragua:

*Barricada Internacional, Barricada* (San Francisco and Managua), biweekly, English and Spanish.

*Envío,* Central American Historical Institute (Washington), monthly, English and Spanish.

*Pensamiento Propio,* Coordinadora Regional de Investigaciones Economicas y Sociales (Managua), monthly, Spanish.

The following books contain valuable background on a wealth of issues important to understanding Nicaragua:

Karl Bermann, *Under the Big Stick* (Boston: South End Press, 1986).

George Black, *Triumph of the People: The Sandinista Revolution in Nicaragua* (London: Zed Books, 1981).

John A. Booth, *The End and the Beginning: The Nicaraguan Revolution* (Boulder: Westview Press, 1985).

Reed Brody, *Contra Terror in Nicaragua* (Boston: South End Press, 1985).

Edgar Chamorro, *Packaging the Contras: A Case of CIA Disinformation* (New York: Institute for Media Analysis, Inc., 1987).

David Close, *Nicaragua: Politics, Economics, and Society* (New York: Pinter Publishers, 1988).

Joseph Collins, et.al., *What Difference Could a Revolution Make? Food and Farming in the New Nicaragua* (New York: Grove Press, 1986).

Michael Dodson and Laura Nuzzi O'Shaughnessy, *Nicaragua's Other Revolution: Religious Faith and Political Struggle* (Chapel Hill: University of North Carolina Press, 1989).

James Dunkerley, *Power in the Isthmus* (London: Verso, 1989).

Patricia Taylor Edmisten, *Nicaragua Divided: La Prensa and the Chamorro Legacy* (Pensacola: University of West Florida Press, 1990).

Richard R. Fagen, Carmen Diana Deere, and José Luís Coraggio, eds., *Transition and Development: Problems of Third World Socialism* (New York: Monthly Review Press, 1986).

Richard Garfield and Glen Williams, *Health and Revolution: The Nicaraguan Experience* (London: Oxfam, 1989).

Dennis Gilbert, *Sandinistas: The Party and the Revolution* (New York: Basil Blackwell, 1988).

Roy Gutman, *Banana Diplomacy: The Making of American Policy in Nicaragua 1981-1987* (New York: Simon and Schuster, 1988).

Richard L. Harris and Carlos M. Vilas, eds., *Nicaragua: A Revolution Under Siege* (London: Zed Books, 1985).

Donald C. Hodges, *Intellectual Foundations of the Nicaraguan Revolution* (Austin: University of Texas Press, 1986).

Peter Kornbluh, *Nicaragua: The Price of Intervention* (Washington: Institute for Policy Studies, 1987).

Richard Millett, *Guardians of the Dynasty* (New York: Maryknoll, 1977).

Jack Nelson-Pallmeyer, *War against the Poor: Low Intensity Conflict and Christian Faith* (New York: Orbis Books, 1989).

Robert Pastor, *Condemned to Repetition: The U.S. and Nicaragua* (New Jersey: Princeton University Press, 1989).

William I. Robinson and Kent Norsworthy, *David and Goliath: The U.S. War Against Nicaragua* (New York: Monthly Review Press, 1987).

Peter Rosset and John Vandermeer, eds., *Nicaragua: Unfinished Revolution* (New York: Grove Press, 1986).

Gary Ruchwarger, *People in Power: Forging a Grassroots Democracy in Nicaragua* (Boston: Bergin and Garvey Publishers, Inc., 1987).

— — —, *Struggling for Survival: Workers, Women, and Class on a Nicaraguan State Farm* (Boulder: Westview Press, 1989).

Gregorio Selser, *Sandino* (New York: Monthly Review Press, 1981).

Holly Sklar, *Washington's War on Nicaragua* (Boston: South End Press, 1988).

Rose J. Spalding, ed., *The Political Economy of Revolutionary Nicaragua* (Boston: Allen and Unwin, Inc., 1987).

Mary Vanderlaan, *Revolution and Foreign Policy in Nicaragua* (Boulder: Westview Press, 1986).

Carlos M. Vilas, *State, Class, and Ethnicity in Nicaragua: Capitalist Modernization and Revolutionary Change on the Atlantic Coast* (Boulder: Lynne Rienner, 1989).

– – –, *The Sandinista Revolution: National Liberation and Social Transformation in Central America* (New York: Monthly Review Press, 1986).

Thomas W. Walker, ed., *Nicaragua: The First Five Years* (New York: Praeger, 1985).

– – –, ed., *Reagan versus the Sandinistas: The Undeclared War on Nicaragua* (Boulder: Westview Press, 1987).

# For More Information

## Resources

Barricada Internacional
P.O. Box 410150
San Francisco, CA 94141

Central America Historical Institute / Envío
Intercultural Center
Georgetown University
Washington DC 20057

Coordinadora Regional de Investigaciones Económicas y Sociales (CRIES) /
Pensamiento Propio
Apartado Postal C-163
Managua, Nicaragua

Environmental Project on Central America (EPOCA)
Earth Island Institute
300 Broadway, Suite 28
San Francisco, CA 94133

## Peace and Justice

Nicaragua Center for Community Action
2140 Shattuck Avenue, Suite 2063
Berkeley, CA 94704

Nicaragua Network
2025 I Street NW, Suite 1117
Washington, DC 20006

Quixote Center / Quest for Peace
P.O. Box 5206
Hyattsville, MD 20782

Witness for Peace
P.O. Box 29497
Washington DC 20017

## Human Rights

Amnesty International
322 8th Avenue
New York, NY 10001

Comisión para la Defensa de los Derechos Humanos en Centroamérica (CODEHUCA)
Apartado Postal 189
Paseo de los Estudiantes
San José, Costa Rica

Human Rights Watch / Americas Watch
36 West 44th Street
New York, NY 10036

## Aid

American Friends Service Committee (AFSC)
1501 Cherry Street
Philadelphia, PA 19102

Comité Evangélico Pro-Ayuda Al Desarrollo (CEPAD)
Apartado Postal 3091
Managua, Nicaragua

Oxfam America
115 Broadway
Boston, MA 02116

## Tours

Global Exchange
2141 Mission Street, Room 202
San Francisco, CA 94110

Marazul Tours
250 West 57th Street, Suite 1311
New York, NY 10107

Tropical Tours
2330 West Third Street, Suite 4
Los Angeles, CA 90057

## Business / Official

Embassy of Nicaragua
1627 New Hampshire Avenue NW
Washington DC 20009

Embassy of the United States in Nicaragua
APO Miami, FL 34021

U.S. State Department
Citizen's Emergency Center / Travel Information
Main State Building
Washington DC 20520

# Also Available

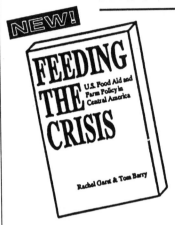